THE ANTHROPOLOGY
OF CANNIBALISM

THE ANTHROPOLOGY
OF CANNIBALISM

Edited by
Laurence R. Goldman

Bergin & Garvey
Westport, Connecticut • London

For Colleen

In order to keep this title in print and available to the academic community, this edition was produced using digital reprint technology in a relatively short print run. This would not have been attainable using traditional methods. Although the cover has been changed from its original appearance, the text remains the same and all materials and methods used still conform to the highest book-making standards.

Library of Congress Cataloging-in-Publication Data

The anthropology of cannibalism / edited by Laurence R. Goldman.
    p.   cm.
    Includes bibliographical references and index.
    ISBN 0–89789–596–7 (alk. paper). — ISBN 0–89789–597–5 (pbk. : alk. paper)
    1. Cannibalism. 2. Ethnology—Methodology. I. Goldman, Laurence.
    GN409.A58   1999
    394′.9—dc21   99–12700

British Library Cataloguing in Publication Data is available.

Library of Congress Catalog Card Number: 99–12700
ISBN: 0–89789–596–7
         0–89789–597–5 (pbk.)

First published in 1999

Bergin & Garvey, 88 Post Road West, Westport, CT 06881
An imprint of Greenwood Publishing Group, Inc.
www.greenwood.com

Printed in the United States of America

The paper used in this book complies with the Permanent Paper Standard issued by the National Information Standards Organization (Z39.48–1984).

10 9 8 7 6 5 4 3 2

At any moment, I gather, a young girl may start up and say to her mother, "I am tired of this feverish and outworn civilisation. I am going out and away to the far places of Mexico to find a strong, vivid, brown-limbed people who practise the old faith of the Mayas. I mean to wander amongst them until they take me away into the mountain fastnesses and drug me with strange herbs, and then at last lead me to the sacrificial chamber. And there, at the moment when the shaft of the sun strikes the altar, they will lay me on the cold stone and sacrifice me, and I shall know a completeness and a contentedness beyond imagination, and beyond dream."

"Yes dear", says her mother; "when do you want to start?"

"This very afternoon."

"I wish you could put it off till tomorrow, dear, because the Smiths are coming to-night, and I had hoped you would arrange the flowers for dinner."

"Witches and Whatnot," E. V. Knox, 1938

Contents

1

From Pot to Polemic:
Uses and Abuses of Cannibalism

Laurence R. Goldman

I do not believe, from what I have been told about this people
[Tupinamba], that there is anything barbarous or savage about them,
except that we call barbarous anything that is contrary to our own
habits. . . . I consider it more barbarous to eat a man alive than eat him
dead. . . . We are justified in calling these people barbarians by
reference to laws of reason, but not in comparison with ourselves, who
surpass them in every kind of barbarity.

Montaigne, "Of Cannibals," Essays, 1581

INTRODUCTION

Michel de Montaigne's Renaissance *essai* "Of Cannibals" has long been regarded within anthropology as a *locus classicus* of how in the representation of
otherness, and most particularly the "exotic," we need to decenter ourselves from
our own culturally shaped morality. His disquisition was emblematic of early
attempts to narrow perceived distances between New World and Euro-Western
practices. In this respect Montaigne's writings are widely appreciated as a pre-
cursor to the development of later ideologies of cultural relativism (Celestin
1990; Geertz 1984; Johnson 1993). Cannibalism is here, as it always has been, a
quintessential symbol of alterity, an entrenched metaphor of cultural xenophobia.
Though enmeshed in philosophies of prelapsarian "natural law," Montaigne
chose cannibalism as a vehicle for reflexive thought not only to subvert conventional wisdoms both within and about his own culture, but as a passageway to

self-enlightenment. Cannibalism was at once a prism that refracts predications of otherness as well as a practice through which the self is situated *vis-à-vis* humanity at large. Importantly, the literary convention of the *essai* became in Montaigne's hands an instrument for experiment; cannibalism was merely the litmus paper to *trial* or *test* [*essai*] one's ethically charged reactions or judgments.

The contributions to this book are very much in the tradition and spirit of Montaigne's essays. Each discloses a portrait of some others' cannibalism, which articulates not simply its grounding in a distinctive cultural logic but its place within their humanistic images of the self. These, then, are essays *"for an anthropology of cannibalism"* in the sense of *trials* by the authors for their subjects, for themselves, and for research about anthropophagy.

Certainly for much of its intellectual history anthropology has been burdened with a public profile often defined in terms of what it has had to say about cannibalism. Few other topics command quite the same level of instant media attention or have the capacity to make or break professional reputations overnight. It is a legacy that has both sensitized the discipline to the fact that its science is never ideologically neutral—images of "others" invariably service political agendas—and sharpened understanding of why it is that people continue to be "scandalized, titillated and spellbound" (Osborne 1997:28) by the subject of cannibalism. The vexed debates about whether, when, who, and where anthropophagy was actually practiced often improperly overshadow the simple fact that cannibalism appears everywhere to have been a matter of some cultural preoccupation. That is, irrespective of whether *people x* or *y* did or did not consume human flesh, the behavioral possibility or potentiality for cannibalism (see Rumsey, chapter 5) appears universally sedimented in some domain of cultural thinking. We have yet to encounter any case of a people bereft of a locally etched understanding of anthropophagy. This much, it seems to me, is indisputable.

Now it is fashionable for anthropologists to indicate that the relative engrossment of the professional academic as against that of the layperson in cannibalism is of a different order. Indeed, that in general anthropologists have rarely made anthropophagy a central part of their studies, or that "no great theories seem to hang in the balance on cannibalism" (Brady 1982:607), reflects less the disappearance of any such practice and more a reticence to perpetuate popular stereotypes and tendentious agendas. But the more anthropologists have dissociated themselves from "popular" dialogue, the more it has appeared that they merely perpetuated the boundary-making exercises that cannibal epithets service. It is not simply that anthropologists have been charged with seeking to maintain the hegemony and identity of their discipline by providing intellectual life-support to the body of the exotic cannibal (cf. Arens 1979; Brady 1982), but that—as Gardner (chapter 2), Ernst (chapter 7), and Zubrinich (chapter 6) eloquently argue here—any talk about cannibalism risks euphemization and distortion and is encumbered by judgmental viewpoints. In the interstitial space between ethnographic enterprises and public preconceptions lies a recognition that cannibalism invariably implies a set of *products, producers,* and *processes.* The point of their convergence, and one explored in greater detail below, is in the discourse of anthropophagy, where producers of all persuasions are playing in structurally similar ways, for similar reasons, with their ingestive metaphors and symbols. Any mooted distance between these mythmakers across history, landscape, or culture is chimerical.

In light of the above remarks, it needs to be emphasized at the outset that readers looking for punch-line conclusions or headline grabs of the type *"yes, x or y culture conventionally consumed human flesh in manner z because . . ."* are likely to miss the intended point of these essays. For the most part, the authors here regard questions about the historical incidence of cannibalism as *passé;* providing answers to skeptics is not a driver in their *trials.* Chasing cannibals is, for them, thus only marginally about exploring why such questions remain so vital or what it is about the questioners that remains so interesting. Collectively these authors proclaim a message of a more profound type: it is that the imaginative commerce of cannibalism—how flesh eating is defined in folklore, cosmology, and world eschatology—provides the only supportive context for evaluating claims about the historical occurrence of anthropophagy and, more importantly, for progressing our understanding of its place and meaning within cultural schemas (Lindenbaum 1983). This mythic instantiation of cannibalism is probably universal; socially sanctioned cannibalism was most certainly not and, some have claimed, quite possibly remains merely an article of belief—a cultural contrivance.

The contributors to this volume have thus seized upon a juncture in anthropology—a time that perhaps witnesses the end to the serious academic exploration of exoticism—to reposition their studies as ultimately about, as well as underpinned by, mythic discourse—see, especially, Rumsey (chapter 5), Pickering (chapter 3), Zubrinich (chapter 6), and Ernst (chapter 7). They all endorse the point that motifs of cannibalism are embedded within imaginative processes that "generate fiction as a modality of historical experience" (Goldman 1998b:174). The resource for their *essais* is the talk of others about cannibalism. Their focus is the way imaginative literature and sacred history are mutually implicative, mutually referential dialogues, not polarized fields of symbolic reasoning. Movements between make-believe and meal, between fantasy and feast, are always conceptually (and therefore culturally) mandated for actors.

However, there is more to these authors' messages than mere contextualization of others' perspectives on flesh eating. Notwithstanding the very real findings that cannibalistic motifs are part of complex calculi about human reproduction, about circumscribing spheres of morality and exchange, and about flesh and food as gendered systems of meaning (Poole 1983; Sanday 1986; Strathern 1982), these essays collectively compel us to acknowledge a second indisputable finding. We have yet to encounter any single case of a culture where the moral turpitude of anthropophagy is not delineated at the level of folktale or folklore. We have good accounts of cases where cannibalism occurred and for which mundane or religious rationales are provided; we have good accounts of cases where cannibalistic themes abound despite the absence of any actual or known practice of cannibalism. What I am suggesting we do not have are fine-grained accounts where, for the same culture, the dimension of folklore is etched in the same detail as the cosmologically contextualized cannibalistic practices. It is surely this very interface (cf. Arens 1979:69; Sanday 1986:x) that is likely to reveal how the shifting and context-sensitive valances of anthropophagy—where it can at once signal the inimical as well as the fecund—are articulated and coexist. This is of course a quite different question to parallel inquiries about the relationship between cultures that did and did not practice cannibalism (Askenasy 1994; Sagan 1974; Shankman 1969; Strathern 1982; see also Rumsey, chapter 5, and Kantner, chapter 4, this volume).

What the contributors here bring to their studies, then, is a more informed disclosure of the relationship between cannibal fact and fantasy in their mythic analyses. Because a single discourse genre may mix elements of the fictive, allusive, allegorical, and factive, they identify how the naive realism of previously untrained commentators has lead to widespread misrepresentations (see Pickering, chapter 3). A failure to speak the local language, to construe the multiple ways in which a verb like "eat" occurs in conversation,[1] and to relate what is being said against the backcloth of real and irreal worlds muddied the understanding of cannibalism in pre- and postcolonial histories. But even where cannibalistic practices are discussed (see Ernst, chapter 7, Zubrinich, chapter 6, Kantner, chapter 4), the accounts here remove the "centeredness" of such behavior for the practitioners. In their human projects, "cannibalism was once important, but never central or necessary" (Ernst, chapter 7). Cannibalism thus emerges as adjunct, augmentative behavior rather than key ritual; it was a means to process ends whose skein of symbolic rationales could be channeled through other outlets when cannibalism ceased. Though the efforts of these authors may indeed narrow the distance of disbelief for some in the historical occurrence of cannibalism, their concern is more fundamentally to "talk out" the very morality of simply writing about the topic given the literary baggage of the tradition in which they work.

It is acknowledged that cannibalism will continue to serve as a mirror for the relationship of anthropology to its wider readership, as well as for images of anthropologists to themselves. This reflects what we have done with the knowledge of anthropophagy when we have had it. Succinctly expressed, attributions of anthropophagy have invariably perpetuated agendas that proclaim that different is dangerous. The literary history reveals the manner in which cannibal claims were embedded within colonial myths variously employed to rationalize subjugation, land aggrandisement, and forms of marginalization. Like it or hate it, that such ideologies persist seems in part a consequence of the impotence of anthropology to effect any revision in the negatively nuanced representations of cannibalism. This reiterates the point drawn above that the moral turpitude of flesh eating has a pan-cultural instantiation. Because flesh eating is imaginatively constructed as larger-than-life behavior, as articulating the sensational, fascinating, and fearsome—at least at the level of folklore—the efforts of anthropologists to act as the public's thought police are invariably diluted or inefficacious. The danger posed by books of this kind then (as discussed by Gardner, chapter 2, Zubrinich, chapter 6, Pickering, chapter 3, and Ernst, chapter 7) is that one inadvertently reproduces the very mythical stereotypes craved by the public. In one sense the discourse about cannibalism entrenches the processes by which musings about consumption become assumption, by which conjecture about calorific predilection transforms into conceptual predisposition.

These *trials* can be read as attempts by the writers to question whether as cannibal *producers* they are not replicating the very structures and representations of anthropophagy they earnestly seek to critique. The key finding—and indeed the solution to such dilemmas—lies in the contributors' recognition that ultimately cannibalism speaks about "what it means to be human" (Zubrinich, chapter 6). On the one hand, as indicated above, fabricators, audiences, and analysts alike are seemingly bound together by a common imaginative commerce in anthropophagic images, at least at the level of fantasy and folklore. On the other hand, producers use their products to engage in discourse processes in seemingly common ways—that is, "cannibalism is not only so good to think about" (Arens 1979:9) but clearly good to say and good to play. This commerce is manifested as conversation, and cannibalism is a resource that agents infuse with poetic artifice. What we know and understand about anthropophagy cross-culturally is thus choreographed by what we might refer to as embedded soundscapes of truth.[2] I am of the opinion that in recognizing cannibalism as fundamentally a product of imaginative discourse, our engagement with the topic will always signal to some extent a ludic journey. In this process, Western media representations—where the salacious and sensational frequently mask the serious (Kidd 1988)—speak no differently to the mythic redactors of the indigenous aboriginal populations considered within.

I want to develop this point about soundscapes of authenticity and imaginative discourse by means of a pointed comparison between patterns typically found in certain Western prose genres and certain non-Western oral traditions with respect to talk about cannibals. Now while it is in the nature of popular media to exploit linguistic artifice in constructing headline grabs, irrespective of topic addressed, the extent to which this has typified the reporting of cannibalism bears comment (cf. Askenasy 1994:236–238; Kidd 1988). The sample shown in Table 1.1, from both science and popular-press journalists, covers many of the cannibal cases discussed in the next section. What is clearly illustrated is the rampant dependence on, and indulgence in, metaphoric play for the delight of readers. Alliteration and assonance are manipulated to foreground the resonant ludic potential

The Anthropology of Cannibalism

Table 1.1.   Headline Statements in Cannibal Journalism

Headline	Source/Date
"A Decent Disposal"	*Australian*, 16 Aug. 1992
"Burnt Bones Point to a Cornucopia of Cannibals"	*Australian*, 5 Aug. 1997
"Why Man Has Been Left off the Menu"	*Australian*, 14 Jan. 1998
"Cavemen Often Had People for Dinner"	*Australian*, 29 Jan. 1996
"Is Cannibalism Too Much to Swallow"	*New Scientist*, 4, 1991
"The People Eaters"	*New Scientist*, 3, 1998
"Ancestral Cannibalism Gives Us Food for Thought"	*New Scientist*, 4, 1992
"A Distaste for Cannibalism"	*Australian*, 1 Aug. 1992
"Cave Clues Suggest Stone-age Cannibalism"	*Science News*, 130, 26 July 1986
"Bones of Contention"	*Scientific American*, 25 May 1986
"Does Man Eat Man"	*Lingua Franca*, 5, 1997
"Butchered Bodies: Food or Fad"	*New Scientist*, 29, 26 Mar. 1987

inherent in the consumptive and homicidal metaphors invoked. It is almost as if the journalists cannot restrain the urge to exploit the punning potential of cannibalism. The following prose examples are fairly representative of what we encounter within the genre:

Did we really nosh on each other's body parts or are we merely feeding on fear and imagination. [Rix 1997]

Cannibalism controversy first reach full boil . . . its existence is hard to swallow . . . questions scholars will be chewing over. [Osborne 1997]

Clearly, commentators are dancing, albeit dangerously,[3] on the borders between fact and fiction, between the sensational and serious, between profundity and jocularity. But if for a moment we agree that this is a topic that uniquely lends itself to such choreography, how far is this really any different to the doings and discourses of the very cultures being reported? How far does the thinking and saying of cannibalism articulate similar patterns of relationships between authors and anthropophagites? It may well be a lot more difficult for even seasoned anthropologists to disengage and disentangle themselves from this artefactual process in which they cannibalize poetic artifice. Perhaps cannibalism plays with them.

I draw here on some previously published data (Goldman 1983, 1998b) on cannibalistic motifs and figures among the Huli of the Southern Highlands of Papua New Guinea. They provide a good case example of what a mythic discourse of cannibalism looks like, as well as providing a broader understanding of how such phenomena are distributed throughout the cultural economy. The Huli never practiced anthropophagy, but, as others in the region, they believed that (a) some of their Strickland-Bosavi and Kutubu neighbors did (see Ernst, chapter 7); and (b) that, like the Duna (Haley 1993), their land was inhabited in the remote past by a giant race of cannibal beings known as *Baya Horo*. These ogres are thus part of the historical and fictional economy of narrativized identities, inhabitants of the *weltmärchen* world shared by bogies, goblins, and other "frightening figures" (Widdowson 1971). In this regard one notes a significant cross-cultural incidence in beliefs about cannibal giants across Asia, Europe, Africa, and India (cf. Aarne 1973; Beecher 1938; Butterworth 1987; Glenn 1971; Mondi 1983; Motz 1982; Page 1955)—often of the one-eyed variety as in the Greek tradition of Polyphemus (the Cyclops legend), the Basque *Tartaro*, or the Greco-Turkish *Tepekózi*. This kind of motific distribution has long beckoned anthropologists to confront issues of cross-cultural similarity (Patton & Doniger 1996:12) and just how cannibalism, for example, might be hard-wired into the architecture of human imaginative structures. Candidate explanations for such universality range from the psychological—Jungian archetypes (Jung 1956), child-engendered projections of parenthood and innate destruction fantasies (Bettelheim 1975; Roheim 1950), and animistic syndromes (Freud 1913)—to pan-cultural "synthetic images" (Kluckhohn 1959; Needham 1978) or socio-ecological responses that generate cannibalistic fantasies (Arens 1979:151).

In their oral traditions of *Baya Horo,* the Huli discriminate between the cycle of tales that are understood as faithful renditions of historical fact—"we also create our rather obscure past as one characterised by cannibalism" (Arens 1998:35)—and a set of fictional tales, incidents, and characters that are appreciated as nonhistorical in nature. In performance the two forms are frequently mixed; audiences discriminate how they are to understand information by reference to familiar story elements and text signals. In either modality, the narratives frequently involve the mythic co-presence of *tricksters* who are generally reported in the literature as "freeing the world from monsters, ogres and giants" (Abrams 1977:145; Basso 1988:296–297; Carroll 1981:305; Eliade 1969:157; Evans-Pritchard 1967:93, 108; Radin 1956:166; Ricketts 1965:327, 342; Street 1972:96) and are invariably anthropophagous (Goldman 1998a). One argument that I proposed in the analysis was that on account of the opposed moral valances of Cannibal Ogre and Trickster, and their symbolic enmeshment with the nexus of antinomies about Life, Death, and Regeneration, there was some co-dependence of these mythic figures in world eschatologies—that, in effect, they represented a primal symbolic complex within Huli imaginative consciousness that was clearly mirrored in other world mythologies.

In line with similarly recorded traditions elsewhere (Arens 1979; Chakravarti 1974; Douglas 1996; Motz 1982), these anthropophagous beings had a pre-cosmic, ahistorical primordiality; they existed in a world that predated human civilization. This universe, while often mythically depicted as some precultural utopia, a golden age, was also bestial, predatory, and baleful. The cannibal race is portrayed as inimical to any continued habitation by humankind until some cataclysmic event, which heralded their complete or partial destruction. Now the first point to be drawn in relation to these data is that such myths "inform us equally about the knowns of this world as well as what can potentially be known . . . this quality of imaginal potentiality imbues myth with the unique capacity to transform tradition and make sense of ever-changing circumstances" (Goldman, Duffield, & Ballard 1998:3). That is, they can be invoked to make narrative sense of ongoing social transformations. This is why, for example, Europeans in both Papua New Guinea (Rumsey, chapter 5) and Africa (Douglas 1996:37) were often seen in the image of cannibal predecessors.

In theorizing about Huli anthropophagites, I talked of a regional subtradition of *Melanesian Cyclops*.[4] Just as Westerners are predisposed to associate cannibalism with the Homeric tale of Polyphemus, so the Huli are culturally conditioned to articulate anthropophagy in the image of *Baya Horo*. Beyond eident similarities in narrative structure, style, and content—gigantic size, remote past, lawless, cave-dwelling, cannibals as ocularly challenged (one-eyedness)—my specific rationale for using this Greek epithet reposed on the manner in which myth and make-believe were indissolubly fused as the basis of Huli historicity. While the Homeric tale of the Cyclopes bequeathed an enduring set of images about anthropophagy, there was clearly also a bidirectional seepage between this poetic fiction and long-established oral traditions (Glenn 1971; Mondi 1983; Page 1955). The Cyclopes tale was based on widely known folklore traditions, which in turn were themselves altered through the specific auspices of the Polyphemus text. Not all Cyclopes, or indeed even Polyphemus, were "one-eyed," and yet we believe they were. The boundaries between the historical and fabled in the Huli tradition of *Baya Horo* is similarly blurred; *mutatis mutandis,* much the same might be said about every culture's consciousness of cannibalism.

Cyclopic ecology is a paradise landscape, a veritable "Garden of Eden." This otherworldly environment is benign, well-ordered, and excessively fertile—a precivilization Utopia. As among the Greek Cyclopes, there appears no public *themistes* [state law], an anarchic polity in which fratricide and endocannibalism occur to satisfy a lust for flesh (cf. Strathern 1982 on "greed for consumption"):

Text 1 [Goldman 1998b:221]

agali bo nana ibaga bialu haga henego au buwa
[Baya Horo] were going around looking for man to kill and eat

agali waga bialu bo nalu agali hangu tai bialunaga henego
searching to kill and eat, looking only for man

Anthropophagy is also mythically developed in terms of the necessity for human sacrifice so as to counter the infertility of land, which is replenished by "blood."[5] Significantly, these cannibalistic figures are asexual. Their powers of rebirth (in the sense of spontaneous recreation of form, mitosis, or fertile remains) are based on anatomical regeneration. In this respect they are symbolically juxtaposed to trickster figures, which are associated with biological reproduction and sexual mores—tricksters are everywhere phallic, gastronomic, and priapic (Goldman 1998a). Within this wider mosaic of themes about life, death, and regeneration, cannibals (like tricksters) represent symbolic play material *par excellence*. Focusing for a moment on what cannibal talk looks like in this culture, I want to examine the name games played in the mythological accounts.

The epithet *Baya Horo* betrays its anthropophagous roots. The appellation is constructed of the terms *baya* ["kill/hit"] + *horo* ["to inter"]. In Huli myths and folk tales we find these terms (the morphs of which are shown in bold in Table 1.2) poetically embellished through various forms of nonconventional reduplication or verbal inflection. Most frequently the name is collocated with some equally contrived form of the verb "consume/ingest" [*na*] to produce a prototypical epithetical string of:

Kill [*ba*] + Inter [*horo*] + Consume [*na*]

This semantic encoding of anthropophagy is part of the soundscape of cannibal truths that bears comparison with the kinds of Western discourse alluded to above. In this poetic portraiture the acme of cannibalistic symbolism is reached in the rhetorical depiction of *Baya Horo* embodiment. Various anatomical parts—presumably cannibalized from humans or other cannibals—function as items of adornment, again emphasizing the disjunctions between human and nonhuman that underpin Huli conceptualizations. The following rhyme is the centerpiece of any ogre narrative, and children as young as 3–4 years old are totally familiar with the composite elements of the cannibal body. The text is constructed on both (a) the striking physical resemblances of body parts to their assigned decorative

Table 1.2.   Ogre nomenclature: *Baya Horo*

Generic Huli terms				
Baya	*Horo*	*Naba*	*Bayaga*	*Horo*
Bayaga	*Horo*	*Nabaya*	*Balu*	*Nana*
Baya	*Horo*	*Nabaliya*	*Balu*	*Nabono*
Balu	*Nolene*	*Nabene*	*Balu*	*Nolene*
Bayaga	*Nalu*	*Nabene*	*Horo*	*Nabu*
Bayaga	*Balu*	*Nolene*	*Nalu*	*Nabiya*

functions—the spleen as an axe, the omentum as a net bag, the trachea as a bow string—and (b) the marked assonance and alliteration (designated in bold) between the anatomical terms and accoutrement terms.

tombene	*tangi*
stomach	(he wears as a) cap
ayuni	*ayu yi*
spleen	(as an) axe he holds
nuni	*nu hene*
omentum	(as a) net bag carried
yabuni	*yandare yi*
anal passage	(as a) spear he holds
gibuni	*gi hondole*
trachea/oesophagus	(he wears as an) arm bracelet
gibuni (variant)	*dandu hibu he*
trachea/oesophagus	used as bow string

Huli adults understand these rhetorical devices to inscribe an imaginary cannibal body. Their belief in the historical *Baya Horo*, however, is not necessarily grounded in the specifics of this anthropophagous identity. Such embellishment is articulated as for the delight and delectation of children. Importantly, much of this folklore tradition of ogres is encoded in sayings that convey both the general sense of cannibals as frightening, gluttonous figures and specific events surrounding individual ogre personalities which provide allegorical resources. For example, children who simply sit and cry for food without doing anything are often reprimanded with the retort that they are like *Baya Horo*. The following restricted selection of proverbial forms encapsulates many of the ogre themes discussed above:

1 *Hogarene Giwi harebe*
Are you becoming Hogarene Giwi?

[Said to a person who pinches another to see if she/he is awake. Recalls a well-known myth in which the Hogarene Giwi used to pinch his victims to ensure they were asleep before cannibalizing them.]

2 *Ogo agi bere ibi dayadabe hondole ya handarebe*
What are doing, checking whether I am ripe?

[Said to a person who feels you over as if he/she is acting like a Baya Horo to see whether you are ready/ripe for eating.]

To these proverbs might be added a gamut of child games in which cannibal role-playing occurs and which are linked to specific etiologic myths (cf. Goldman 1998b).

These cannibalistic themes are developed through a depiction of which anatomical parts are inserted into bamboo tubes for roasting, the sizzling sounds [*kodo kodo*] that will be heard as the human flesh cooks, and the manner in which they will be served as food to children (see Text 2). Much of the ethnography here resonates with themes inherent in the Jack cycle of stories in Western folklore and the giant whose signature refrain is "Fe Fi Fo Fum I smell the blood of an Englishman." Typically, cannibal victims were carried back to caves or houses, where they were either dismembered or ripened (cf. Wagner 1978:172 on Toro ogres among the Daribi) by continual feeding with cucumber [*bambo*: *cucumis sativus*] before they were consumed. This equivalence of "humans/ cucumbers = ogre food" has a number of resonances in Huli culture. Cucumber is recognized as a food type associated with the earliest epoch of Huli history, which again temporally dislocates cannibals from the "time of man" [*agalinaga*]. Equally, cucumbers are believed to grow in the Hades land where dead spirits go—*Humbirini*. What is brought together in Huli thought here are the paramount lines of association between the "otherworldly" status of ogre existence, cannibalism, and "outside/marginal" domains like *Humbirini* or the Huli's cannibal neighbors.

TEXT 2 (cf. Goldman 1998b:210)
Informant: Alembo, Tari 1993
Recounted routine verbal formula on cannibal actions as told to children

> *ibu ainya bo yalu puwa Bayaga Horome*
> he [the ogre] killed and carried his [the child's] mother away, Baya Horo
>
> *Bo yalu ayu ibirabe*
> having killed is he [the ogre] bringing her now?
>
> *Yawi ibirabe hondole bedo lowa*
> is he bringing her tomorrow, I am waiting to see it is said
>
> *ogoni i ainyanaga bayene kodo kodo lara*
> your [the child's] mother's thigh is sizzling [in the bamboo on the fire]
>
> *abeyene kodo kodo lara*
> the side of the stomach meat is sizzling
>
> *kuabeyane kodo kodo lara lalu*
> the rib meat is sizzling it is said
>
> *ibu ainyanaga andu pugu wowa*
> his mother's breast has been cut off
>
> *wandari igiri emene biago nelo mialu howa*
> he [the ogre] gave those things to little children to eat
>
> *bo yalu piaga lene*
> he used to kill and carry off like this it is said
>
> *waneigini dugu biragola ani laga*
> when the children are crying it used to be said like that

Huli ogres kill parents and in particular mothers by first cutting off their breasts and then feeding them to the children. As these data show, the motif of cannibalism in Huli is culturally inflected across a wide arena of behavioral and conceptual phenomena. There is little doubt that the ogre conveys a vision of control analogously encapsulated in Western frightening figures like the "bogey-man" or "little green monster" used to coerce, frighten, or cajole children into obedience. But this external threat does not symbolize that of an authority figure punishing misdemeanors. The fiction as transformed history is not only—or even primarily—a vehicle for policing operations. However, because the ogre quite fundamentally frame-shifts as a being who is between fact and fiction, it stands apart too from comparable Western "imaginary" figures or companions like the Sand Man, Jack Frost, Easter Bunny, Man in the Moon, Tooth Fairy, or Father Christmas, who most often are invested solely with a "second-world" reality.

The insulation of cannibalism within an earlier historical epoch and projected as a practice belonging to the "other" is, of course, a common cultural phenomena (Arens 1979). But such images of precivilization existence are dual: cannibalism is at once something anathema to humans and an expression or embodiment of "strength." These resonances impinge directly on children because they are encoded in nursery rhymes used to promote child growth. Text 3 is a nursery rhyme made to a female baby from Dugube (a congeries of Strickland-Bosavi peoples feared for their supposed cannibalism), in which the mother alludes to the anthropophagous behavior of Dugube people, who are also regarded as the source of all dangerous and powerful sorcery. The mother wants to instil this kind of "strength" into the child

TEXT 3:   Nursery rhyme—Yaluba 1993 [Goldman 1998b:214]

Ainyali balu naga ara wane
O mother, daughter of people who used to kill and eat [humans]

Hengeda Pupigi Pogai wane
daughter of Hengeda, Pupigi, Pogai

balu naga Hulu wane
daughter of people who used to kill and eat [humans]

These kinds of data, then, address two concerns. (a) They provide some insight into both how cannibal motifs percolate through a range of interactional fields, and what cannibal discourse looks like in the popular traditions of another culture. Clearly, as Ernst also notes in his insightful chapter on Onabasulu cannibalism (chapter 7), there is no "ethnographic oddity" (Arens 1979:69) in understanding anthropophagy as resonating opposed valances—somehow evil and abhorred, somehow attractive and desired. (b) Across most of the cultures described in this volume, the cultural experience of cannibalism is scaffolded by its simultaneous habitation of imaginative literature and sacred history. Cannibalism as a model of antipathetic agency shifts between phenomenal domains. Narrative discourse here heightens the boundaries between human and nonhuman, civilized and barbarian, male and female, and utopian and entropic worlds. The human predicament and condition, seen within an historical context, is disclosed. Equally, the structural homologies in reproducing these cannibal artefacts through talk are foregrounded for producers everywhere. There is more to the topic of cannibalism, then, than mere considerations of flesh eating.

A SYNOPSIS OF RESEARCH ISSUES

The contributors to this volume work against a background of questions and issues that may be entirely unfamiliar to those first encountering the research field of cannibalism. With this in mind I shall make a highly selective raid on the vast literature to provide a brief overview (cf. also Anglo 1979; Arens 1979; Askenasy 1994; Davies 1981; Farb & Amelagos 1980; Hogg 1962; Pickering 1985; Sanday 1986; Tuzin & Brown 1983).

Far more so than Herodotus or Homer, the popular Western imagination of cannibalism has been shaped by the accounts of early explorers, missionaries, colonial officers, travelers, and others. In this melting pot are the commonly cited accounts of the South American Tupinamba Indians (Staden 1928), the Carribean Cariba—the term cannibal is itself a corrupted form of "carrib"—of St. Vincent, St. Croix, and Martinique (Columbus 1968), and the South American Aztecs (Alvardo 1963; Cortés 1962; Diaz del Castillo 1970; Durán 1964, 1971; Gómara 1964; Sahagón 1951–1957). These were followed by numerous reported incidences in Africa (Evans-Pritchard 1965; George 1968; Kalous 1974), Polynesia, Australia, and Papua New Guinea, about which more is said below. A compendium of case citations is unnecessary here, since the focus is on background issues associated with these accounts.

Without doubt, a defining moment in the whole study of cannibalism arrived when William Arens—"I never wanted to be Mr. Cannibalism" (Osborne 1997:38)—cast a shadow of skepticism over the entire corpus of literary accounts that claimed that society *x* or *y* indulged in this practice. So pervasive—some would argue, so pernicious (Gardner, chapter 2)—and influential has been Arens' critique that most authors subconsciously engage in some debate with his arguments when writing about the topic. In part, the simplistic elegance of his position in which there is no fence-sitting or equivocating—ritual cannibalism is for Arens a "myth"—acts like a solicitation to engage in academic controversy. Based on his considerations of various written accounts, which are shown to be of uneven quality, reliant on secondhand reports and hearsay, and where the reporters were often beacons of bigotry steeped in fundamentalist and ethnocentric ideology, Arens (1979) boldly declared that

I am dubious about the actual existence of this act as an accepted practice for any time or place. [9]

I have been unable to uncover adequate documentation of cannibalism as a custom in any form for any society. [21]

... the idea of "other" as cannibals, rather than the act, is the universal phenomenon. [139]

Arens' pointed revisionism moved the debate from the cliched "pot" of colonialism to the cauldron of postcolonial polemic. Ensuing controversies were as much about the use, reliability, and authenticity of such archival evidence as about the professionalism of practitioners writing on the topic. Like any attack on conventional wisdoms and cherished mentors in anthropology, Arens provoked ascorbic responses in exchanges to which one might easily and aptly append the gloss of "sex, lies, and videotapes." Reflecting nearly two decades later on what became a minor cottage industry, Arens noted that "convincing colleagues that there might be no cannibals was like trying to persuade a convention of UFO buffs that there are no aliens visiting us" (1998:35). All of this was in and of itself "good copy" as scientific journalists prompted the question of "why does the issue of cannibalism's very existence drive the people dedicated to its study into opposing camps?" (Osborne 1997:37). Equally, the manner in which such disputes exposed fundamental issues about anthropological science and methodology helped to constitute the topic of anthropophagy as de rigueur in introductory first-year undergraduate programs. Here was an issue about human behavior that allowed for multidisciplinary approaches, begging questions about epistemology and knowledge gained through historical reconstruction, which provided a window on how anthropologists do ethnography.

Although no generally accepted typology is used in cannibalism research, a number of descriptive phrases have currency and allow us to refine the categories of behavior most in dispute. Survival cannibalism, in which people eat human flesh in emergency starvation situations, is certainly accepted as fact. The most commonly documented and referred-to cases include those of the 1846 Donner Party in the American Navada and the South American athletes stranded in 1972 in the Andes for 70 days (which became the subject of the film Survival). Exocannibalism refers to consumption of "outsiders," such as enemies of war, and frequently includes some form of perimortem mutilation and use of skull trophies (headhunting). Endocannibalism is the consumption of flesh from a member of one's "insider" group (possibly kinship or descent) and seems most usually associated with ideologies about the recycling and regeneration of life-force substances, discussed further below. Most of the debates about the actual practice of cannibalism refer to these latter two categories.

With the passage of two decades since Arens aired his critique (though he clearly still adheres to the same opinions), the quantum increase in ethnographic accounts in areas such as Papua New Guinea has tended to work against any widespread acceptance of his views amongst Melanesian anthropologists (Knauft 1999; Sillitoe 1998). Although most researchers would agree that archival sources leave much to be desired, the inferential passage to the "inexistence" of cannibalism is considered unacceptable (see Rumsey, chapter 5, Gardner, chapter 2, and Ernst, chapter 7, this volume). In particular, the restriction of what can constitute adequate documentation to "personally observed" (Arens 1998) firsthand accounts rather threw the baby out with the bathwater. Given the virtual disappearance of the practice in this region, videotaped evidence would seem impossible to obtain. Moreover, "under the careful scrutiny of sceptics armed with rules for 'scientific evidence,' most 'eyewitness' accounts are hard to believe" (Brady 1982:595). Now the epistemological problem of what constitutes anthropological knowledge is too complex to pursue in detail here. Suffice it to remark that establishing a line in the sand between "observed" vs. "recounted/ reconstructed" cases—as data different in kind—fails to acknowledge the singular importance that patterns of inference play in both types of account. There is no such thing as "self-evident" data on cannibalism since all human actions require interpreters and interpretation to make sense. Most anthropologists construct ethnographic accounts with reference to practices that no longer obtain, or which they did not encounter, but which are reliably held to be part of present memory or discourse in that culture. "If you have people in a group cogently telling you, one after the other, 'this is how we eat man, this is how we do it'— and you can cross-check—either there is a very large collective myth going on in that group or they are telling the truth" (McLancy, cited in Ripe 1992:4). None of this should be taken as in any way minimizing the problems faced by ethnographers, even those fluent in the native language, in locating the phenomenal levels at which cannibalism has meaning for a people. In this endeavor, however, even the best researchers can easily be fooled.[6]

The dilemmas posed by methodological reflexivity went hand in-hand with more "personally" targeted attacks that reflected both the centrality of the topic in anthropology and in the public consciousness and how these are profoundly related to professional reputations. In 1992 Tim White suggested that 800-year-old skeletal bone fragments retrieved from the Anasazi site at Mancos in southwest Colorado exhibited classic footprints of cannibal activity. Arens (1995) commented that White had been "seduced" by the holy grail of anthropophagy. A negative case result would not be newsworthy, so the temptation is to make a positive case of the find. White retorted that he found such imputations of fortune hunting "personally offensive" (quoted in Rix 1997). The Arens–White controversy is enmeshed with opposing perspectives about expectations that hard science delivers neutral truth (cf. Rix 1997) when, as noted in the Introduction above, all anthropology is part-advocacy of some form.

Arens also mounted a challenge to Dr. Daniel Gajdusek's claims of a cannibal etiology to the outbreak of *kuru* (a fatal disease of the nervous system) among the Fore people of Papua New Guinea. Gajdusek, assisted by Shirley Lindenbaum and Robert Glasse, was interested in the transmission of a disease related to Creutzfeldt-Jacob, Bovine Spongiform Encephalopathy (BSE)—"mad cows' disease"—and Gertmann–Staussler–Scheinker syndrome. *Kuru* was attributed to prions, first discovered by neuroscientist Professor Prusiner, which are an endogenous form of cell destruction. Gajdusek's work won him a Nobel Prize in 1976. Arens charged that the photographic evidence of human flesh produced by Gajdusek was falsely described—that it was, in fact, pig's meat—and that therefore "he had not observed cannibalism 'in the flesh'" (Arens 1998:36). While other explanations have been canvassed for transmission of this disease, including contamination from merely handling human body parts, Arens was later to reiterate his doubts on Gajdusek's work by *ad hominem* innuendo. Thus Gajdusek's subsequent arrest for the sexual abuse of minors is directly referred to in Arens' (1998) own overview of the *kuru* debates in a manner that could hardly be described as inadvertent, naive, or innocent.[7]

While the case that orientalist impulses often cloud what should otherwise be unbiased reporting is well made by Arens, the same charge is less easily upheld in relation to modern ethnographers, such as those who have worked in Papua New Guinea since the early 1970s. As Ernst ably demonstrates, two decades of research have revealed consistent, repeated confirmations of precolonial cannibalism among the Strickland-Bosavi groups that amount to a regional pattern. Quite paradoxically, the reputation of Papua New Guinea societies for cannibalism directly influenced the reporting of such practices in neighboring Australia. Both Pickering (1985) and Richard Buckhorn have kept up crusade-like efforts against the persistent stereotyping of Aborigines as previously cannibals. Pickering's essay speaks of the politically nuanced manner in which such claims are voiced, and his subsection title, "Please Explain?" will have a special resonance for Australian readers in the context of the political party One Nation and its often claimed racial platform. Of equal interest have been Buckhorn's (1992a, 1992b) letters to the media and book presses against misuse or misconception of historical sources claiming Aboriginal cannibalism. To one such claim of historical inaccuracy by E. Rolls (1992) in his book *Sojourners,* the following response was received. It shows how misconceptions about cannibalism in other regions are easily transported to new areas.

Some of the Cape York tribes were akin to natives from Papua New Guinea. There was a long established trading association—the routes were probably thousands of years old. And customs have always been traded with goods. That might have accounted for the increased cannibalism among Cape York tribes as well as the periodic shortage of food. [Buckhorn, private correspondence]

The evidential quagmire represents only one of a number of sources for polarized perspectives about cannibalism and its reputed historical occurrence. There has been much controversy, too, concerning what kind of social conditions and what kind of rationales underpinned the practice. One school of thought is of the opinion that anthropophagites are ingesting positively valued qualities in either exo- or endocannibalism. Sanday (1986) posits that such practice was linked to the maintenance of systems of belief about life reproduction, regeneration, and human identity. Cannibalism is here a means for processing life-generating substances often linked to ideas about feminine reproductivity as among the Gimi (Gillison 1983) and Hua of Papua New Guinea. Similar themes appear to fit other cases such as the Daribi (Wagner 1967) and Bimin-Kukusmin (Poole 1983). Strathern (1982), in particular, attempted to link such ideas to marriage distribution patterns and symbolic equivalences between humans and pigs. In the Papua New Guinea Highlands, which evidence a distinct absence of past cannibal practices,[8] pig sacrifices are theorized as performing similar functions. Ernst (chapter 7) develops an allied theme, which shows that flesh eating may also be a way in which actors reconvert the egocentered immorality of witches to the sociocentered exchange behavior of the kin group as bounding discrete moral universes.

A second strong line of argument posits that exocannibalism can be an expression of hostility, violence, or domination toward the victim, as in the cases discussed by Kantner (chapter 4). A third line of explanation, most notably invoked to explain Aztec cannibalism (Harris 1977, 1979; Sahlins 1978), has it that large-scale survival cannibalism is related both to hunger and to an appreciation of the nutritional value of such human consumption. On the basis of Harner's (1977) earlier thesis, Harris suggested that Aztec anthropophagy was the natural and rational response to the material conditions of their existence, which included protein depreciation due to dwindling livestock (cf. Dornstreich & Morren 1974; Farb & Amelagos 1980; Garn 1979; Garn & Block 1970). Ritual sacrifice and cannibalism, common in Mesoamerica well before the Aztecs arrived in Mexico, was mediated by state-sponsored agents as a response to ecological and subsistence problems. Sahlins (1978) countered that the materialist reductionism of Harris had given insufficient recognition to the role, place, and nature of cosmological beliefs and rationales about the relationship between people and land renewal. The protagonists each drew on various other historical sources (Berdan 1982; Ortiz de Montellano 1978) as support for their positions, leaving the general reader with the distinct impression that here the evidence is quite equivocal.

While the above strands might be said to be prominent in the research literature, they are by no means exhaustive. Any search through the World Wide Web under "Cannibal" reveals numerous unpublished papers, email exchanges, and what we might refer to as "lunatic-fringe" theories. For example, one lively letter chain develops an "anthropophagocentric" version of evolution to argue that primates developed bipedalism to better eat other primates. Still other contributors draw on the psychological profiles of famous serial cannibals like Jeffrey Dahmer, Albert Fish, or Nikolai Dzhurmongaliev to propagate their politically inflected theories of social anomie. By contrast, other sites contain lively debates concerning the kinds of definitional quandaries and moral dilemmas posed by corneal grafts, transplants, blood transfusions, and spare-part surgery, which is euphemistically referred to as medical science (Rumsey, chapter 5) but which might easily be glossed as cannibalism.

None of the above is to suggest in any way that cannibalism is some oasis for cultural anthropology. In palaeontology/archaeology the musings of research scientists over the significance of their osteological evidence has similarly contributed to the making and breaking of myths. Here, too, there prevailed "well-entrenched" (White & Toth 1991:119) predispositions to sensationalize findings (Bahn 1991, 1992:40) in the context of inferred cannibal practices. The recorded instances of such skeletal interpretations are legion, and Kantner (chapter 4) here provides a state-of-the-art synopsis of the cases for one region. The sites referred to most frequently range from 400 to 780,000 years ago and include Sierra de Atapuerco (Spain), Arizona Polacca Walsh, Gough's cave at Cheddar Gorge Somerset (U.K.), Guattari Cave at Monte Circeo (Italy), Fontbregoua cave in Southern France, and Krapina in Yugoslavia. Tim White's (1992) account of the twelfth-century site at Mancos, in which he examined the skeletal trauma signatures of bone markings, disarticulations, and breakage patterns, is one of the most detailed in this genre. Succinctly stated, the cut marks on his sample bones were indicative of defleshing; only the long leg bones had been targeted for marrow extraction, while others were simply discarded (indicative of native recognition of their superior nutritive value); pot polish occurred as abrasions from boiling bones to extract fat and grease. In many of these resects the assemblages were different from mortuary finds in the same area.

From this large and complex research field it is sufficient simply to indicate here that alternative explanations have been mooted for the same skeletal evidence and discard patterns. These include (1) mortuary rituals and secondary burial; (2) extraneous damage through natural disaster; and (3) animal interference (see Bahn 1992; Buckhorn 1992b; Gibbons 1997; Pickering 1992; White 1992). In many ways the history of radically opposed interpretations on the Guattari cave craniums, which were "icons for Neanderthal mortuary practices" (White & Toth 1991:118)—but whose marks were subsequently attributed to natural disaster and interference by hyenas—is a legacy that still haunts claims of Palaeolithic cannibalism. As Kantner remarks in chapter 4, postdepositional processes of perimortem mutilation as a taphonomic features are susceptible to other explanations or causes. For many, the jury is still out on much of the skeletal evidence.

CONCLUSIONS

Readers will no doubt be struck by the fact that most of the present essays are heavily weighted, as are those in the earlier Tuzin and Brown (1983) volume, in favor of Melanesia. In part this may reflect my own geographic biases. But equally it is also a sign that we regard Papua New Guinea as the locale that marks the tombstone for Arens' denial of cannibalism. It is somewhat ironic, therefore, that Arens had characterized this island as "anthropology's last remaining laboratory of classic primitives" (1979:96), "the 'final frontier' of western cultural contact" (1998:35). It would certainly strain credulity were it not to be acknowledged that many of the early reports display the same predisposition to exoticism already commented upon for other areas. Book titles such as *Unexplored New Guinea: A Record of the Travels, Adventures and Experiences of a Resident Magistrate among the Headhunting Savages and Cannibals of the Unexplored Interior of New Guinea* (Beaver 1920), *Eight Bells: A Tale of the Sea and of the Cannibals of New Guinea* (Nisbet 1889), *Two Years among New Guinea Canni-*

bals (Pratt 1906), or *Where Cannibals Roam* (Taylor 1924) are typical of this period.[9] Equally the early colonial field officers' reports might (less charitably) be taken as representing the "potential limits of contemporary anthropology in New Guinea" (Arens 1979:101)

The following text example from an early Government Patrol report comments on raids between Irumuku and Morere people in the Kikori basin in Gulf province.

The people have been classified as Papuan, and all, except those under control, practise headhunting and cannibalism. . . . Before a house can be occupied or a canoe launched it is the custom to sprinkle the building or boat with human blood . . . the heads of people are slain and collected . . . bodies are cut up, cooked in various ways and eaten. Thus the Government in its work of civilisation is faced at the outset with the formidable task of suppressing a practice of homicide which occupies a fundamental place in the social and religious fabric of the people. . . . In October 1916 the villages of Moreri (Morere) were visited for the first time. The people were living in one large house, which was entered by my party at dawn while the Moreri were eating the bodies of Irumuku natives they had killed. [Chinnery 1920:448–449]

But there is a world of difference between these types of accounts, some of the earliest findings by trained anthropologists in the area—Mundugumor (Mead 1950), Jale (Koch 1970), Asmat (Zegwaard 1968), Fore (Berndt 1962), and Keraki (Williams 1936)—and the now burgeoning ethnographic confirmations of precolonial cannibalism among the Bimin-Kukusmin (Poole 1983), Gimi (Gillison 1983), Hua (Sanday 1986), Mianmin (Morren 1974), Foi (Weiner 1988), Daribi (Wagner 1967), and Stickland-Bosavi peoples such as the Kaluli, Etoro, Bedamini, Samo, Gebusi, Kubor, and Onabasulu (see Knauft 1993, 1999; Strathern 1982; see also Ernst, chapter 7, this volume). This articulation of regional patterns based on linguistic and historical associations between cultures (see Biersack 1995; Goldman & Ballard 1998; Weiner 1988) compel us to appreciate that the case for past cannibalism in parts of Papua New Guinea is no longer an issue for the majority of Melanesian scholars.

Where there is still much work to be done in the research field of anthropophagy is on amplifying how the various perspectives and historical readings of such past behavior are now understood and used by later generations exposed to alternative value frameworks. To give some indication of the modern reception of versions of their own history, I want to conclude by briefly referring to one of the most famous cannibal incidents in Papua New Guinean (PNG) history. On 7 April 1901 James Chalmers (*Tamate*) and his colleague O. Tomkins were supposedly "killed and eaten" (Haddon 1918:180) at Dopima village on Goaribari Island. In the retributive raids that followed, Rev. H. M. Dauncey reports, between 4 and 700 skulls were found in each of the men's houses [*dobu*] destroyed, yielding a total count of some 10,000 skulls burnt in this raid. The present lower Kikori basin population stands at approximately 4,000 people, and there is no oral evidence of raiding by Goaribari people with all of the lower Kikori settlements in precolonial times.[10] This figure, were it to be credible, therefore suggests a precolonial population of immense scale slowly decimated by fighting and cannibalism. The Chalmers' incident has passed into national PNG folklore as part of their understanding of a past engagement with colonialism. Recently, two articles appeared in the PNG daily newspaper *The Post Courier*. The first concerned a remark made by Prince Philip of Britain when awarding a student in Sydney with the Duke of Edinburgh medal for trekking across the Kokoda Trail. He is reported to have said: "You managed not to get eaten, then." Letters of protest appeared in the 23 April (p. 2) and 24 April (p. 4) 1998 editions of the paper, in which it is reported that Prime Minister "Mr Skate . . . was saddened by suggestions that cannibalism is still practiced in PNG." Official apologies were sought from the Crown representative for misrepresentation of Koiari and Popondetta peoples. Two months later, however, the prime minister opened a new school in the Gulf province—in which Goaribari lies—which had been partly funded as an infrastructure project by oil industry representatives. During his speech, Prime Minister Skate sought further commitment to the region from the representative companies by admonishing them in the following manner:

> Don't give wrong signals, if you want to pack up and go, tell me honestly and go. . . .
> I am prepared to take my ancestors' place. I'd rather take my people back to my
> *tumbuna* [ancestral] days where *Tamate* killed a white man and ate him. [*Post
> Courier* 22 May 1998, p. 2]

Though muddling his names somewhat, reference to the Chalmers incident is clearly invoked to signal strength, self-reliance, survival, and ultimately threat to outsiders. It builds on the symbolism of cannibalism and its place within the colonial mind as well history of the colonial encounter. In an important sense Prime Minister Skate is expressing a collective *essai*, or *trial*, as to how the cultural significance of a past practice—so long an icon of outsiders' images of the indigenous peoples—can be reconfigured to make sense of changing circumstances. The historical incident passes through folklore to become a morality tale; this possibility is always open because cannibal myths encapsulate imaginal potentialities whereby the past can be linked to the present.

In much the same way the essayists here are not waiting for some messianic moment that will yield up incontrovertible proof to skeptics. They know that any postmortem on this topic will always and inevitably be a fusion of part science, part autobiography, and part biography. Their discourses on cannibalism are acknowledged as historically inflected and situated; their concern, however, is to *test* their versions of humanity by looking for the present in the past.

NOTES

1. There are innumerable figurative or metaphoric usages parasitic on the ingestive sense of "eat" in most languages. For example, in Huli (Papua New Guinea) the same verb, "eat" [*na*], occurs in constructions that mean "to cover distances rapidly," "to win or beat someone else,"

"to have sexual intercourse," or "to be consumed by pain." As Pickering (chapter 3) notes, it may be that accounts by nonnative speakers frequently confused the literal and metaphorical in relation to cannibalistic confessions.

2. To give but one example, the background music to Rhys-Jones' narrative on Anasazi anthropophagy in the documentary *Cannibals* (1995) is a slow dramatic dirge reminiscent of a Hitchcock horror movie. The sound markers deliver archaeology as entertainment, playing on the widespread associations between death and "exotic" cultures. The film here invokes musical textures long associated with the dramatic portrayal of mystery thrillers.

3. More abhorrent examples can be found in recent Australian newspaper reports on the supposed consumption of Chinese settlers by Australian aborigines, which have been referred to as a "sweet and sour" relationship.

4. I am reminded here of what the Arawak told Columbus about their neighbors, who were "men with one eye . . . who ate men" (Arens 1979:45).

5. See Sahlins (1978) for parallel interpretations of Aztec cannibalism and symbolism.

6. Assessments made by those in allied disciplines are particularly subject to error in this regard. Tim White, commenting on Gajdusek's *Kuru* findings, says, "I believe the disease was contracted through ingestion because the ethnographers who concluded that are familiar with New Guinea and watched this practice taking place" (quoted in Rix 1997). As a test of reliability or veracity this appears suspect. For example, Robert Glasse (one of the ethnographers being referred to) who worked far longer amongst the Huli than the Fore, is known to have made major errors of factual attribution in his Huli ethnography. Imbuing a misplaced concreteness to information that is "just talk," in the sense of popular sayings or adages, is a trap most anthropologists (including myself) would confess to having fallen into at some time.

7. Rumors about the professional conduct of other researchers who have written on cannibalism circulate in academic circles, often similarly casting doubt on the credibility of their field data.

8. Strathern (1982) in talking about Melpa ideology explicitly refers in his note 7 to a corpus of early cannibal tales, which, he suggests, would repay further investigation. Notwithstanding Rumsey's remarks on Ku Waru and Melpa ideas of prehistory (see Rumsey, chapter 5, note 8), there may be belief traditions similar to that described here for the Huli among these Highlands societies which further enlighten us as to why cannibal practices were absent.

9. The popular press continues to project these kinds of images with headlines like "The People Eaters" (McKie 1998). Interestingly, the photographic montage illustrating this particular headline shows only Huli people. Accuracy of representation is here subsidiary to the intent to sensationalize and shock the magazine readers.

10. One point worth making here is that Harris (1979) has talked of the unique scale of Aztec sacrifice based on a count of 136,000 heads. But if the Goaribari report is similarly to be believed, then on a proportional population count Goaribari cannibalism would dwarf that of the Aztecs.

REFERENCES

Aarne, A. (1973). *The Types of the Folktale*. Helsinki: Helsingin Liikek Irjapaino.
Abrams, D. (1977). A developmental analysis of the Trickster from folklore. In P. Stevens (ed.), *Studies in the Anthropology of Play: Papers in Memory of B. Allan Tindall* (pp. 145–154). New York: Leisure Press.
Alvardo, P. de (1963). Two letters of Pedro de Alvardo. In P. de Fuentes (ed.), *The Conquistadors (pp. 182–196)*. New York: The Orion Press.
Anglo M. (1979). *Man Eats Man*. London: Jupiter Books.

Arens, W. (1979). *The Man-Eating Myth. Anthropology and Anthropophagy.* New York: Oxford University Press.

Arens, W. (1995). *Cannibals.* VHS videocasette, Archaeology Series, Sydney, NSW.

Arens, W. (1998). Why man has been left off the menu. *The Australian* (14 Jan.): 35–36.

Askenasy, H. (1994). *Cannibalism: From Sacrifice to Survival.* Amherst, NY: Prometheus.

Bahn, P. (1991). Is cannibalism too much to swallow. *New Scientist* 27: 30–32.

Bahn, P. (1992). Ancestral cannibalism gives us food for thought. *New Scientist* 4: 40–41.

Basso, E. (1988). The Trickster's scattered self. *Anthropological Linguistics* 30 (3): 292–308.

Beaver, W. N. (1920). *Unexplored New Guinea.* London: Seeley, Service.

Beecher, L. (1938). The stories of the Kikuyu. *Africa* 11: 80–87.

Berdan, F. F. (1982). *The Aztecs of Central Mexico.* New York: Holt, Rinehart and Winston.

Berndt, R. M. (1962). *Excess and Restraint.* Chicago, IL: University of Chicago Press.

Bettelheim, B. (1975). *The Uses of Enchantment: The Meaning and Importance of Fairy Tales.* New York: Alfred A. Knopf.

Biersack, A. (1995). *Papuan Borderlands: Huli, Duna and Ipili perspectives on the Papua New Guinea Highlands.* Ann Arbor, MI: Michigan University Press.

Brady, I. (1982). The myth-eating man. Review article. *American Anthropologist* 84: 595–611.

Buckhorn, R. (1992a). Eating at home. *The Australian* (6 Aug.), Letters.

Buckhorn, R. (1992b). Cannibal quarrel. *New Scientist,* 15 (8): 11.

Butterworth, E. (1987). The tales Odysseus told Alkinoos, and an Akkadian Seal. In K. Atchity (ed.), *Critical Essays on Homer* (pp. 181–186). Boston, MA: G. K. Hall.

Carroll, M. (1981). Lévi-Strauss, Freud, and the Trickster: A new perspective upon an old problem. *American Ethnologist,* 8: 301–313.

Celestin, R. (1990). Montaigne and the cannibals: Towards a redefinition of exoticism. *Current Anthropology* 5: 292–313.

Chakravarti, P. (1974). The ogre-killing child: A major theme of Papua New Guinea folklore. *Gigibori* 1 (1): 12–20.

Chinnery, E. (1920). The opening of new territories in Papua New Guinea. *Geographical Journal* 55: 439–459.

Columbus, C. (1968). *The Journal of Christopher Columbus* (trans. Cecil Jane). London: Anthony Blond.

Cortés, H. (1962). *Five Letters 1519–1526* (trans. J. B. Morris). New York: W. W. Norton.

Davies, N. (1981). *Human Sacrifice.* New York: William Morrow & Co.

Diaz del Castillo, B. (1970). *The Discovery and Conquest of Mexico* (trans. Irving A. Leonard). New York: Octagon Books.

Dornstreich, M. D., & Morren, G. E. D. (1974). Does New Guinea cannibalism have nutritional value? *Human Ecology* 2: 1–12.

Douglas, M. (1996). Children consumed and child cannibals: Robertson Smith's attack on the science of mythology. In L. Patton and W. Doniger (eds.), *Myth and Method*. (pp. 29–51). Charlottesville, VA: University Press of Virginia.

Durán, F. D. (1964). *The Aztecs: The History of the Indies of New Spain* (trans. & ed. D. Heyden & F. Horcasitas). New York: Orion Press.

Durán, F. D. (1971). *Book of the Gods and Rites and the Ancient Calendar* (trans. & ed. F. Horcasitas & D. Heyden). Norman, OK: University of Oklahoma Press.

Eliade, M. (1969). *The Quest: History and Meaning in Religion*. Chicago, IL: University of Chicago Press.

Evans-Pritchard, E. (1965). Zande cannibalism. In *The Position of Women in Primitive Societies and Other Essays in Social Anthropology* (pp. 133–164). London: Faber and Faber.

Evans-Pritchard, E. (1967). *The Zande Trickster*. Oxford: Oxford University Press.

Farb, P., & Amelagos, G. (1980). *Consuming Passions: The Anthropology of Eating*. Boston, MA: Houghton Mifflin.

Freud, S. (1913). *Totem and Taboo*. New York: W. W. Norton.

Garn, S. M. (1979). The non-economic nature of eating people. *American Anthropologist* 81 (4): 902–903.

Garn, S. M., & Block, W. D. (1970). The limited nutritional value of cannibalism. *American Anthropologist* 72: 106.

Geertz, C. (1984). Anti anti-relativism. *American Anthropologist* 84: 263–278.

George, K. (1968). The civilized west looks at primitive Africa 1400–1800: A study in ethnocentrism. In A. Montagu (ed.), *The Concept of the Primitive* (pp. 175–193). New York: The Free Press.

Gibbons, A. (1997). Archaeologists rediscover cannibals. *Scientist* 277: 635–637.

Gillison, G. (1983). Cannibalism among women in the eastern highlands of Papua New Guinea. In D. Tuzin & P. Brown (eds.), *The Ethnography of Cannibalism* (pp. 33–50). Washington, DC: Society for Psychological Anthropology.

Glenn, J. (1971). The Polyphemus folktale and Homer's Kyklôpeia. *Transactions and Proceedings of the American Philological Association* 102: 201–208.

Goldman, L. R. (1983). *Talk Never Dies*. London: Tavistock.

Goldman, L. R. (1998a). A Trickster for all seasons: The Huli *Iba Tiri*. In L. Goldman & C. Ballard (eds.), *Fluid Ontologies. Myth, Ritual and Philosophy in the Highlands of Papua New Guinea* (pp. 87–124). Westport, CT: Bergin & Garvey.

Goldman, L. R. (1998b). *Child's Play. Myth, Mimesis and Make-Believe*. Oxford: Berg.

Goldman, L. R., & Ballard, C. (eds.) (1998). *Fluid Ontologies. Myth, Ritual and Philosophy in the Highlands of Papua New Guinea*, Westport, CT: Bergin & Garvey.

Goldman, L. R., Duffield, J., & Ballard, C. (1998). Fire and water: Fluid ontologies in Melanesian myths. In L. Goldman & C. Ballard (eds.), *Fluid Ontologies. Myth, Ritual and Philosophy in the Highlands of Papua New Guinea* (pp. 1–13). Westport, CT: Bergin & Garvey.

Gómara, F. L. de (1964). *Cortés: The Life of the Conqueror by His Secretary* (trans. & ed. L. B. Simpson). Berkeley, CA: University of California Press.

Haddon, A. C. (1918). The Agiba cult of the Kerewa culture. *Man (OS)* 18: 177–183.

Haley, N. (1993). *Altered Texts and Contexts: Narrative, History and Identity among the Duna*. Unpublished Honours Thesis, Macquarie University.

Harner, M. (1977). The ecological basis for Aztec sacrifice. *American Ethnologist* 4: 117–135.

Harris, M. (1977). *Cannibals and Kings*. New York: Random House.

Harris, M. (1979). Cannibals and kings. An exchange. *New York Review of Books* 26 (11): 51–52.

Hogg, G. (1962). *Cannibalism and Human Sacrifice*. London: Pan.

Johnson, N. B. (1993). Cannibals and culture: The anthropology of Michel de Montaigne. *Dialectical Anthropology* 18: 153–176.

Jung, C. G. (1956). On the psychology of the Trickster figure. In P. Radin (ed.), *The Trickster: A Study in American Indian Mythology* (pp. 195–211). London: Routledge & Kegan Paul.

Kalous, M. (1974). *Cannibals and Tongo Players of Sierra Leone*. Auckland: Kegan Paul, Trench, Trubner.

Kidd, J. S. (1988). Scholarly excess and journalistic restraint in the popular treatment of cannibalism. *Social Studies of Science* 18: 749–754.

Kluckhohn, C. (1959). Recurrent themes in myth and mythology. *Daedalus: Journal of the American Academy of Arts and Sciences* 88: 269.

Knauft, B. (1993). *South Coast New Guinea Cultures: History, Comparison, Dialectic* Cambridge: Cambridge University Press.

Knauft, B. (1999). *From Primitive to Postcolonial in Melanesia and Anthropology*. Ann Arbor, MI: University of Michigan Press.

Knox, E. V. (1938). Witches and Whatnot. In J. W. Marriott (ed.), *Modern Essays and Sketches* (pp 170–175). London: Thomas Nelson.

Koch, K.-F. (1970). Cannibalistic revenge in Jale warfare. *Natural History* 79: 41–50.

Lindenbaum, S. (1983). Cannibalism: Symbolic production and consumption. In D. Tuzin & P. Brown (eds.), *The Ethnography of Cannibalism* (pp. 94–105). Washington, DC: Society for Psychological Anthropology.

McKie, R. (1998). The people eaters. *New Scientist* 157: 43–46.

Mead, M. (1950). *Sex and Temperament in Three Primitive Societies*. New York: Mentor Books.

Mondi, R. (1983). The Homeric Cyclopes: Folktale, tradition and theme. *Transactions and Proceedings of the American Philological Association* 113: 17–38.

Montaigne, Michel de. (1958). *Essays* (trans. J. M. Cohen). Harmondsworth, Middlesex: Penguin.

Morren, G. E. B., Jr. (1974). *Settlement Strategies and Hunting in a New Guinea Society*. Ph.D Thesis, Department of Anthropology, Columbia University.

Motz, L. (1982). Giants in folklore and mythology: A new approach. *Folklore* 93 (1): 70–84.

Needham, R. (1978). *Primordial Characters*. Charlottesville, VA: University Press of Virginia.

Nisbet, H. (1889). *Eight Bells: A Tale of the Sea and Cannibals of New Guinea.* London: Ward & Downey.

Ortiz de Montellano, B. R. (1978). Aztec cannibalism: An ecological necessity? *Science* 200: 611–617.

Osborne, L. (1997). Does man eat man? Inside the great cannibalism controversy. *Lingua Franca* (May), 29–38.

Page, D. (1955). *The Homeric Odyssey.* Westport, CT: Greenwood Press.

Patton, L. L., & Doniger, W. (1996). Introduction. In L. Patton & W. Doniger (eds.), *Myth and Method* (pp. 1–26). Charlottesville: University Press of Virginia.

Pickering, M. (1985). *Cannibalism amongst Aborigines? A Critical Review of the Literary Evidence.* Lit.B. Thesis, Australian National University, Canberra.

Pickering, M. (1992). Cannibal quarrel. *New Scientist* (15 Aug.): 11.

Poole, F. J. P. (1983). Cannibals, tricksters and witches: Anthropophagic images among Bimin-Kuskusmin. In D. Tuzin & P. Brown (eds.), *The Ethnography of Cannibalism* (pp. 6–32). Washington, DC: Society for Psychological Anthropology.

Pratt, A. E. (1906). *Two Years Among New Guinea Cannibals.* London: Seeley.

Radin, P. (1956). *The Trickster.* London: Routledge & Kegan Paul.

Ricketts, M. L. (1965). The North American Indian Trickster. *History of Religions* 5: 327–350.

Ripe, C. (1992). A distate for cannibalism. *The Australian* (1–2 Aug.): 12.

Rix, K. (1997). Interview with Tim White. *Salon Magazine* 14: 22–29.

Roheim, G. (1950). *Psychoanalysis and Anthropology: Culture Personality and the Unconscious.* New York: International Universities Press.

Rolls, E. (1992). *Sojourners: The Epic Story of China's Centuries-Old Relationship with Australia.* St. Lucia, QLD: University of Queensland Press.

Sagan, E. (1974). *Cannibalism: Human Aggression and Cultural Form.* New York: Harper & Row.

Sahagón, Fray B. de (1950). *Florentine Codex: General History of the Things of New Spain. Book 1: The Gods* (trans. C. E. Dibble & A. J. O. Anderson). Santa Fe, NM: The School of American Research.

Sahagón, Fray B. de (1951). *Florentine Codex: General History of the Things of New Spain. Book 2: The Ceremonies* (trans. C. E. Dibble & A. J. O. Anderson). Santa Fe, NM: The School of American Research.

Sahagón, Fray B. de (1952). *Florentine Codex: General History of the Things of New Spain. Book 3: The Origin of the Gods* (trans. C. E. Dibble & A. J. O. Anderson). Santa Fe, NM: The School of American Research.

Sahagón, Fray B. de (1953). *Florentine Codex: General History of the Things of New Spain. Book 7: The Sun, Moon, and Stars and the Binding of the Years* (trans. C. E. Dibble & A. J. O. Anderson). Santa Fe, NM: The School of American Research.

Sahagón, Fray B. de (1955). *Florentine Codex: General History of the Things of New Spain. Book 12: The Conquest of Mexico* (trans. C. E. Dibble & A. J. O. Anderson). Santa Fe, NM: The School of American Research.

Sahagón, Fray B. de (1957). *Florentine Codex: General History of the Things of New Spain. Book 4: The Soothsayers; Book 5: The Omens* (trans. C. E. Dibble & A. J. O. Anderson). Santa Fe, NM: The School of American Research.

Sahlins, M. (1978). Culture as protein and profit. *New York Review of Books* 25: 45–53.

Sahlins, M. (1979). Cannibals and kings. An exchange. *New York Review of Books* 26 (11): 52–53.

Sanday, P. (1986). *Divine Hunger: Cannibalism as a Cultural System*. Cambridge: Cambridge University Press.

Sillitoe, P. (1998). *An Introduction to the Anthropology of Melanesia*. Cambridge: Cambridge University Press.

Shankman, P. (1969). *Le roti et le boulli*: Lévi-Strauss' theory of cannibalism. *American Anthropologist* 71 (1): 54–69.

Staden, H. (1928). *Hans Staden: The True Story of His Captivity 1557* (trans. Malcolm Letts). New York: Robert M. McBride.

Strathern, A. (1982). Witchcraft, greed, cannibalism and death. In M. Bloch & J. Perry (eds.), *Death and the Regeneration of Life* (pp. 111–133). Cambridge: Cambridge University Press.

Street, B. (1972). The Trickster theme: Winnebago and Azande. In A. Singer & B. Street (eds.), *Zande Themes* (pp. 82–104). Oxford: Blackwell.

Taylor, M. M. (1924). *Where Cannibals Roam*. London: Geoffrey Bles.

Tuzin, D., & Brown, P. (eds.) (1983). *The Ethnography of Cannibalism*. Washington, DC: Society for Psychological Anthropology.

Wagner, R. (1967). *The Curse of Souw: Principles of Daribi Clan Definition and Alliance*. Chicago, IL: University of Chicago Press.

Wagner, R. (1978). *Lethal Speech*. Ithaca, NY: Cornell University Press.

Weiner, J. (1988). *The Heart of the Pearl Shell: The Mythological Dimension of Foi Sociality*. Berkeley, CA: University of California Press.

White, T. (1992). *Prehistoric Cannibalism at Mancos 5MTUMR-2346*. Princeton, NJ: Princeton University Press.

White, T., & Toth, N. (1991). The question of ritual cannibalism at Grotta Guattari. *Current Anthropology* 32 (2): 118–138.

Widdowson, J. (1971). The Bogeyman: Some preliminary observations of frightening figures. *Folklore* 82: 95–115.

Williams, F. E. (1936). *Papuans of the Trans-Fly*. Oxford: Oxford University Press.

Zegwaard, Rev. G. A. (1968). Headhunting practices of the Asmat of Netherlands New Guinea. In A. P. Vayda (ed.), *Peoples and Cultures of the Pacific* (pp. 421–450). Garden City, NY: Natural History Press.

2

Anthropophagy, Myth, and the Subtle Ways of Ethnocentrism

Don Gardner

INTRODUCTION

In 1868, Mark Twain published his famous short story, "Cannibalism in the Cars," in which the narrator strikes up a conversation with the gentleman sitting opposite him during a train journey. The gentleman, who turns out to be an ex-congressman, recounts the events that occurred on a journey he had taken some years earlier, during which the train had remained stranded in a furious snowstorm for many days, somewhere between St Louis and Chicago. He tells how, after seven days of ever more desperate hunger, the 24 hapless men stranded on the train nominated daily which of them would die "to furnish food" for the remainder of the company. The horror of the story depends in large part on the disengaged manner in which the ex-congressman details the intricate bureaucratic procedures, evidently modeled on those of congressional committees, which resulted in the nomination of the next meal. The effect is compounded by the absence of any account of the actual demise of those "successful candidates" elected by these procedures, while the debates, spirited but polite, that were a prelude to the killings are scrupulously recounted, as are the narrator's subtle gastronomic assessments of the quality of each meal. Indeed, he reports, the refined gourmet later wrote letters of appreciation to the widows of those whose flesh had provided special gustatory delight. A final and valedictory detail the cannibal provides concerns the marriage between one of the survivors and the widow of the man who had provided the first fast-breaking, meal for the company.

The narrator reporting the ex-congressman's extraordinary account tells us that he could not doubt the man's narrative, could not "question a single item in a statement so stamped with the earnestness of truth as his." But when he asks the train's conductor who his fellow traveler was, and learns that he had in fact been stranded for many days but had merely been unhinged by the experience and now frequently travels that route telling others the story of cannibalism in the cars, the narrator tells of his inexpressible relief at learning that he had "only been listening to the harmless vagaries of a madman instead of the genuine experiences of a bloodthirsty cannibal."

The horror that Mark Twain's hero felt at the idea of organized cannibalism is shared—or so I will argue—by William Arens, who published *The Man-Eating Myth* in 1979. Indeed, Arens finds the thought so horrific that he cannot even entertain seriously the possibility that there has ever been a society in which cannibalism was routinely practiced. He concedes that people facing starvation sometimes do, under enormous duress, and with reluctance, consume their fellows, but he regards the idea of anthropophagy as a cultural practice as a product of the mythic imagination. Arens, whose arguments and methods (as Michael Pickering pointed out to me) seem to have been influenced by Evans-Pritchard's careful scrutiny of reports of cannibalism among the Azande (1965), does not exactly rule out such a practice as a matter of principle. On the contrary, he portrays himself as a dispassionate and open-minded analyst: he concludes his study by reminding the reader that he has "consciously avoided suggesting that customary cannibalism in some form does not or has never existed," for he knows that "it is not possible to demonstrate conclusively that a practice does not exist" (1979:180–181). Accordingly, he confines himself to showing that cannibalism is "unobserved and undocumented" (181), and arguing that "the cannibal complex" is more plausibly interpreted as a mythic dimension of cultural worldviews (especially that of the West) than as a conclusion of proper empirical investigation. Arens is, then, the very antithesis of a dogmatist, and nobody can point to statements in which he categorically asserts that organized cannibalism has never existed. Rather, he sets the evidential bar so high, and sets it in accord with such rankly empiricist precepts, that it comes out that we have no good grounds for believing that cannibalism ever was a cultural practice—anywhere, at any time. Attributions of cannibalism are, instead, best seen as an expression of "the thinly disguised prejudices of Western culture about others" (1979:10), or, in his most recent statement, an expression of our desire "to deny the stranger our time, and its prevailing sensibilities" (1998:35).[1]

I propose to discuss Arens's claims about the mythical nature of anthropophagy. His book has been roundly and rightly criticized ever since its publication in 1979; it is an unsatisfactory book—methodologically flawed, dependent upon false oppositions and some pretty scandalous rhetoric, and very unreflective—and probably would not be worth extended discussion, except: (a) as Arens shows, there is ample evidence that, for many peoples, attributions of cannibalism to alien others is an effective instrument of demonization; (b) as it happens, reliable European eyewitness accounts are hard—but not impossible—to come by (although, given the historical circumstances that normally obtain, this may not be surprising); and (c) how a people are characterized ethically is often of considerable political consequence, especially in colonial contexts. For example, Hugh Morgan, the executive director of Western Mining Corporation, has suggested: "that the public should reject Aboriginal claims to sacred sites in the same manner as it has refused to sanction other features of early Aboriginal life such as cannibalism, infanticide and cruel initiation rites" (*The Australian*, 3 May 1984; quoted in Pickering 1985:1). And, more significantly, when Pauline Hanson—the leader of the Australian right's newest (and worryingly successful) movement, the One Nation Party—raised the issue of Aboriginal cannibalism, many of her Aboriginal and non-Aboriginal opponents responded with Arens-like arguments about the lack of evidence, colonialism's demonizing discourses, and so on.[2] Whatever the merits of Arens's case, then, the issue he has raised is of some contemporary relevance.

My strategy is, first, to introduce ethnographic material that addresses the evidential issues (explicitly raised by Arens) and then to pose the ethical questions that his position raises indirectly. Finally, I consider the general question of the epistemological and ethical constraints on cross-cultural characterizations. Having raised and—I hope—dealt with the empirical issue in the context of a particular people of New Guinea, the remainder of the discussion will focus on the ethical context in which the arguments about cannibalism are embedded. The chapter argues that a consideration of Arens' case, its unsoundness and implausibility notwithstanding, throws light on a more general pattern of argument sometimes employed by anthropologists and other specialists and on its ethical presuppositions.

MIANMIN CANNIBALISM

The ethnographic material I present concerns the Mianmin, one of the Mountain Ok peoples of central New Guinea, whom I first visited in 1975. They make a good case study for my purposes, since they have had a reputation for outstanding "savagery" ever since Europeans first encountered them. This reputation, though, was partly produced by the intercourse between Europeans and the Mianmin's neighbors, which took place before any direct contact between these newcomers and the Mianmin (hence the name given to them by the colonial administration). The lurid and gruesome picture painted of the Mianmin by their neighbors might not have become entrenched but for the fact that the first official European patrol into the area—the celebrated Hagen-Sepik patrol of 1938—was attacked by the Mianmin, who took it to be a raiding party of their enemies (Gammage 1998). With this event, the negative picture of the Mianmin was assured wider currency through the official and unofficial channels of European communication.

Nevertheless, that the Mianmin have a reputation for relentless savagery among their neighbors seems clear. Numerous patrol reports state how fearful this or that neighboring group is of the Mianmin who raid and terrorize them. One patrol officer estimated that 138 people, in a population of about 1,000, had been killed or captured by Mianmin over an 11-year period. Ethnographers reinforce these reports. Poole, for example, states that the Bimin-Kuskusmin, who themselves practice ritual cannibalism, say that the Mianmin, whom they regard with fear and horror, pursue "the search for human flesh as an end in itself . . . [and see] humans . . . as food in the ordinary [nonritual] sense . . . comparable to pigs and marsupials" (1983:7). Similar views are held among other neighboring groups—Telefolmin, Atbalmin, Owininga, and Abau.

Not long after I had begun fieldwork among the western Mianmin, a friend kindly sent me a prepublication copy of Frederick Barth's (1975) *Religion and Knowledge among the Baktaman of New Guinea*, which also concerns one of the Mountain Ok peoples. Barth discusses Baktaman cannibalism, which occurs after the successful slaying of enemies, in both secular feasts and certain ritual contexts. Barth notes that "cannibalism is an escalation of the war against the enemy, and is done in anger and lust for revenge" (1975:152). He also remarks on "an apparent callousness in these practices, and in the way informants speak about them" (1975:152). Barth finds it relevant that some people reported that they were unable to eat human flesh and vomited when they tried it. And although he gives some graphic descriptions of raids and the slayings and cannibalism that these entailed, he goes to some lengths to suggest that the Baktaman were not really enthusiastic cannibals (153–154). Rather, the subjectively felt humane impulses he believed he had detected lacked the "cultural codification" that could help the Baktaman articulate these attitudes or formulate them into moral imperatives; in the absence of such codification "men are easily moved and can act in a mood of dominant, unrestrained anger" (154).

By the time I received Barth's book, I had collected several accounts of Mianmin raids on both the Atbalmin, another Mountain Ok group on the western side of the Sepik River, and the Abau-speaking Upper Sepik people who lived north of the western Mianmin. In all of these accounts, the details of the number of deaths and the number of bodies carried back for consumption loomed large. I was intrigued, therefore, to pursue the implications of Barth's treatment of Baktaman cannibalism, and I questioned my informants about their ideas and feelings concerning the consumption of the others. Uniformly, the men I questioned said that they had no qualms whatsoever about eating dead Atbalmins or Abaus. They asked me why on earth they should leave "good meat" lying around if, at great risk, they had gone to the trouble of traveling considerable distances in order to kill their enemies. "It is not as though they were our friends or relatives," a man told me, "No, the Atbalmins were our game."[3]

Such statements are, of course, unlikely to cut much ice with Arens, so I shall concentrate on a specific event, which can be presented from several different points of view. First, I will reproduce the relevant section of an official 1959 report written by the patrol officer who led the investigation of a Mianmin raid on a lowland people known as the Owininga that resulted in a number of deaths.

Some time in January 1959 a large group of Mianmin men raided the small Owininga settlement of Suwana . . . near May River Patrol Post. Three Suwana men: Apomiga, Kogoreniga and Wabuo; as well as one adult female, Lausabo, were killed; and the Suwana women Bibabaisabo, Pamsibu, Orowi, Eigabei, Sunagei and Yalei were abducted. These women were taken back to the Mianmin area. Later Eigabei escaped from the Mianmin and came to the May River Patrol Post [to report what had happened]. Another woman, Sunagei, was murdered at Mianmin while trying to escape.

The Mianmin raiding party consisted of 17 men from the Usage [River] settlement and several men from the Itema river area. The Usage men were Kikekaua, Bogugsep, Damo, Atoningo, Nagosuo, Ttitmaua, Bigigwidabo, Kalamaua, Tofu, Fafato, Didepmonabo, Kwini, Walantuwo, Kalaliwena, Nagarame, and Kapma. The number of Itema men involved and their names are difficult to ascertain. It would appear that the Itema men only played a minor part in the raid except Kasikaua and Orisak. These two men played a major part in the attack.

The Usage group involved in the raid live in a small settlement of three houses known as Aiyuliavip. This settlement is 5 hours and 20 minutes walk up the Usage River, which a right bank tributary of the May River. The Itema River is also a right bank tributary of the May River and is about 10 miles upstream from the junction of the Usage and May Rivers. Neither the Usage nor Itema groups have been visited by patrols in their villages, but Messrs. Aisbett and Fenton passed through the area in 1958 and people from both groups visited patrol camps. There were also people from this area involved in the Atbalmin massacre in 1956.[4] Some Mianmins are serving prison sentences in Wewak as a result of A.D.O. Neville's patrols subsequent to the massacre.

The raiding party assembled at the junction of the Usage and May river and slept the night there. The following morning they built several rafts . . . and commenced drifting down the May river. They slept for two nights en route and arrived at [the settlement known as] Aimi on the third day. Aimi is a small Burumai [Tunap Iwam] settlement on the left bank of the May River about one mile upstream from the main Burumai village. They stayed that night at Aimi with Namoi, a "big man" from Aimi. On the fifth day the raiding party crossed the May River with a group of six Burumai men as guides, and set out to locate the Suwana settlement. The raiding party stopped some distance from an old Suwana settlement while the Burumai men went ahead to locate the Suwana group. The scouts returned in the late afternoon, announced that they had found the new Suwana settlement, and spent the night with the main body of the Mianmin party in the bush.

At dawn the following day a large number of the Mianmin raiding party surrounded the Sowana settlement and hid in the bush. The settlement consisted of one large communal house divided into sections for individual families. The Mianmins were accompanied by Maye, an adult female originally from Suwana, who had been abducted during a previous Mianmin raid and had married Nagarame of Usage. Maye [entered the cleared the area in front of the house first and] called out to her half-brother Sowasa to come outside. Sowasa came out of the house with three men

Apomiga, Wabuo and Kogoreniga; two women, Orowi and Bibabaisabo: Olowi's daughter, Pamsibu, [also came out]. The other Sowana women remained in the house. Maye immediately went to her brother and held him by the wrists, pulling him to the edge of the village clearing, apparently to prevent him being killed.

A Mianmin man whose name cannot be ascertained then held Apomiga and Bogugsep of Usage hit him twice with a tomahawk: once on the head and once again in the neck. Apomiga fell down dead. Wabuo and Kogoren attempted to run away but they were completely surrounded and were shot with arrows. Kwini of Usage shot Kogoreniga in the side with a bamboo pointed arrow and he fell dead. Kalamaua shot Wabuo in the side with another bamboo pointed arrow and when he fell another Mianmin, Kalaliwena, shot a second arrow into him.

The raiding party then commenced cutting up the bodies with bamboo knives, and some men went into a house and dragged the women outside. The women they pulled outside Sunagei, Lausabo, Eigabei, and Yalei. This made a total of seven women in all as Orowi, Bibaisabo and Pamsibu were already outside. The Mianmin then decided amongst themselves who would take which woman. . . .

The Mianmin left the heads and entrails of the victims and carried the rest of the bodies away to be eaten. The party set out for Mianmin with [Sowasa,] the seven abducted women, and the bodies of their victims. One woman, Lausaba, was a cripple and had difficulty keeping up with the rest of the party. Therefore, she was killed by Kaitap and Yumap and parts of her body taken to be eaten late. Lausabo was killed on the track near the Bigu Canal which runs into the May River. The Mianmin party continued up the right bank of the May River and passed a group of Burumai men in two dugout canoes near the Neiyeipi Lake. These Burumai men were Naiu, Umbo, Sunaiyo, Namau, Naiti, Naganau, Masio and Widinigi. [The raiders] did not speak to the Burumai group and continued on and made camp on a ridge on the right bank of the May River. That night they ate the livers and other small portions of their victims.

The following evening the raiding party arrived at the Usage settlement of Aiyuliavip. The remains of the bodies were cooked with taro and eaten.

After two nights [months?] at the Usage settlement, Eibagei, the woman whom Kalimau had claimed as his share of the spoils, escaped and made her way to May River Patrol Post. Sunagei, the woman whom Kasikaua had taken, was later killed at Usage and eaten. (It is difficult to ascertain the time). At the time Sunagei was murdered a group of Mianmins were living in some caves in the side of a hill on the northern side of the Usage Valley. Titamau, the leader of the Usage group, was mourning the death of his child. In his sorrow he decided to kill Sunagei. He told some other Mianmin men of his decision and the group went to the river where Sunagei was working. Titimau fired a bamboo pointed arrow into Sunagei's side and Atoning, Walantuwo, Fafato and Bogugsep also shot arrows into Sunagei's body. The body was later cut up and eaten. [Mater 1959:8–9]

On 16 May 1960, 16 Mianmin men were put on trial for this raid. They all pleaded guilty and were sentenced to death for murder—a sentence that was later commuted to a term of imprisonment. The account given in the patrol report was later revised somewhat; in particular, it became evident that Eigabei, the woman who escaped to May River Patrol Post to raise the alarm, had actually spent two months with the Mianmin and only left after the husband who took her captive had died. The judge, in his account of the trial, reports that Eigabei would have been happy to stay with the man who had captured her had he not died. "She told me that if the captor husband had survived she would not have wanted to escape or be rescued and sent home. She said to me 'What would be the use of my going back to my people—I have no man there?'" Maye, the Owininga woman who had been captured earlier on and who was involved in the raid—she had lured her brother from the house and drawn him out of harm's way—also told the judge that she was quite content to remain with the people who had captured her, regarding herself as one of them.

The judge was clearly fascinated by the raiders ("who are well known as being amongst the fiercest and wildest natives in the Territory"). As a result of their experience, they had:

acquired a very good understanding of applied psychology. Apparently they have to rely on raids of this kind to obtain wives for their young men, and that the killing, cutting up and eating of the women's husbands appears to be accepted by the women as something inevitable and final, so that they simply accept the position and generally make no attempt to escape. The cannibalism involved was not merely ritualistic and was not made the occasion of any very obvious form of celebration. On the other hand, it was evidently not solely a matter of obtaining a supply of fresh meat. [Mann 1960]

The Suwana raid concerns eastern Mianmin people, of whom I met only a few in my earlier periods of my fieldwork among Mianmin of the Aki River area. In 1994 and 1995, however, I spent several weeks in the community concerned in these reports.[5] Most of the young men who took part in the raid, and a good proportion of the older men who organized it, are still alive, and I was able to confirm, and indeed amplify, the main events contained in the reports of the patrol officers and the judge. During that same period, I also worked briefly among Owininga people, where I spoke to Sowasa, the only man to have survived the raid. His account also agreed with the report, but he was also able to explain the presence of the Iwam men who accompanied the Mianmin, and why the heads of the victims were not carried back to Usage.

Other raids in Mianmin history can be triangulated between different accounts in the same way as the Sowana raid can. Furthermore, evidence of raids like that made against Suwana is provided by the number of captives still alive today. In a 1995 survey that covered some 1,300 individuals (about 95% of the East Mianmin population), 3.5% of marriages involved captured women. When Morren conducted his first field trip in the mid-1960s, however, 14% of the extant marriages among the powerful Kimeilten group involved captives, while 11% of all Kimeilten were born of a captured woman (1974:122–125). An estimated 15% of one western Miyan group's living members are either of Atbalmin birth or are the children of an Atbalmin captive. On the other side, among the Owininga, just one of the small interfluvial lowlands groups the Mianmin had raided (comprising today just 333 individuals), I collected genealogies that recorded a total of 600 deaths. Of these, 85 were reported to have been killed by raiders, 67 at the hands of the Mianmin, who invariably carried away the bodies of the slain. In addition, at least nine captured Owininga women were still living in Miyan communities.

The Miyan informants I questioned after reading Barth's book did have reservations, ranging from mild disapproval to something approaching disgust, at the idea of eating somebody one had known, even though they acknowledged that men who had become extremely angry did consume and not merely kill those who had angered them. Later, I gathered accounts of conflicts in which this sort of thing did occur. One concerned Imefoob, a man who lived in the village where I was working; it recounted how Krikiyendre, the leader of Imefoob's own group, who with numerous accomplices had slain Imefoob's mother's brother son and consumed the boy's body, then induced Imefoob to eat his cross-cousin's penis. (Krikiyendre was enraged by the dead boy's father, his wife's brother, who had intimated that the leader had had a hand in the death of his wife. Imefoob cut rather a sad figure: physically frail, childless, and a frequent victim of small unkindnesses; his childless wife had the wickedest tongue in the village and exercised it most frequently on her husband. His relatives explained his predicament by reference to his inadvertent consumption of a maternal kinsman's organ of procreation.) Consider another example, related to me by several living witnesses to the events:

In the mid-1950s, group of nine Kari people, returning to their settlement at the head of the Tabo River, after a feast at a Usali community, stopped in an abandoned garden to rest and consume some of the food that they had been given by their hosts. A sudden strong gust of wind blew down a gigantic tree, which had been ring-barked in the course of gardening; it fell upon the assembled party, killing three people instantly and crushing the leg of the man who had led the group. That man, Sifun, later died of his injuries. There were many repercussions from this event, including a raid by the kin of the dead upon the settlement of the group that had invited him to the feast. (These raids, which were customary, often resulted in injuries, albeit of a minor kind, and only came to an end when the offending group had offered some compensation.) However, Sifun's wife had been captured as a child on a raid on the Atbalmins, and spirit mediums as well as others in the community formed the idea that the freak accident had in some way been precipitated by the Atbalmins or their spirits. One of the dead was a boy called Dokonab. His mother's brother, Betenab, upon hearing of the accident and the current opinion assigning responsibility for the accident to Atbalmins, took up his bow and arrows and shot the young girl, Nakgon, through the chest at short range. This girl had been adopted by Betenab and his wife many years before, when, as a very young child, she was brought back from a raid on the Atbalmins. In short, then, the girl was his daughter, and she was not far from being of marriageable age. Betenab's anger was such that he butchered and cooked the girl, then shared her flesh with the rest of the village.

Finally, I will turn to Hereba, a preeminent man who lived in a house opposite mine throughout my first period of fieldwork, in the village of Iboliofib. I knew Hereba very well—or thought I did. He had spent a great deal of time in my house during my first field trip, and I in his (he was a fount of knowledge about the most northerly Mianmin, who differed considerably from those in higher altitudes to the south of Iboliofib). Some months into my second field trip, Hereba was suffering from chronic toothache. One night, during a casual conversation with some young men, including Hereba's younger brother, I asked what steps Hereba might have taken to cure his toothache if Western analgesics had not been available. They named some plants that were found to be of some help and described some other techniques that might be used; then one of them remarked that Hereba's toothache was not an ordinary ailment, but the result of his having eaten relatives and co-residents.[6] That night I took notes on 12 killings that Hereba had committed during the 25 years that he had been an adult. All of them were people he knew, most of them intimately (including his allegedly adulterous second wife and the husband of the woman who became his third wife), and of these he had cooked and eaten five. (To my astonishment, one of the victims had been the younger brother of another very important man of Iboliofib, whose house was no more than five meters from Hereba's.) Later, Hereba and I discussed these events in a casual sort of way. He confirmed that the accounts were true and also agreed with the diagnosis of his current problems.

It is relevant to note, in a chapter such as this, that it would be possible to continue giving examples of gruesome cannibalistic events (as well as to give gorier accounts of those already presented). I could also describe, for example, the way Mianmin treat wild birds and mammals, and compound thereby the impression, which the foregoing accounts will probably have inclined readers to form, that the Mianmin are—or were—a cruel people. Like many anthropologists, though, I have reservations about providing information that might rationalize such inferences. Indeed, I was beset by a mixture of sadness and anger when an old friend, with whom I had cooperated on two projects among the Mianmin, recently published a popular account of his adventures in New Guinea that was larded with regrettably sensational and exoticizing accounts of their lives (Flannery 1998). For a little while, at least, I found myself wishing that Arens had managed to show that all such characterizations were mythic fantasies. But, *pace* Arens, the Mianmin case, as well as much other ethnographic and historical material, indicates that this is a forlorn hope. The ambivalence that anthropologists often feel in such contexts is relevant to the discussion below.

As it is, it seems that the material presented here is hard to account for except on the assumption—which Occam's razor would also dictate—that Mianmin did in fact raid their neighbors, capture women and children, and slay, carry off, and consume men and recalcitrant or unwanted women.

It would also be possible to present mythic and ritual material showing that the practice of cannibalism does not stand alone in Miyan life and thought but articulates with many profound aspects of their take on the world. That exo-cannibalism is associated with reproductive practices should not be surprising, given that it frequently occurred in conjuction with the abduction of women and children. Equally, it would also be possible to present material on Miyan attitudes and values concerning domesticated animals, and other humanly produced valu-ables, that bespeak their place in densely textured affective and conceptual fields that sit ill with a notion that humans—as a category—are ontologically, ethically, and emotionally separated from other beings. A variant of this notion is implicit in Arens's perspective.

Such materials would tend to support Sahlins's argument (1983), made in a wonderful conspectus of the Fijian material, that cannibalistic practices and mythic contexts are indissolubly linked (they presuppose one another). While this is true of particular historical settings, and is in any case a general tenet of the Lévi-Straussian perspective Sahlins adopts, some caution is necessary in charac-terizing the link. On the one hand, there are peoples among whom crucial social practices are mythically associated with cannibalism but yet who do not practice it—for example, the Duna (Modjeska 1983:106) and, of course, Christians. On the other hand, I can only think of question-begging reasons why it should be inconceivable that a people might practice cannibalism yet assign it no special mythic significance. In any case, having presented what I take to be sufficient evidence for concluding that the Mianmin practiced cannibalism, my principal goal now is to interrogate the ethical context of Arens's position; and if there is an issue about the ethical characterization of a practice, which I will suggest *is* a significant part of what underpins Arens's case, it cannot be made to disappear by any amount of material on myth, ritual, or cosmology, even though, of course, it would be relevant to questions of mitigation. Accordingly, I will leave the Mianmin data and turn to the question of Arens' characterizations of cannibal-ism. I propose to tackle directly his claims about the unreality of cannibalism and, more importantly, the underlying ethical characterization that his position pre-supposes.

ARENS'S ARGUMENT AND ITS RAMIFICATIONS

I have already alluded to the rhetoric of disinterestedness that Arens frequently uses when characterizing his own position. Yet a closer inspection of the way he interrogates reports of cannibalism and deals with the anthropological material (especially that from New Guinea) belies this rhetoric.[7] What measured reading of the anthropological literature, for example, could lead one to conclude that "almost every anthropologist considers it a sacred duty to report that the people studied and lived among were in the past or until just recently eaters of their own kind" (1979:10)? What disinterested and informed reader of the New Guinea ethnographic corpus could agree that in "our own era . . . it is scarcely possible to pick up a book on New Guinea without finding a series of references to cannibalism in the index" (97)? The plain fact is that there are numerous New Guinea ethnographies that do not attribute cannibalism to the people with whom they deal—a fact that Arens should find embarrassing, given his own diagnosis concerning the origin and motivation of "the cannibal complex," which may explain why it goes unmentioned.

Another methodological problem concerns his treatment of informants's statements and the use of them made by anthropologists. Thus, while he accepts anthropological reports of informants's denials of the suggestion that they practiced cannibalism as evidence that they were not (142–143), he omits to mention the numerous anthropological reports of informants who do state that they had practiced it, which, by parity of argument, should be taken, other things being equal, as evidence that they had.

It would be tedious to continue arguing over specifics and, if I am correct in the case I am about to pursue, redundant as well. So let us turn to the general position.

First, though, let us acknowledge that someone—say, a philosopher like Russell—could find cannibalism (construed literally as the ingestion of human flesh) relatively innocuous in comparison to the act of cold-bloodedly killing someone and yet find it necessary to debunk hearsay reports that it occurred among a particular people precisely on the grounds (which all acknowledge) that many people are inclined to see cannibalism as both fascinating and horrible and therefore an apt way of expressing their negative view of that people. This, perhaps, is how Arens thinks of himself and is probably how most people would see their inclinations to debunk reports of witches' covens. A consideration of Arens's polemic, though, suggests a different picture, or so I hold.

We can begin by observing the oddity of a position that purports to combat our deepest tendencies to ethnocentrism and yet makes authenticated Western eyewitness accounts the yardstick of evidential adequacy in cross-cultural enquiries. It is as though Arens had carefully sifted reports of cannibalism not just to scotch the unacceptable precept "no smoke without fire," but to establish the proposition that "there are only ever smokescreens." What would lead him to set the evidential bar so unreasonably high?

The answer becomes apparent, I suggest, if we note a clear—if unstated— counterfactual running through his book—one that implies that Westerners' demonization of cannibals would have been appropriate, or had at least some justification, had they in fact indulged in a practice "repugnant to us" (22). In other words, had anthropophagy been an actual, rather than mythical, practice, then Queen Isabella of Spain might have had some grounds for decreeing that Spaniards could legally enslave American Indians who practiced cannibalism, or Pope Innocent IV for promulgating a doctrine that defined cannibalism as a sin meriting punishment by Christians through force of arms (Conklin 1997:68).

Arens, like Hugh Morgan, seems unable to conceive of circumstances wherein one could acknowledge that cannibalism was institutionalized among a people and yet refrain from adopting an attitude of censure toward them. On the other hand, though, Arens is wedded to liberal anthropological precepts that require respect—if not something stronger—for other cultures. The cognitive dissonance engendered by these two irreconcilable attitudes is resolved, in Arens's case, by denying that cannibalism has ever been routinely practiced.

Arens seems to share the initial view of Joseph Banks, who found it hard to "debase human nature" by admitting that reports that Maoris relished human flesh might be true (quoted in Barber 1992:256). (So much, one might observe, for the omnipresent *ethno*centrism of the Western world-view.) Banks, as a careful sifter of evidence and despite his reluctance to accept circumstantial evidence of cannibalism (which he shared with Cook, and the astronomer William Wales), eventually accepted that Maoris practiced cannibalism (Barber 1992). Arens, however, finds himself unable to accept any such thing.

If we ponder the tension here, it becomes obvious that it depends upon a suppressed premise: to wit, that—as Arens phrases it—"our time, and its prevailing sensibilities," provide the appropriate benchmark for according respect to other cultures. Yet it seems clear that anthropology's place among the humanities rests on its capacity to raise questions precisely about prevailing sensibilities. By putting the widespread abhorrence of cannibalism beyond the bounds of ethical consideration, by refusing to interrogate our reactions to the phenomenon, Arens has painted himself into a corner that almost all regard as untenable. Yet, as I will presently suggest, the usefulness of considering the difficulties of Arens's position is not exhausted by showing (yet again) the dangers of uncritical ethnocentrism. For Arens's professional sensibilities are widely shared amongst anthropologists, even if many of them do not endorse his arguments about cannibalism. Rather than endorse Arens's denial of the reality of cannibalism in the face of most Westerners' negative reaction to it, most anthropologists' disciplinary habits tend to lead them to seek to contextualize it, to show that it is "'symbolic' even when it is real" (Sahlins 1983:88), or otherwise show that it needs to be understood as "meaningful." I also share this disposition and regard as appropriate a colleague's suggestion that I would have strengthened my inclination to reject a negative ethical characterization of the Mianmin by, exactly, providing the broader cultural context of their anthropophagy that I set aside above. Yet my concern in this chapter, aside from providing evidence that the practice did occur among the Mianmin, is precisely with the broad ethical context of the discipline. The remainder of this chapter is, therefore, concerned with the possibility that this contextualizing move, too, can be sustained by ethical orientations uncomfortably close to those characteristic of people who would condemn cannibalism out of hand. This occurs, I shall suggest, when a euphemizing impulse leads to what I dub a sylleptical redescription, rather than a proper contextualization, of practices.

OF SYLLEPSIS AND EUPHEMISM

In this section I set out four possible responses that any person might have after experiencing a spontaneous and ethically charged reaction to a practice such as cannibalism: (a) a reflexive response involving deliberation about the reaction and its aptness; (b) a response, based on varying degrees of reflection, that ends with an endorsement of the attitude evinced in the reaction; (c) what I will call a euphemizing response; and (d) a response that involves the denial of the phenomenon provoking the reactive attitude. My aim is to set out a framework within which it is possible to locate Arens's position on cannibalism and those of other anthropologists, as well as those of persons without any particular professional or political commitments. I shall argue that only the first response can ground a discipline like anthropology, while the last three share crucial negative ethical orientations and, consequently, embody subtly ethnocentric attitudes. I shall also suggest that some established anthropological approaches (some of the time, anyway) represent a species of the third—ultimately ethnocentric—approach rather than the first, appearances notwithstanding.

It seems that every person has reactive attitudes: things strike one as amusing, charming, revolting, disgusting, distasteful, frightening, puzzling, and so on. These reactive attitudes are central to much of ordinary life, from self-perception to interpersonal relations, and the appreciation of jokes or art. While such reactive attitudes manifest intentionality, in the sense of being about something under a specific description, neither their onset nor their expression is, usually, a process present to consciousness.[8] Nevertheless, reactive attitudes—especially negative ones associated with blame and positive ones associated with admiration—are central to ethical practices.[9] In relation to matters at hand, it is crucial that we recognize that circumstances, actions, persons, and so on that evoke negative reactive attitudes are a central part of what constitutes the realm of the ethical. The Umeda of New Guinea who recoiled in horror and disgust when Alfred Gell (1979) sucked the blood flowing from his cut finger expressed ethically relevant reactive attitudes no less than did the medieval Christians revolted by tales of cannibalism.

If one thinks about the reactions a person might have to an account—a detailed one, let us say—of an act of cannibalism, there seem to be several possibilities. One might react with such revulsion that one seeks to block it out of one's thought and memory—although, given our historical interest in the practice, we would probably be surprised at someone who reacted thus. (We would be less surprised, however, if someone were to respond in this way after witnessing such an act.) At the other extreme, someone might, conceivably, react hardly at all, expressing nothing but indifference to the account. (We should, I suppose, find it much harder to imagine what degree of world-weariness might lead someone who witnessed such an act to respond in this way.) Between these extremes fall those who do react and then ethically deliberate upon their reaction and on the act itself. It is with this middle range of responses that I am concerned.

If, without deliberation, you condemn or censure a person for some action, it seems straightforward that you have a negative reactive attitude to it.[10] Yet the reaction and subsequent ethical deliberation need not pull in the same direction. Reflection afterwards, perhaps on one's response and values as much as the action, can, in principle, lead one to modify one's reactions (or, perhaps more realistically, to want to do so), or it might only serve to reinforce the initial negative response by assimilating it to general ethical patterns or to explicit precepts. Of course, people's reactive attitudes are occasionally so strong that they cannot even bring themselves to reflect upon the offending actions, but I will leave such individuals aside for the time being and focus only on those who are inclined to deliberate about their reactions and the actions that provoke them. For my purposes, then, there are two possible responses to deliberation on the expression of a negative reactive attitude: one that leads to reflection on the attitude itself (a reflexive response) and one that endorses that reaction through the censure of the state of affairs that evoked it (a confirming response). The reflexive response has an elective affinity with attempts to flesh out an understanding of the context of the ethically questionable practice that might explain or excuse it. Indeed, a reflexive response might be engendered precisely because an act calls forth peculiarly strong negative reactive attitudes. (It goes without saying, I hope, that these distinctions are intended as argumentative idealizations and not descriptions of psychological processes: if deliberation takes place at all, it is almost certain that reflection on the attitude will occur, if only momentarily.)

So far, we have noted the reflexive and the confirming responses to practices that provoke negative reactive attitudes: but they are not—at first glance, anyway—the only ones possible. Someone might strive, in the face of their own or other's reactive attitudes, to reinterpret the practice (*X*, say) as some other practice (*Y*) that does not tend to provoke a negative attitude and so to short-circuit the reaction that does, *prima facie*, raise the question of our attitude to the practice. A familiar paradigm here is the everyday euphemization of bodily functions ("Joyce is in the bathroom" vs. "Joyce is crapping"). By contrast, anthropology has been highly successful in contextualizing and redescribing practices that do or might evoke negative reactive attitudes without euphemizing them. Even simply learning that such an action is an instance of a general cultural practice is relevant to subsequent reflection, even if it is not always decisive. Whatever else we might think of, say, genital mutilation, learning of its cultural significance is subversive—I take it—of an inclination to see a particular instance of it as an act of *wanton* cruelty. (Hereafter I will stick to actions that do instantiate institutionalized cultural practices, since it is these forms that are at issue).

The proper cultural contextualization of a practice can sometimes actually achieve what the euphemizing redescription only mimics through a collusive decision to agree that it has succeeded. Thus, for example, a woman marries in exchange for valuables, and an observer is inclined to speak of her as having been "sold," a description very likely to evoke negative reactive responses among Westerners, whereupon an ethnographer points to the cycle of reproductive gift exchanges of which the marriage is part and underscores the decisive dissimilarities between standard purchases and the bridewealth transaction. But anthropologists' contextualizing redescriptions do not always reconfigure ethical issues by preempting negative reactive responses in this way. Consider, for example, a cultural ecological explanation of cannibalism: even the most convincing demonstration that human flesh makes a decisive contribution to protein intake (Dornstreich & Morren 1974) cannot, of itself, address the concerns of those whose reactive attitudes the practice engages (any more than showing the economic importance of narcotics trafficking will allay the reactions of those who object to it). Indeed, part of the perennial fascination of such topics as cannibalism is just the difficulty of providing accounts that might subvert the phenomenological starkness of people's negative reactive attitudes to them.

Anthropologists who would repudiate Arens's arguments (and, *a fortiori,* those of people ready to straightforwardly condemn cannibalism) sometimes write, especially for fellow professionals, as though they thought that contextualizing an ethically questionable practice, by showing it to be meaningfully embedded in its cultural milieux, or—in an earlier phase—to be socially functional, is tantamount to resolving the ethical issue: as though showing, for example, that an act is not an instance of wanton cruelty sufficed to show that it was not an act of cruelty at all. From the point of view of those who recognize that ethical questions are raised by acts like cannibalism (almost everyone, including seasoned anthropologists—even if most have a professionally practiced blind eye), such a maneuver will seem question-begging, or the outright avoidance of the central ethical issue. So far, I have argued that Arens, in denying the existence of cannibalism, evinces values close to those held by unselfconsciously ethnocentric souls who condemn the practice. I have also drawn a distinction between euphemizing and proper contextualizing redescriptions of practices, which may or may not neutralize negative reactive attitudes. I want to suggest now that there is sometimes a kinship between those who would demonize and those who would contextualize ethically questionable practices. For although most anthropologists would see their contextualizing interests as the heart of the discipline's antiethnocentric, reflexive posture, contextualization can take the form of a euphemization of practices, which tendency is encouraged by anthropology's abiding concern with cultural wholes meaningfully or functionally integrated. Of course, anthropology is as keen to contextualize or thickly describe all practices, from food production to death rituals, not just those that raise ethical concerns. However, euphemization, like Arens's foolhardy denial of the reality of cannibalism, is a particularly attractive strategy when the ethical issues are pressing.[11]

So far we have noted a variety of postdeliberative responses to negative reactive attitudes occasioned by practices: (a) reflexive; (b) confirming (of the attitude evinced); (c) euphemizing; and (d) denying (the reality of the phenomenon provoking the reactive attitude). The cultural contextualization of such practices may be a crucial dimension of the reflexive response and vice versa, but, as I have also suggested, such contextualization may be inflected by the urge to euphemize a practice.

All these responses, it is important to point out, are equally related to the brute facticity of negative reactive attitudes: all (implicitly or explicitly) acknowledge that, *prima facie* and relative to the historically developed set of social mores, certain practices provoke negative reactive attitudes. If we consider the third, euphemizing, response, however, it can seem that those attracted to it, like those with Arensish commitments to the fourth, share with those inclined to condemn the act the conviction that the negative reactive attitude does indeed provide grounds for evaluating X negatively; that is why such a person is motivated to redescribe X as Y. In this respect, the confirming, the denying and euphemizing, responses contrast with the first, which assumes that it is possible for someone to have a negative reactive attitude toward the practice X and yet regard it as an open question what should be made of it ethically. The first copes with the question, raised *prima facie* by the negative reactive attitude to X, by bracketing the response and, typically, seeking cultural–historical circumstances that makes X-ing reasonable (in the narrow sense of that term: as being done for reasons, as opposed to being done for what reflection would necessarily endorse as good reasons). One reason why responses other than the reflexive are unsatisfactory is that whatever their tactical appeal, they are not very successful as strategies, or so I shall presently try to argue. Another, related, reason is that they are insufficiently radical and cannot effectively ground a fundamentally critical discipline like anthropology. In fact, I think even this way of putting it is too weak. I want to suggest that anthropology is not a discipline that can guide our ethical deliberations by providing evidence, or otherwise addressing them—as it were—from the outside; rather it is, or should be, part of those ethical deliberations.

If we compare Arens and Evans-Pritchard on cannibalism (1965: Chap. 6), the difference between earlier and more recent anthropology becomes apparent. Evans-Pritchard had fewer qualms about Zande cannibalism than does Arens. This is not just because he sifted the evidence more carefully and without preconceptions one way or the other, but because he could take for granted an experience-distant, functionalist perspective that facilitated ethical disengagement. The implicit move here—if the polemic be allowed—is something like the following: don't ask about the ethical characteristics of a practice, for they will only involve difficult issues; ask instead about its function [or its cultural meaning], and if you do that often enough, and set up some shibboleths about relativism, you won't even notice that there are ethical issues. In short, it is a euphemizing move, this time in the characteristic anthropological guise of re-descriptions of practices that amount to a form of the trope known as "syllepsis" (or "zeugma"): a man performs a complex ceremonial procedure involving impassioned pleas to his father's father for garden fertility; perplexed, a person asks what the man is doing, whereupon the anthropologist proffers, in explanation, the observation that he is performing a garden fertility ritual and an act augmenting the solidarity of the descent group. (Compare: "At the meeting this morning John managed to get on the steering committee and everybody's nerves.") In short, the anthropologist's description, like the trope, plays fast and loose with the vital conceptual boundary between what is and what is not properly attributed to the act as intentional behavior.[12]

Nothing, perhaps, promises to get the anthropologist off the ethical hook with such ease as the sylleptical formulations of holism (whether of the structural–functionalist or the culturalist variety). It was feminism, as much as anything else, that made this move become less and less respectable over the last few decades. And yet the impulse still thematizes anthropology; we see echoes of it, I believe, in resistance theory and in aspects of Marilyn Strathern's rich and multidimensional writings (1988). Syllepsis is still the first resort of those attracted to a euphemizing anthropology. The motivation for this, I have suggested, is an ethical characterization of alien practices that goes beyond reactive attitudes to converge with those who would censure or condemn them. I have been arguing that we must face up to these reactive attitudes and the responses that people think they entrain, mostly because we have little choice: there seems no possibility—short of radical dehumanization—of blocking reactive attitudes. What we can do, however, is to try to subvert the link between these negative reactive attitudes and any further, stronger ethical characterization.

If the reader will indulge me, I would like to give just one more example in an effort to make my position clearer. This time it concerns a cognitive rather than an ethical reactive attitude, yet it exemplifies my arguments quite well. Consider a low-level descriptive statement such as "the Nuer say of [human] twins that they are birds." Such a statement can and does evoke reactive attitudes: the embedded statement, baldly made, expresses an odd belief, which is why anyone, including anthropologists, deem it worthy of consideration. Those so inclined might go on to suggest that the Nuer are therefore daft, cognitively impaired, typical Africans or what have you. Anthropologists, rightly appalled by such judgments, have sometimes sought to euphemize such statements by suggesting that they do not express beliefs, and so are not up for cognitive assessment; rather, they are to be read as symbols of this or that aspect of social structure, human experience, or what have you. (I hasten to add that I am not suggesting that there is no link between such statements and these other features of life: I am only claiming that they should not be linked to them *as opposed to* expressing beliefs.) Today more complex, possibly less coherent visions underpin the idea that statements and actions are primarily symbolic, but the chronic ambiguity of the term still suits those who yield to the euphemizing impulse, fearing, it seems, that negative reactive attitudes not only produce, but warrant, inclinations to censure or condemn practitioners. I am suggesting that to euphemize a practice is to backhandedly support precisely those straightforwardly ethnocentric judgments that appalled us. I do not wish to argue that the euphemizers necessarily or always actively endorse censuring moves of the ethnocentric. The mistake here, I think, stems from the forlorn hope that, on such topics as anthropophagy, anthropologists might be able to avoid giving ammunition to politicians and others appealing to certain fears and anxieties in the population: to—let us call them— the "baddies." (And it *is* a mistake: when, for example, did racist demagogues ever base their responses and arguments on evidence?) To try to stop giving the baddies material that they take to be ammunition, simply because they *do* take it to be ammunition, is misguided. The baddies are wrong to think ethnographic material is ammunition, except perhaps for a public relations campaign. (I would agree, in passing, that such campaigns do require a response. However, the response should be a matter of tactics rather than of principle.) Worst of all, though, is that in trying to repackage such material in order to stymie the bad guys, we imply that they were correct to take it as ammunition. So, if we seek to deny or euphemize the cannibalistic practices of a people because we are anxious about the leverage a proper contextualizing description is imagined to provide those seeking to stigmatize that people, we implicitly endorse the view that such people are indeed rightly stigmatized on such patently ethnocentric grounds.

I said earlier that it is possible for someone to have a negative reactive attitude toward a practice and yet forbear to condemn it. This, I said, seems to be the position of someone intent on understanding or excusing the practitioner. Such an intention may seem to betoken a paternalistic or condescending attitude: alternatively, though, one could see it as a necessary condition of a properly microhistorical understanding. Resistance might also be felt to the reflexive move on the grounds that it would entail excusing the inexcusable—what we might call the John Major response.[13] Here, I would counter with the suggestion that nothing is necessarily inexcusable in the absence of all the ethically relevant information.

So, even after we have tidied up the factual errors and other misconceptions that undergird particular inappropriate reactive attitudes, we still face genuine questions about many practices. Reactive attitudes and broader ethical issues concerning what people are up to and why are unavoidable, arising as they do in the course of life as we work prereflectively in the world: they are—to use Heidegger's phrase—"ready to hand." And if, subsequently, our answers to the questions raised by reactive attitudes themselves raise questions, so that the practices of reflecting upon and responding to these attitudes become issues for us—become what Heidegger called "present at hand"—we have no option but to tackle them, and in so doing raise questions about our initial reactive attitudes. But nothing here makes it possible to ignore those attitudes, and nothing here need motivate us to try to do so. It is only, I suggest, when we want to block the unreflective entrainments of our reactive attitudes, yet feel reluctant to put them in question, that we will resort to denials or euphemisms. If this seems to be "a plea for excuses"—albeit of a very different sort from the one made by Austin—

then we shall have to live with that. But, it seems to me, we can console ourselves for the unwelcome connotations of such a characterization with the thought that this position is as near as we can get in a general intellectual orientation to the stark challenge of those who would respond to our reactive attitudes with "so what?"[14] Unlike the standard moves I discussed earlier, this one has the advantage of making ethical sense of those who take terms—like "nigger," or "queer"—that have been used against them and make them their own; they become radical activists, attacking reactive attitudes at their source, rather than miracle-workers.

Perhaps another way of stating all this is simply to take seriously the notion that anthropology is one of the *geisteswissenschaften*—the moral disciplines. Simply put, the characteristic modality of such disciplines is not only the study of their objects, but an ethically relevant engagement with them. Indeed, "characteristic" is too lame, for it suggests the possibility of a contingent association, whereas engagement is constitutive of such disciplines (Rorty 1982: Chap. 11). So anthropology is not just a response to questions that arise in an ethical realm beyond its boundaries, but is itself an ethical response to ethical questions, and disengagement is only ever a contrivance. What appeals about the move to excuse practices that—in the nature of things—engage reactive attitudes is that it enjoins us to become reflective about our attitudes, to question the role they ought to have in guiding our behavior, and even to seek a context of understanding that might diminish the strength of those reactions.

CONCLUSION

Some four centuries ago, Montaigne considered a wide range of ethical questions, including those posed by cannibalism. His essay "Of Cannibalism" contains a passage that has often been quoted by anthropologists defending relativism (for instance, Geertz 1984:264): "each man calls barbarism whatever is not his own practice; for indeed it seems we have no other test of truth and reason than the example and pattern of the opinions and customs of the country we live in" (Montaigne 1965:152). Yet, in order to extract a relativist moral from this passage, one would need to add something like "and what seems to be the case, is the case, and we therefore cannot but use the example and pattern of opinion and customs of the country in which we live." Montaigne, though, continues this passage with an ironical suggestion that our country, of course, always contains "the perfect religion, the perfect government . . . " and so on. He then goes on to contest an understanding commonly held to follow from our reactive attitudes that would characterize cannibals as wild or savage. His case, though, is quite different from one that might be made by a modern relativist: in his ceaseless search for intellectual balance (what the Greek Sceptics he admired so much called "equipollence")—a point that will enable us to avoid making everything slide to one side or the other—he goes on to say (with a stress on the first person):

I am not sorry that we notice the barbarous horror of [these cannibalistic] acts, but I am heartily sorry that, judging their faults rightly, we should be so blind to our own. I think there is more barbarity in eating a man alive than in eating him dead; and in tearing by tortures and the rack a body still full of feeling, in roasting a man bit by bit, in having him bitten and mangled by dogs and swine. . . , than in roasting and eating him after he is dead. [155]

Montaigne, less weighed down than twentieth-century thinkers by the notion that ethical exploration should result in a moral judgment, was freer to compare and contrast without the impress of a need to reach a definitive verdict. Were we to follow his lead—as, in effect, I have tried to suggest we should—we might come to reflect on our horror of cannibalism without denying or euphemizing what it involves, in the context, for instance, of our general unconcern at our (Western medicine's) consumption of the blood and organs of the world's poor—but without denying that this traffic, too, needs to be understood.

NOTES

1. In part, Arens's recent reiteration of his position seems to be his response to the legal difficulties of Dr. Daniel Gajdusek, whose work on *kuru* was the most celebrated hurdle facing the original thesis. (For a comprehensive and measured account of the investigation of this disease, see Nelson 1996.)

2. For example, Charles Perkins declared the suggestion that Aboriginal people had practiced cannibalism to be "dangerous and untrue" (*The Australian*, 23 April 1997), while Professor Henry Reynolds, a leading scholar of postinvasion Aboriginal history, denounced such claims as without evidence and "*profoundly insulting* to Aboriginal people" (*The Sydney Morning Herald*, 22 April 1997: emphasis added). My point here is not to suggest that the claims about Aboriginal cannibalism made in Pauline Hanson's extraordinary book are defensible (for they clearly are not), but only to underline the way some of her opponents responded to the "charge" of Aboriginal anthropophagy (see Pickering 1985, and chapter 3, this volume, for a careful and specific enquiry into this question).

3. Bercovitch, who has since worked among the Atbalmin, reports that they say exactly the same about the Mianmin (1989:341). Interestingly, Bercovitch also found that the participants in the raid that produced human flesh were the least likely to consume it: more generally, he reports, "the main consumers of human meat were women and children" (1989:340).

4. The Mianmin mounted two raids in 1956, which, together, resulted in the deaths of twenty Atbalmins—four from the first raid and sixteen from the second. Both were in retaliation for the slaying of four Mianmin men who had sought to establish friendly relations with their former enemies after government patrols had declared that all raiding was at an end. The Mianmin mounted the second raid after a patrol from Telefolmin sent to investigate the first round of killings had shown some leniency to both sides in view of the equality in numbers killed on each side and the relatively recent contact they had had with the colonial administration. Their determination *not* to accept numerical equality, their ruthless disregard for the edicts of the authorities, and the scale of the second raid once again propelled the Mianmin into the spotlight in the guise of wanton killers and cannibals.

5. The different groups referred to in the report, along with some others, have now settled together at the Hotmin Airstrip, on the Usage–May junction.

6. Sahlins reports that Fijians also held that endocannibalism caused dental problems in Fiji (1983:78).

7. Actually, something less than a close inspection of the way Arens constructs his case is sufficient to raise doubts about how disinterestedly he has made it: can anthropologists unpersuaded by Arens's arguments aptly be likened to "a convention of UFO buffs [asked to accept] that there are no aliens visiting us" (1998)?

8. The qualification is necessary because, for example, one sometimes frowns *in order to* express disapproval. Nevertheless, it seems clear that one can only do this because, in the right circumstances, frowns spontaneously express disapproval.

9. I do not intend, as will shortly become clear, to suggest that blame or admiration are only matters of reactive attitudes. One can conclude, after a process of deliberation, perhaps involving detailed analysis, that an action or practice is blameworthy or admirable. In the context of crosscultural evaluations, however, it seems that it is the reactive attitudes that loom largest, for familiar Bourdieuian reasons.

10. Famously, of course, Durkheim gave such attitudes analytical pride of place in his discussion of the *conscience collective* (1949).

11. For those wary of abstractions, let me try to me try to exemplify the point I am making (although the example does not concern anthropophagy). At a conference I attended several years ago, the question of what to make of eighteenth- and nineteenth-century Polynesian women who had sexual intercourse with European sailors became something of an issue. It was strenuously—and largely successfully—argued by several conferees that although these liaisons were an aspect of the women's interests in valuables of various sorts, it was improper to describe them as prostituting themselves, since such a transaction is only properly described as occurring in commodity regimes, whereas the women in question were acting within a gift regime. It seemed clear that the argument was not simply about finding the semantically appropriate verb, but about the aptness of stigmatizing Polynesian women by describing them as indulging in prostitution. Leaving aside the other issues that might arise from the debate, my main reservation concerned where this argument left prostitutes in Harlem, Soho, or King's Cross. The implication seemed to be that they *could* be stigmatized for having sex with men in exchange for valuables. A more radical anthropology would question the very idea of stigmatizing someone—anyone at all—by merely suggesting that they exchanged sex for valuables. (That characterizing these Polynesian women as "having sex with Europeans" is often a description thin to the point of distortion, in that they were seeking *mana* rather than, or in addition to, sensuous pleasures, does not alter the effect of the point I am trying to make.) By implicitly accepting that a prostitute is *ipso facto* ethically impugned, and seeking to euphemize the activities of Polynesian women to avoid this, the conferees, it seemed to me, were endorsing, rather than merely taking note of, the "prevailing sensibilities" of our times. Moreover, they did so by relying on a traditional anthropological move, one that conceives of cultures as integrated wholes within which any general practice or value has its rationale. Whatever the theoretical and methodological merits of such a perspective, when it is invoked in relation to genuine ethical concerns, it amounts to a sort of plural Panglossianism.

12. One way to think of this suggestion is as an alternative formulation of the critique of objectivism made by Bourdieu (e.g., 1977).

13. When he was the British prime minister, John Major once stated that "we should condemn more and understand less" (quoted in Irvine Welsh 1996:x).

14. Once, in London, I witnessed an angry and abusive young man respond to an authority figure who was attempting to morally disarm him by observing that he evidently thought it "clever to swear" with the dialogue-stopping, "Yeah! So fucking what?"

REFERENCES

Arens, W. (1979). *The Man-Eating Myth.* New York: Oxford University Press.

Arens, W. (1998). Why man has been left off the menu. *The Australian* (14 Jan.).

Barber, I. (1992). Archaeology, ethnography, and the record of Maori cannibalism before 1815: A critical review. *The Journal of the Polynesian Society* 101: 241–292.

Barth, F. (1975). *Religion and Knowledge among the Baktaman of New Guinea.* New Haven, CT: Yale University Press.

Bercovitch, E. (1989). *Disclosure and Concealment: A Study of Secrecy among the Nalumin People of Papua New Guinea.* Ph.D. Thesis, Department of Anthropology, Stanford University.

Bourdieu, P. (1977). *Outline of a Theory of Practice.* Cambridge: Cambridge University Press.

Conklin, B. A. (1997). Consuming images: Representation of cannibalism on the Amazonian frontier. *Anthropological Quarterly* 70: 68–78.

Dornstreich, M., & Morren, G. E. B., Jr. (1974). Does New Guinea cannibalism have nutritional value? *Human Ecology* 2: 1–12.

Durkheim, E. (1949). *The Division of Labour in Society* (trans. G. Simpson). Glencoe, IL: The Free Press.

Evans-Pritchard, E. E. (1965). *The Position of Women in Primitive Societies and Other Essays in Social Anthropology.* London: Faber and Faber.

Flannery, T. (1998). *Throwim Way Leg.* Melbourne: Text Publishing.

Gammage, W. (1998). *The Sky Travellers.* Melbourne: Melbourne University Press.

Geertz, C. (1984). Anti anti-relativism. *American Anthropologist* 84: 263–278.

Gell, A. (1979). Reflections on a cut finger: Taboo in the Umeda conception of the self. In R. H. Hook (ed.), *Fantasy and Symbol.* London: Academic Press.

Mann, A. H. (1960). *Extract from a report by His Honour, The Chief Justice of the Supreme Court of the Territory of Papua New Guinea, Mr Justice A. H. Mann.* Issued at Wewak, TPNG, 16 May 1960.

Mater, J. H. (1959). *Ambunti Patrol Report No. 13, 1959/60.*

Modjeska, N. (1983). Production and inequality: Perspectives from central New Guinea. In A. Strathern (ed.), *Inequality in New Guinea Highlands Societies.* Cambridge: Cambridge University Press.

Montaigne, M. (1965). *The Complete Essays of Montaigne* (trans. Donald M. Frame). Stanford: Stanford University Press.

Morren, G. E. B., Jr. (1974). *Settlement Strategies and Hunting in a New Guinea Society.* Ph.D thesis. Dept. of Anthropology, Columbia University.

Nelson, H. (1996). Kuru: The pursuit of the prize and the cure. *Journal of Pacific History* 31: 178–201.

Pickering, M. P. (1985). *Cannibalism amongst Aborigines.* Lit.B. Thesis, Australian National University, Canberra.

Poole, F. J. P. (1983). Cannibals, tricksters and witches: Anthropophagic images among Bimin-Kuskusmin. In D. Tuzin & P. Brown (eds.), *The Ethnography of Cannibalism.* Washington, DC: Society for Psychological Anthropology.

Rorty, R. (1982). *The Consequences of Pragmatism.* Brighton, Sussex: Harvester Press.

Sahlins, M. (1983). Raw women, cooked men, and other "great things" of the Fiji Islands. In D. Tuzin & P. Brown (eds.), *The Ethnography of Cannibalism*. Washington, DC: Society for Psychological Anthropology.

Strathern, M. (1988). *The Gender of the Gift*. Berkeley, CA: University of California Press.

Twain, Mark (1985). *Mark Twain's Short Stories*. New York: Signet Classics.

Welsh, I. (1996). *The Marabou Stork Nightmares*. London: Vintage.

3

Consuming Doubts:
What Some People Ate?
Or What Some People Swallowed?

Michael Pickering

INTRODUCTION

Few countries have such a preoccupation with the eating habits of its indigenous peoples as does Australia. "Bush tucker" is all the rage, with articles, books, and restaurants serving up the latest indigenous dishes. Perhaps it should come as no surprise, then, that Australia continues its 200-year love affair with the notion of Aboriginal cannibalism. Unlike other indigenous culinary phenomena, however, this particular dish may be unfit for popular consumption.

So what is cannibalism? This question could be debated for some time, with the direction of debate strongly influenced by the complexity of the definitions of cannibalism applied. We could, for example, identify and debate distinctions between ritualized cannibalism and gustatory cannibalism; we would touch on auto-cannibalism and survival cannibalism, debate blood transfusions and heart transplants, and agree to disagree on Christian transubstantiation. For the purpose of this study, cannibalism is defined in its popular context, as the eating of human flesh. Further refinement is, however, essential given the nature of contemporary applications of the term. Modern popular usage usually sees the term applied as a term of abuse, not of individuals, but of entire societies. Historically, the argument has been that cannibalism was a cultural trait of Australian indigenous societies. The claim of popular history, therefore, is that Aboriginal cannibalism was institutionalized; that it was a tradition and custom of Australian Aboriginal societies.

I argue here that there is no reliable evidence to support the claim that Australian Aboriginal societies engaged in institutionalized cannibalism. This is evident through the critical examination of the most popular and available literary sources—those that colored, and color, public opinion, and those that are most relied upon by contemporary commentators and researchers. I describe the poor quality of early reports, the paucity of evidence, the lack of consistency between descriptions, and the contextual questions that underlie the most graphic descriptions. I then consider why such accounts should prove so popular to writers and readers alike.

PREVIOUS RESEARCH

My interests in the question of Aboriginal cannibalism developed when I was a young and naive anthropology postgraduate. I shared the popular belief that it had indeed been a common practice in the past; after all, all the past greats of Australian anthropology said so. I intended to choose a nice example, one full of detail, and analyze it for its ritual, symbolic, or even economic content. To do this, of course, I needed a good example. It was not long before I realized I could not find one. I was asked to believe in Aboriginal cannibalism on faith rather than on argument. This led me to start questioning whether the phenomenon really existed. When I approached a supervisor with this observation, I was advised, first, not to do any research on topics associated with Aboriginal violence; second, not to worry about assessing the evidence but rather, to look at why people did it as a prelude to looking at the symbolism of cannibalism. Even before starting my research in earnest it was, therefore, clear that prominent anthropologists were already convinced of the reality of institutionalized Aboriginal cannibalism. As a hard-core empiricist I was of the opinion that, in any study, it is essential that the quality of the evidence be considered. Any theoretical developments based on invalid evidence are useless.

Previous research into cannibalism can be classified according to approaches. These are not mutually exclusive. First, there are popular works, characterized by sensational and often lurid anecdotes (e.g., Anglo 1979; Hanson 1996; Hogg 1962); second, there are the "social evolutionary" studies, which see cannibalism as a cultural trait reflecting a stage of humanity's moral and social development (e.g., Hanson 1996; Helmuth 1973; Tannahill 1975); third, there are the cultural materialist arguments, which discuss cannibalism as an economic nutritional phenomenon (Dornstreich & Morren 1974; Farb & Amelagos 1980; Harris 1977); fourth, there are the psychological analyses, which consider the motivation factors for cannibalism (Askenasy 1994; Davies 1981; Freud 1913, 1950; Helmuth 1973; Levi-Strauss 1966; Sagan 1974; Tannahill 1975); fifth, there are the symbolic interpretations, which are concerned with beliefs associated with cannibalism and the symbolic and ritual means through which these beliefs are expressed (Gillison 1983; Lindenbaum 1983; Kilgour 1990; MacCormack 1983; Poole 1983; Sahlins 1983; Sanday 1988; Tuzin 1983); finally, there are the historic/critical writings, which emphasize the careful examination of sources as a necessary preliminary to any further examination (Arens 1979; Evans-Pritchard

1960). It is a characteristic of the first five approaches that the source data are rarely subject to critical analysis prior to analyses. All of the approaches provide insights into the study of cannibalism and associated phenomena, but research has certainly suffered through the unqualified use of inappropriate "evidence." It is only the historic/critical approach that has procedurally addressed the accuracy and reliability of sources.

While there are numerous popular and academic accounts alleging Aboriginal cannibalism, there have been very few research-oriented investigations into the phenomenon. Those studies that have been attempted usually make a token concession to the potential unreliability of historic sources, acknowledging bias, misinterpretation, lies, and so on but then usually continuing to treat their particular examples as reliable and irrefutable facts (e.g., Bridges 1971; Brockwell 1977; Heap 1967; Hobhouse, Wheeler, & Ginsberg 1915 [1965]:242–243; Howitt 1904; Meehan 1971). The fundamental premise in these studies is that *their* sources are accurate.

The critical assessment of information on Aboriginal cannibalism has not, however, been totally neglected. One characteristic of all studies of cannibalism (including this one) is that they rely on sources where cannibalism is described rather than on those accounts where cannibalism is not reported or is even specifically denied. This is particularly evident where the account is in response to questionnaires, a common means of collecting data during the nineteenth and early twentieth centuries (Curr 1886; Howitt 1904; Smyth 1876; Taplin 1879). Such questionnaires were sent out to pastoralists, police, missionaries, and so on. A typical example is that of Curr (1886:194), who explicitly asked:

35. Are your blacks cannibals? Please mention the grounds of your opinion or belief in this subject.
36. If they are cannibals, to what extent; and what are their practices with respect to cannibalism?
37. Please state any facts you know on the subject.

Despite such leading questions, examination of the responses shows that the majority of respondents either denied that the Aborigines were cannibals or failed to respond to this question (Bates papers in National Library; Curr 1886; Howitt papers in Museum Victoria). One notable example is Constance Petrie, who, despite believing in Aboriginal cannibalism, nonetheless criticized several popular writers acknowledged as contemporary "experts" on things Aboriginal. About Lang (1861), who argued that human sacrifice was a practice, Petrie (1904:19) commented, "There is no truth in this statement: it is just hearsay . . ." stating elsewhere that it was ". . . another case showing the mischief which is done by casual visitors putting into circulation sensational accounts of savage customs" (correspondence in Howitt papers Box 2, Folder 2, Paper 6). About claims by

Smyth (1876), Lang (1861), and Curr (1886) of the deliberate killing of people for food, she stated:

> I think the writers you quote are all mistaken and have just gone on "hearsay". R. Brough Smyth gives no proof—he has very likely just heard things said, and the same with Dr. Lang. Then E. M. Curr may have taken things up wrongly. Hearing of the flesh hunger he doubtless jumped to conclusions. [Petrie, letter to Howitt 23–11–1902, Box 2, Folder 2, Paper 6]

Naturally, such explicit and implicit denials rarely rate a reference or consideration in the procannibalism literature.

Recent research in which the evidence for Aboriginal cannibalism has been critically addressed includes Shankman (1969), Loos (1978), Anderson and Mitchell (1981), Buckhorn (1994), Howie-Willis (1994), and Pickering (1985, 1995a, 1995b). Pickering (1985) critically assessed the literature on Aboriginal cannibalism, examining 440 accounts of cannibalism contained in 298 published and unpublished sources. My conclusions were that there was very little evidence that institutionalized cannibalism was a characteristic of any Australian Aboriginal society. Despite the 14 years that have elapsed between the initial study and this chapter, and my continued informal research into Aboriginal cannibalism in literature and field study, I have yet to meet with an Australian example, either literary or oral, that does not have a parallel considered in Pickering (1985).

READING CANNIBALISM:
UNSOURCED AND SECONDHAND ACCOUNTS

The majority of literary accounts of cannibalism were characterized by being unsourced and largely unsubstantiated. These accounts provided little or no evidence to support their allegations of Aboriginal cannibalism. Sometimes they were simple affirmations, sometimes they were graphic. Most important, however, is the fact that they failed to state whether the writer had actually observed the act or derived the information from a second- or thirdhand source. While unsourced accounts cannot immediately be dismissed as fabrications, equally they cannot be accepted at face value as accurate descriptions of a situation. The next-most-common accounts are those based on secondhand sources, either published or verbal. These range from accounts that refer to unsourced and unsubstantiated accounts to those in which the original commentator was claimed to be a witness.

Most of the literary accounts (e.g., 72% according to Pickering 1985) were probably derived from unsourced and secondhand sources—an important consideration when a popular misconception today is that the frequency of references in the literature indicates the reality and frequency of cannibalism. The problem with such accounts is, of course, that one original account was often multiplied and modified by repetitive telling, greatly exaggerating the alleged frequency of the act. Incautious repetition and misquotation similarly led to fictions, misinterpretations, further misquotations, errors, and abuse quickly becoming established and accepted as facts. A good example of this can be found where Sturt (1833:222–223) recounts hearing of an act of cannibalism of an infant. Sturt's account is cited by Mackenzie (1852:117), who states that Sturt had seen the act. Mackenzie's account, in turn, is cited by Strachan (1870), who has the perpetrator "greedily devouring" the infant. The same Mackenzie (1852:127), providing a secondhand account of an event allegedly observed by a "respectable man named Morrice," is later cited by Andrews (1920:33) as being the observer of the event.

It may be argued that, in suggesting that unsourced and secondhand accounts should be considered inadmissible as evidence, many are being harshly criticized for their literary style, leaving out that information which is now considered important but, at the time of writing, was seen as unimportant. It is possible that some of these accounts do have their basis in observations of real behavior, though not necessarily of cannibalism. Similarly, however, there can be no doubt that the majority of the accounts were based on hearsay and on popularized, fabricated, exaggerated, and misinterpreted evidence. If any of the unsourced and secondhand accounts were ever based on real acts of cannibalism rather than on manufactured mythologies of reporters, these events have certainly become exaggerated in their frequency through repeated telling and the subsequent acceptance of each retelling as a specific event. As a result, unsourced and secondhand accounts must be dismissed as primary evidence for or against the reality of cannibalism.

READING CANNIBALISM: FIRSTHAND ACCOUNTS

It is only with alleged firsthand accounts that anthropology can really begin to come to grips with some of the phenomena associated with accounts of cannibalism. These accounts throw light on what may be latent in unsourced and secondhand sources. For analytical purposes, firsthand accounts are considered to be those based on alleged personal experiences of the author or of the author's Aboriginal informants.

Aboriginal Informants

Accounts by Aboriginal informants are the most common form of firsthand report. These consist of Aboriginal people referring either to others actions to which they were witnesses, or to their own actions. There is no reason to doubt that most colonial recorders of these accounts provided close-to-literal reproductions of what they were told. There is, however, reason to suspect that the relationships between what was said, what was meant, and what actually happened, were considerably different. There was certainly usually more to the interpretation of Aboriginal accounts than was appreciated by European reporters.

Accounts of members of one group accusing members of another group as being cannibals may not reflect experiential reality. Accusing alien people—those outside the immediate social universe of the informant—of cannibalism is the most commonly encountered account. (This is not a phenomenon exclusive to Aboriginal people.) Keppel (1853 [2]:155), for example, wrote: "One of the tribes, distant from Port Essington about sixty miles, is said to be composed of very bad men, cannibals; they are very much afraid of them." Helms (1893:282) similarly wrote that his informant "asserts that his tribe never practiced cannibalism. . . . But he tells me that the Bardocks up to quite recent times indulged in this terrible practice," while Dahl (1926:93) recounts: "I very often asked the blacks if they practiced the eating of human flesh. They answered almost invariably that they did not do it themselves but the neighboring tribes did it." Bates (e.g., 1928, 1932) drew most of her evidence for cannibalism from the accusations of one group toward another, usually in unconventional meetings at missions or ration stations. Meggitt (1962:36) describes Warlpiri distrust of distant neighbors in that ". . . most Warlpiri are convinced that these people, in their own countries, make a practice of killing strangers and eating their kidney fat." Ancillary to this are accusations by people who, while not aliens, are outside a restricted social class—for example, children or youths (e.g., uninitiated males) reporting on the habits of elders, or men reporting on the secret habits of women, and vice versa. Thus informants recount their experiences as children where they observed or were informed of the alleged private cannibal habits of their elders. When they are adults, however, cannibalism is no longer practiced (e.g., Bates 1911, 1928, 1947). Similarly, old men told tales of an epidemic of infanticide and cannibalism practiced by women (Bates 1930).

The belief that outsiders are cannibals appears to be an unconscious but effective mechanism for maintaining self-identity, social superiority, and "humanness" at the cost of the identity, social status, and "humanness" of aliens. What is particularly notable about such accounts is that they are *always* derogatory, the Aboriginal informants seeing the presumed cannibalistic habits of aliens as "wrong" behavior. As Shankman (1969:59) observed: ". . . cannibalism is one of the nastiest things that can be said about others. People who are feared and distrusted are sometimes ascribed a general syndrome of disgusting behavior of which cannibalism is a part." Most anthropological studies of cannibalism have come up with variations on this theme (e.g., Arens 1979; Evans-Pritchard 1960; MacCormack 1983; Pickering 1985; Poole 1983; Tuzin 1983; Tuzin & Brown 1983).

There are also accounts by people who admit to participation in the act or admit to it being a practice of their direct forebears. Such accounts cannot be dismissed as fabrications, but neither can they be unquestioningly accepted as reflecting experiential reality. Acceptance of these accounts is complicated by phenomena characteristic of Aboriginal societies—in particular, the significance of cannibalism in myth (compounded by the interpretation by Europeans of myth as history), belief in the reality of cannibalism through metaphysical experience (dreams, trance, etc.), and the use of metaphors. Mythological ancestors were perceived as being the direct ancestors of informants. Thus the actions of those ancestors were perceived as real events. These ancestors were often cannibals, their actions described in graphic accounts (see, e.g., Beveridge 1889; Hiatt 1975:13–14; Howitt 1904; Massola 1968:92–102; Roheim 1974:70–73; Spencer & Gillen 1927:309, 335–336; Tonkinson 1978:108, 110). Informants thus provided statements along the lines of "We don't do it now, but we used to." This interpretation of myth as history by informants is compounded by European reporters similarly interpreting myth as being rooted in historical events outside living memory (Hiatt 1975:13–14; Spencer & Gillen 1899:475, 1927:365–366), effectively transubstantiating the symbolic into the material.

Statements of historic cannibalism were usually seen by reporters as evidence of how European intrusion had brought about cessation of the practice (Salvado 1851, 1977:84), rather than of references to the imputed actions of sacred "ancestors." It is again notable, however, that in such tales the cannibalism is ultimately considered inappropriate, wrong, or maladaptive behavior, and the guilty ancestors are described as ultimately having suffered for the deed.

Aboriginal perceptions of concurrent metaphysical worlds—the worlds of dreams, trances, and spirits—must be acknowledged. Experiences whilst dreaming or in trance states were seen as real events involving the spirit of a person (Berndt & Berndt 1977:304–331; Tonkinson 1978:111). Thus sorcerers traveled "out of body" to extract and consume the kidney fat of a victim. "Victims" dreamed that they had been cannibalized by sorcerers. Evil spirits were cannibals, waiting to prey on the living. These were—and still are—very real experiences to Aboriginal people and were recounted as such. Metaphor was also an important element in Aboriginal communications, with the variety of common metaphors including some that could be confused by an inexperienced recorder as evidence of cannibalism. Roheim (1974:245), for example, noted that central desert groups used the metaphor "have you eaten" to mean "have you had sex," with girls being described as "unripe" or "cooked" as a measure of their sexual availability. Tonkinson (1978:74) describes an action during initiation in which the young boy, having swallowed his own foreskin, is told that ". . . he has eaten his own boy. . . ." Rose (1984:194–195), writing of the Victoria River district of northern Australia, describes a ceremony called ". . . 'cooking the baby' which is performed from one to three times for newborn infants, both male and female . . ." in which the baby is rubbed with a slurry of ant bed and water. This contributes toward the bestowal of rights to a child's mother's country. Rose describes people asserting ties to their mothers and mothers' mothers' country by referring to themselves as "cooked" in that country. The 1983 transcript of the Murranji Land Claim in the Northern Territory independently records one claimant, in describing this ceremony, as saying, "Get that baby, cook him" (Aboriginal Land Commissioner 1983:75–76). In this metaphoric frame of reference, one in which the context of the metaphor is made clear, certain historical "admissions" could be interpreted as describing activities altogether different from cannibalism. For example, Dahl (1926:93) wrote, in connection with eliciting information about cannibalism:

Once when this question was asked they looked sniggering at one of my younger men—the scamp Jingo—hinting that he had some experience in this field. Jingo then reluctantly, but at the same time with a certain pride, admitted that he had been one of a group that had eaten a fat woman.

There is, therefore, clear evidence of the tendency to confuse metaphoric allusion with literal description. This was aggravated when informants were speaking to reporters in Aboriginal English—the language of most communications between informants and early European reporters. The problem is not exclusive to cannibalism and sex. Most contemporary "Australianist" anthropologists will note field experiences with such concepts as the distinction between "kill 'im," meaning to hit or wound, and "kill 'im dead," meaning to kill (e.g., Layton 1995:216).

While some authors may have had basic proficiency in the language of the groups they were describing, there is little evidence that they were as proficient in the identification of the different systems of meaning, metaphor, and allegory inherent in Aboriginal language. Figurative statements, both in "language" and in Aboriginal English, were taken literally. Questions and answers were misunderstood by both sides, aggravating the confusion.

A largely ignored, but key, consideration in the assessment of Aboriginal admissions is the methodology of the interrogator. Many accounts appear to have involved the badgering of informants until they provided an answer satisfying the observers' preconceptions; leading questions were often asked. Take, for example, the detailed account of Lang (1861:386–387), writing of the Aborigines of Wide Bay in Queensland:

After talking with the black for some time, it struck me that I had then an excellent opportunity of questioning him as to the practice of cannibalism amongst his tribe, and I proceeded to take advantage of it by asking him, without comment or preface, if the bodies had been eaten. He pretended disgust at the bare idea of such a thing, and denied that the Wide Bay Blacks were ever cannibals. I merely asked, in reply to his denial, "if the bodies had been cut up, and when they would be eaten". He now evidently supposed that I knew all about the matter, but would not give a direct reply to my questions. He fairly committed himself, however, by saying, "two of the bodies belonged to old men and were therefore put in a hole". I asked, then, if the third man had been cut up, and he replied in the affirmative; stating in answer to other questions, that the rite of cannibalism would be observed on the morrow . . . I had to speak to the black before me in such a manner as to assure him that I did not question in order to mock or upbraid; for I desired to get at the whole truth, which I perceived could not be taken by storm, but must be arrived at by stratagem. He told me, first, with regard to human flesh, that he had never eaten human flesh; afterward that he did not like the taste of it, and again, on my giving him a little encouragement to speak plainly, that it was "good and close up bullock," or much like beef.

It is quite incredible how many authors judged a reticent response to be the result of shame at performing the act rather than shock at being asked the question (e.g., Beveridge 1889:28; Horne & Aiston 1924:47; Roth 1901:30). Smyth, for example, commented:

It is creditable to them that they are ashamed of the practice. They usually deny that they ever ate human flesh, but as constantly allege that "wild blacks" are guilty of the crime. It is sad to relate that there are only too many well-authenticated instances of cannibalism; and the fact is apparent, too, that not seldom the natives destroyed the victim under circumstances of peculiar atrocity. It was not always done that they might comply with a custom, or that by eating portions of a body they might thereby acquire the courage and strength of the deceased. They undoubtedly on some occasions indulged in the horrible practice because they rejoiced in the savage banquet.

Unlike many other offences with which they are justly charged, but which because of their ignorance or because of the pressure of their necessities cannot be called crimes, this one in general they knew to be wrong. Their behaviour, when questioned on the subject, shows that they erred knowingly and wilfully. That they were not so bad as the men of Fiji and New Zealand is undoubtedly true, and so much perhaps may be said in their favour. [Smyth 1876 (1):xxxviii]

Spencer (n.d., Box 16, Folder 1, 83) similarly noted:

Nothing is more common than for the members of one tribe to accuse a distant tribe of eating the dead and to deny that they themselves do it whilst all the time it may be a regular custom among them.

Elsewhere Spencer wrote more formally:

As can be imagined, it is a subject on which the natives are very reticent: in fact, unless you know them fairly well, they will, when questioned on the matter, either know nothing about it, or deny the existence of the practice in their own tribe whilst admitting, at the same time, that it does exist amongst others. [Spencer 1914:253]

Sturt, in recounting a tale of cannibalism told to him under duress, concluded:

Many of my readers may probably doubt this horrid occurrence having taken place, as I have not mentioned any corroborating circumstances. I am myself, however, as firmly persuaded of the truth of what I have stated as if I had seen the savage commit the act . . . Be that as it may, the very mention of such a thing among these people goes to prove they are capable of such an enormity. [Sturt 1833:222–223]

If, as Sturt suggests, the very mention of the topic is proof of its practice, then colonial writers on the subject must have been ravenous.

Given the disbelief in which their testimony was held, it is remarkable that Aboriginal people were ever asked to comment. Aborigines, therefore, had the limited options of being described either as admitted cannibals or as liars.

Colonial Commentators

The second form of firsthand accounts are those by authors who claim to have personally witnessed the event. Such claims are actually very rare (e.g., of the 440 accounts in Pickering 1985, only 8% explicitly claimed this experience). There are two main types of firsthand accounts by whites: (a) those where some fragment of behavior, or some material evidence, is observed and presumed to have been part of a cannibal act, and (b) those that claim to have actually observed preparation or consumption of the body. The first type is the most common of the firsthand accounts by Europeans (5% of the sample). These reports typically describe some human remains in an unusual state or context, such as broken, burnt, or in a fire (Bates 1928; Dalrymple 1874; Forrest 1876: 314; Gregory & Gregory 1884; Jardine & Jardine 1867:183; Meston 1924; Palmerstone 1883; Petrie 1904; Searcy 1912:164); the observation of Aborigines eating or handling what was presumed to be human flesh (Campbell 1847:249; Murray 1898:4); the observation of identifiably human remains in the possession of an Aboriginal (Byrne 1848 [2]:278; Le Souef 1878:296; Searcy 1909:193); or the observation of unusual mortuary rites that, it was presumed, would eventually lead to a cannibal conclusion that was never actually observed (McDonald 1872, 1873).

The question that arises from these accounts is whether the observation of suspected human remains is conclusive evidence of a past or intended cannibal act. The assumption of most authors is that human remains would not be treated in such a manner unless cannibalism was involved. While we cannot dismiss the possibility of cannibalism, there are other, better-documented, possibilities: Aborigines were known to have carried body parts as charms or mementos, or as part of the mourning process (Howitt 1904:459–460); various mortuary processes included ritual cooking, smoking, drying, dismemberment of bodies, defleshing of bones, and breaking of bones (Basedow 1935:230; Berndt & Berndt 1977:465; Davidson 1948:78–79; Maddock 1982; McDonald 1872:218; McKenzie 1980; Meehan 1971; Peterson 1976:107; Pickering 1989; Roth 1907:402). While such customs were, for Europeans, unusual, they were not cannibalism.

Of lateral interest is the number of accounts of a reporter having discovered Aboriginal remains within a fireplace (e.g., Bates 1928; Dalrymple 1874; Gregory & Gregory 1884; Jardine & Jardine 1867:183; Meston 1924; Palmerstone 1883; Petrie 1904; Searcy 1912:164). Dalrymple (1874:18), for example, wrote:

From the discoveries we made in their camps we all heartily rejoiced at the severe lesson their unwarrantable hostility has brought upon them . . . In every camp along the beach for two miles unmistakable evidence of wholesale cannibalism were discovered: heaps of human bones and skulls were found in each camp, and in some, roasted and partially eaten bodies were found beside the fires at which they had been cooked. Lumps of half-eaten human flesh were found in the gin's dilly bags.

Searcy (1912:164), after "dispersing" a group of Aborigines, similarly wrote:

. . . judge of our horror when, on reaching the fire, it was discovered a cannibal feast had been interrupted. I leave the details to the imagination of the reader. We were filled with loathing for the brutes who had escaped us and with pity for their victims, the remains of whom were scattered around.

In each case the evidence followed unprovoked assault by hostile Europeans. What is of interest in interpreting these accounts is that it was the common practice of Europeans in the colonial frontier to pile up the bodies of massacre victims and set fire to them. Allen (1839), for example, wrote how, after the killing of two Aborigines by his station staff, he ". . . ordered them to be burned which was done I understand in the morning." Under the law of the time it was also not possible to effectively prosecute offenders if their victims could not be identified (e.g., Parliamentary Papers 1839). The question remains, therefore, as to whether reports like those of Searcy and Dalrymple (obviously hostile witnesses) describe acts of cannibalism or, alternatively, elements of mortuary rites or attempts to recover the remains of murdered and burnt family members.

Finally, there are the accounts of reporters who claim to have witnessed acts of cannibalism. Accounts of this type are extremely rare (Basedow 1935; Chaseling 1957; Meston 1955; Mowbray 1886; Sievwright 1844). Despite their claims, their descriptions often lack any consolidating evidence, or it emerges that they were at the site either before or after the presumed act, and hence their claims of being witnesses are based on their presumption rather than on substantiated descriptions.

The only "substantiated" account to have emerged from the 440 that I read initially (Pickering 1985) and from numerous others since—one in which the author claims personal experience and gives a complete description—is that of Sievwright (1844; for an easily accessible copy of the account, see Eyre 1845: 256–258). Sievwright provided a detailed description of alleged Aboriginal cannibalism at Lake Terang in Victoria. The reported context involved a woman who died as a result of a fight. Signs were made to Sievwright that the body would be eaten. The body was disembowelled, and the liver, kidneys, and heart were eaten and the blood drunk. The flesh was cut from the body and the body dismembered, the limbs being placed into baskets. Sievwright was offered a foot, which he refused; he then left. This account is the most detailed I have come across in the Australian literature. It would appear from this account that Sievwright actually witnessed an act of cannibalism, with consumption of body parts. Sievwright's description cannot be challenged on the basis of the evidence it contains. There are, however, some issues to be applied in considering Sievwright's evidence. Sievwright, a "Protector of Aborigines," had a poor reputation. He has been accused, over the years, of being an "unmitigated liar" (Bridges 1972:58), an imprudent gambler, imprudent (Hankey 1838), a poor husband and father (Cannon 1983:365; Robinson 1839), and inept and reluctant to do his duties (Christie 1979:97; Clark 1990:97; Robinson 1841b), and of misconduct and immorality [adultery and incest] (Christie 1979:97–98; Lakic & Wrench 1994:19–20; Rae-

Ellis 1988:190–191; Robinson 1839). Sievwright's observation, dated 24 April 1841, coincided with a visit to the region by Robinson, his superior and the Chief Protector, who had left the site two days before the alleged event. Robinson and Sievwright were not on good terms. Sievwright's poor performance was part of the reason for Robinson's visit (Robinson 1841a, 1841b), and only a few days before this episode Robinson had ordered Sievwright to move his camp, an order Sievwright opposed. Bridges (1972:58) says of Sievwright:

In the voluminous report tendered in answer to the Colonial Office instructions, various strong assertions were given the lie direct by La Trobe, Robinson and Parker. The papers as a whole establish satisfactorily the fact that Sievewright [sic] was an unmitigated liar as well as an inefficient and insubordinate Protector and magistrate. As Chief Protector Robinson said at the time of Sievewright's suspension, his connection with the department was unfortunate and the sooner dissolved the better.

While these criticisms alone are insufficient evidence upon which fully to discredit Sievwright's account, it must be conceded that strong doubts remain about Sievwright's reliability and motives.

READING CANNIBALISM: A SUMMARY

The collection of accounts of cannibalism and their attendant characteristics is best visualized as a pyramid, at the very tip of which lies the very small number of detailed accounts—those that make at least some effort to substantiate their allegations. Forming the base and body of the pyramid are the larger number of unsourced accounts and blanket assertions.

Though it is not made explicit in the accounts themselves, unsourced accounts are most likely to be derived from the same sources as alleged second- and firsthand accounts. The secondhand accounts, in turn, are likely to be derived from the same sources as unsourced and alleged firsthand accounts. It is quantifiably clear, therefore, that the bulk of the sources in which Aborigines are charged with cannibalism is based on unsubstantiated hearsay, secondhand and thirdhand reports, exaggeration, misquoting, and deliberate lying. The evidence simply does not exist. Indeed, so many accounts are so demonstrably unreliable and subject to more likely alternative explanations (e.g., mortuary rites) that doubts are strengthened concerning the reliability of the "good ones" as actually representing real acts of cannibalism.

PLEASE EXPLAIN?

The question arises as to why cannibalism was such a popular topic. Indeed, why does it remain such a popular topic today? Historical documents must be assessed in the light of the contemporary theories—scientific, popular, political, and religious—that prevailed at the time and may have influenced the authors. Studies of indigenous populations in the nineteenth and early twentieth century were particularly influenced by the rise of social evolutionary theory. The theory of natural selection and evolution in natural history was appropriated and misapplied to human history to provide a political and moral justification for conquest and rule. There had already been a strong belief in Western Europe in the moral inferiority of other cultures. Such beliefs had already been used to help justify the decimation of indigenous, non-Christian cultures for hundreds of years. The publication of Darwin's *Origin of Species* in 1859 did not initiate theories of social evolution but merely provided "scientific proof" of an already popular idea. The impact on the fledgling science of anthropology, itself partially a product of colonial experiences, was the firm establishment of schools of social evolutionary theory that emphasized the definition and study of technological, economic, political, social, moral, and religious development of societies, each stage of development characterized by particular institutions. Thus societies were presumed to have "evolved" from uncivilized to civilized, and cannibalism was presumed to be one of the institutions characteristic of the most "primitive," "uncivilized" stage of human social development, the act progressively giving way to other symbolic representation (e.g., sacraments, icons). The situation existed wherein while cannibalism was to be considered proof of a primitive stage in human development, any group exhibiting a perceived primitive (aboriginal) stage of human development [read: almost any alien group] was therefore to be considered a cannibal. The argument was that cannibals were aborigines, therefore aborigines were cannibals. Early reporters went into the field raised on this belief and, in the main, expected to find the real thing. As Street (1975:182), summarizing the popular appeal of social evolutionary theory, states, it:

enabled the European to accept the unity of mankind without the intellectual discomfort of ascribing to "primitive" customs the same value and significance as those of Europe. An evolutionary relativism accommodated "primitive" peoples at an earlier stage of development than the European with institutions sharing the characteristics of European institutions in much less sophisticated form.

Such theories were also particularly convenient at a time of colonial expansion. At best, it was much easier to justify alienation of lands and destruction of alien societies when motivated by the belief that the dispossessed would benefit from the technological, political, social, religious, and moral superiority of the invader. At worst, a base motive of "survival of the fittest" ensued.

It is to be expected that the Australian literature of the nineteenth and early twentieth centuries should similarly reflect contemporaneous social and political theories. Stanner (1969, 1974:36), writing of early Australian studies, observed that "few people who wrote at that time doubted that men and institutions everywhere must have developed through a fixed sequence of set stages from savagery and barbarism to civilization." This belief is frequently expressed by authors of cannibal accounts: Aborigines are argued as being "lowest in intellect" (Leigh 1839:159), "lowest samples of the human race" (Westgarth 1848:159), "the lowest grade of barbarity" (Helms 1893:237), "a crude race" (Banfield 1918:7). The list goes on and on.

The alleged inferiority of Aboriginal society was used to justify interference. Howitt (1854:301), for example, argued that

their cannibalism, their practice of infanticide, and their strange superstition that everyone who dies a natural death has died from the evil acts of an enemy who has eaten his kidney fat, and therefore must be avenged, would, had not the white man come, in time have exterminated the race.

Reverend Love (1922:20), in a review of Aboriginal culture for school children, wrote:

I am afraid, that I must admit that the blacks were, and still are, in some places cannibals in a very horrible way.

These things are very repulsive; but then you must remember that these people do not know any better. Why, if they had no horrible habits, they would not need any help from us, who do know better.

And remember, too, that with all their bad habits, they have a great many characteristics that are good and lovable, and that makes it possible to do work among them to lift them to higher things.

Would you expect savages, who have lived in ignorance for countless years, to be good and attractive in every way? Yet again even the lowest of men have in them much that is good and the possibility of becoming better.

Many of the early writers on Aboriginal culture were dilettantes. Their casual observations of aboriginal culture, combined with a degree of literary skills, led them to issue statements in books or journals. An interest or a publication was often all that was required to be considered an authority. For example, Helms, a naturalist on the Elder Scientific Expedition of 1891, admitted to making fragmentary notes on Aborigines out of casual interest rather than professional inquiry. Nonetheless, as the only person on the expedition to do so, he was given the task of writing the anthropological section of the expedition's report (Helms 1893:232). As Barwick (1984:103) has observed:

The nineteenth-century gentlemen whose ethnographic publications influence modern research were not mere scribes: their jealousies, ambitions, loyalties and roles in colonial society shaped their inquiries and the content of their publications. They cannot be blamed for the ignorance which blinded them and others of their time to the complexity of indigenous concepts of identity and land ownership. But we should not forget that they wrote for a contemporary audience and their views were, sometimes, mere propaganda in the contemporary political context of Aboriginal dispossession.

At the same time that casual observations were being reported in the popular press, some scholars were starting to take a more intellectual interest in the study of Aboriginal social institutions. Social evolution was still the rage, and these scholars were concerned with the origins and development of human societies. Frazer, for example, in the preface to Spencer and Gillen's *The Native Tribes of Central Australia* (1899), was to applaud the study of Aborigines, describing them as "approximating most closely to the type of absolutely primitive humanity" (Frazer 1899:viii). A concern with cannibalism as a characteristic of primitive societies still prevailed. There is no doubt that the works of nineteenth-century authors like Taplin, Curr, Howitt, Smyth, Roth, Mathews, and Spencer and Gillen contained valuable information and bought Aboriginal societies to anthropological prominence. However, there is also no doubt that while they did not share all of the aggressive prejudices of Australian colonial society (e.g., settlers, missionaries, police), they did share some of the same basic conceptions regarding the status of Aboriginal people as low on the scale of human social evolution. Many of their interpretations of observations are thus colored by preconceptions as to what institutions and practices were to be expected. Cannibalism was one such institution, and these authors were to write prolifically on the subject. Conjecture became an established method of inquiry in Australian professional anthropology.

Although these "more serious" researchers may have been less biased and more objective than lay writers, they often relied heavily on information provided by the general public, pastoralists, local officials, missionaries, journalists, and others. Thus, although their works may have been more serious scholarly endeavors, the data upon which some of their interpretations were based are sometimes suspect. Most lay correspondents and popular authors of the time had little real interaction with the groups they were describing and failed to identify the group or to describe other aspects of Aboriginal societies. It is also common that the only reference to a group being cannibals was from a single account—insufficient evidence from which to make definite conclusions. The question remains as to how much evidence is necessary to confirm an observation. Indeed, quantitatively speaking, any statistician would agree that there is no evidence for cannibalism. It must be acknowledged, however, that some of the data may be unfairly treated by such an analysis, and, when examined qualitatively, there is some circumstantial evidence that some accounts might have some basis in real acts, though, I would maintain, not necessarily of *institutionalized* cannibalism.

CANNIBALISM OR MORTUARY RITES

While for many accounts the interpretations drawn by reporters may be suspect, the observations on which they are based, and which were reported, sometimes share consistencies and similarities that support their being descriptions of real acts, though not necessarily of cannibalism. The reports that are most consistent in content are those that report cannibalism as an element of mortuary ceremonies. I suspect that many of the more detailed accounts of cannibalism have their roots in observations or reports of mortuary rites entailing an unusual, though not materialistically cannibalistic, treatment of human remains.

The mortuary practices of Australian Aboriginal peoples reflected complex metaphysical beliefs, in particular a belief in the dualities of body from spirit and of flesh and bone. Aboriginal people achieved the separation of body and spirit, flesh from bone, through both symbolic and material means. The symbolic means involved metaphysical beliefs, the material means involved ritual and, often, a treatment of the body. Such treatments were diverse, depending upon the belief systems of the subject groups. Queensland appears to have been an area in which mortuary practices were frequently mistaken for cannibalism. McDonald (1872, 1873), for example, wrote in detail on the mortuary proceedings he observed in the Upper Mary River area. The body was reportedly skinned and decapitated, the legs were cut off at the knees and thighs and the arms removed. The anatomical portions were then defleshed through scraping and cutting. The bones were broken to get out the marrow, not for eating, but as part of the flesh disposal process. The flesh was then buried, while the scraped bones were distributed amongst relatives. McDonald believed that in the past the meat would have been eaten, though there is no evidence for this. Roth (1907:402) described the treatment of a tree burial, where, after the corpse had rotted, ". . . it was taken down by two old women, opened out, the skull, jaw, pelvis and limb-bones cleaned up and rubbed with charcoal, while the remainder of the corpse . . . was burnt." Dalrymple (1874:18), Meston (1924:11), Palmerstone (1883:20), and Petrie (1904:164) all described episodes in Queensland in which human remains were found in various stages of flensing and disposal. Each immediately concluded that a cannibal act was about to occur or had occurred. In Arnhem Land in the Northern Territory, Basedow (1935:230) described a woman cooking her dead child and removing the flesh from the bones; the flesh was buried back in the camp, while the bones were deposited in a log coffin. Arnhem Land mortuary ceremonies include the scraping of bones and their being smashed prior to placement in a log coffin (McKenzie 1980; Peterson 1976; see Pickering 1989).

The consistency between these accounts suggests that the process was a part of institutionalized mortuary rites and not institutionalized cannibalism. This treatment of the corpses involved ritual performances that, to the uninformed, uninitiated alien, were extremely unusual. Preconditioned by a prevailing ideology of Aboriginal cannibalism it is perhaps not surprising that reporters, confronted by dismemberment, "cooking," defleshing, or cracking of bones, made the allegations of cannibalism that they did. It is, however, surprising that modern audiences, both popular and academic, still prefer to adhere to interpretations of such phenomena as acts of cannibalism rather than noncannibal mortuary rituals, despite the evidence to the contrary.

CONCLUSIONS

Why did early reporters have such a fixation with Aboriginal cannibalism? Perhaps they did not. Perhaps it is only those authors writing on Aboriginal cannibalism who were so fixated (I include myself here). Having read hundreds of accounts of cannibalism, it is sometimes hard to remember that there are thousands more where cannibalism was explicity or implicitly denied or not mentioned at all. Accounts describing cannibalism thus probably constitute a very small percentage of the total literature of Australian Aboriginal societies. This in itself is an implicit reflection of the relative insignificance of cannibalism in comparison to other better-substantiated Aboriginal culture phenomena. This, correspondingly, adds to the doubts that must exist concerning its status as a social institution and, indeed, its very existence as a real act.

When subjected to critical analysis, the majority of reports of Aboriginal cannibalism can be demonstrated to have their basis, at one end of the scale, in innocent misunderstanding and misinterpretations and, at the other end of the scale, in deliberate lies and attempts to belittle, denigrate, and dehumanize Aboriginal people and their cultures, usually as a prelude to denying them basic human rights and to usurping their lands. While it is possible to demonstrate that an overwhelming majority of accounts of cannibalism in the Australian literature have little basis in fact, I cannot objectively conclude that acts of cannibalism never occurred; some accounts may be rooted in real acts. Nonetheless the evidence, or rather the lack of evidence, is more than sufficient to refute arguments that cannibalism was a traditional institution in Aboriginal societies. There may have been occasional acts, but, as in all societies, these were likely to have been the result of the pathological behavior of individuals or small groups acting under stress. That such trauma can induce cannibalism is well documented in other first- second-, and third-world societies (see, e.g., Askenasy 1994 [American settlers, criminals, air crash survivors]; Simpson 1984 [British mariners]; Tuzin 1983 [Japanese soldiers]). In indigenous communities such stress may well have been induced through frontier contact, with its attendant violence, disease, and massacres—the collapse of their universe as they knew it.

There has been a tendency, usually not deliberate, among many researchers who rely heavily on historic texts for information about Aboriginal people to avoid the critical consideration of the original social and/or historical contexts of their sources, just as many historic reporters neglected the social and cultural contexts in which their reported observations occurred. The result is that many inaccurate or questionable interpretations of cultural phenomena are accepted and perpetuated as demonstrated facts. Nowhere is this truer than in the case of alleged Aboriginal cannibalism.

There is no excuse for failing to assess methodically the quality of accounts prior to further research. Regardless of ultimate conclusions, workable theoretical and methodological parameters for the analysis of sources have been well established (Arens 1979; Buckhorn 1994; Evans-Pritchard 1960; Pickering 1985,

1989,1995a, 1995b). Objective assessment of sources and information is thus an easy and necessary preliminary to any study. Regardless of the direction discussions may take, any article that fails to provide an initial statement as to the evaluation of sources is open to severe criticism.

The question of whether cannibalism was ever really practiced or whether it was manifest only through ritual and symbolic expressions is a real one, worthy of investigation. By arguing that there is very poor evidence for institutionalized cannibalism involving the actual consumption of human flesh, other avenues of investigation are opened, particularly in relation to the significance of metaphors of cannibalism. For example, what is the significance of the belief in cannibalism in Aboriginal society? What is the significance of the belief in cannibalism in European society? Is there any real difference in the significance?

In all societies where cannibalism is a belief, one aspect of the belief is to demarcate symbolic boundaries between the religious and the secular, between "us" and "them," and between humans and nonhumans. Metaphors of incorporation are endemic in most societies (Kilgour 1991). What becomes clear is that cannibalism, real or symbolic, cannot be considered in isolation from other social phenomena. The most informative and relevant investigations are those that address beliefs about cannibalism through the systematic examination of the symbolic, metaphoric, and physical manifestations of such phenomena within the social universe of the subject group. It is the examination of the metaphors of cannibalism rather than the "acts" of cannibalism that is most called for in light of the evidence and is most likely to provide accurate insights into human societies.

NOTE

Early drafts of this paper were commented on by Ann Robb, Nancy Ladas, Dr Ron Vanderwal, Dr Gaye Sculthorpe, Dr. John Morton, among others.

REFERENCES

Aboriginal Land Commissioner (1983). *Transcript of Proceedings at Murranji Bore on Tuesday, 9 August 1983, at 9.45 AM.* Commonwealth of Australia.
Allen, W. (1839). Declaration before C. W. Sievwright J.P. In Mary Lakic & Rosemary Wrench (n.d.), *Correspondence of G. A. Robinson Chief Protector of Aborigines and the Assistant Protectors of the Port Phillip District 1839–1841* (p. 15). Aboriginal Studies Department, Museum of Victoria.
Anderson, J. C., & Mitchell, N. (1981). Kubara: A Kuku-Yulanji view of the Chinese in North Queensland. *Aboriginal History* 5 (1): 20–37.
Andrews, A. (1920). *The First Settlement of the Upper Murray.* Sydney: Ford Press.
Anglo, M. (1979). *Man Eats Man.* London: Jupiter Books.
Arens, W. (1979). *The Man-Eating Myth.* New York: Oxford University Press.
Askenasy, H. (1994). *Cannibalism: From Sacrifice to Survival.* Amherst, NY: Prometheus Books.
Banfield, E. J. (1918). *Tropic Days.* London: Fisher Unwin.

Barwick, D. (1984). Mapping the past: An atlas of Victorian clans 1835–1904. *Aboriginal History* 8 (2): 100–131.

Basedow, H. (1935). *Knights of the Boomerang*. Sydney: Endeavour Press.

Bates, D. M. (1928). Aboriginal cannibals: Mothers who eat their babies. *Adelaide Register* (8 March).

Bates, D. M. (1930). Aboriginal savages. Central Australian natives: Lawless cannibals. *Adelaide Advertiser* (2 January).

Bates, D. M. (1932). Cannibals along the east–west railway. *Adelaide Mail* (17 September).

Bates, D. M. (1947). *The Passing of the Aborigines*. London: Murray.

Bates, D. M. (1911). Fanny Balbuk-Yooreel: The last Swan River (female) native. *Science of Man* 13 (5): 100–101; (6): 119–121.

Bedford, Jean (1983). The secret life of Daisy Bates and the Breaker. *The National Times* (11–17 November), 28.

Berndt, R. M., & Berndt, C. H. (1977). *The World of the First Australians*. Sydney: Ure Smith.

Beveridge, P. (1889). *The Aborigines of Victoria and Riverina*. Melbourne: Hutchinson.

Bridges, B. J. (1971). Aboriginal cannibalism. *Royal Australian Historical Society Newsletter* 109: 7–8.

Bridges, B. J. (1972). G. W. Sievewright and the Geelong District of the Aborigines Protectorate. *Investigator* (Geelong Historical Society), 7 (1): 21–22, 54–59.

Brockwell, C. J. (1977). *Cannibalism in Queensland*. B.A. Hons Thesis, Australian National University, Canberra.

Buckhorn, R. (1994). A taste for Chinese. *The Skeptic* 14 (1): 30–32.

Byrne, J. C. (1848). *Twelve Years' Wanderings in the British Colonies* (2 vols.). London: Beatley.

Campbell, C. A. (1847–1848). Letter to the South Australian Register. Reprinted in J. C. Byrne, *Twelve Years Wanderings in the British Colonies* (2 vols.). London: Beatley.

Cannon, M. (1983). *Historical Records of Victoria, Volume 2b: Aborigines and Protectors 1838–1839*. Melbourne: Victorian Government Printing Office.

Chaseling, W. S. (1957). *Yulengor: Nomads of Arnhem Land*. London: Epworth Press.

Christie, M. F. (1979). *Aborigines in Colonial Victoria 1835–86*. Sydney: Sydney University Press.

Clark, I. D. (1990). In quest of the tribes: G. A. Robinson's unabridged report of his 1841 expedition among western Victorian Aboriginal tribes: Kenyon's "Condensation" reconsidered. In *Memoirs of the Museum of Victoria* 1 (1): 97–130.

Curr, E. M. (1886). *The Australian Race*. Melbourne: Ferres.

Dahl, K. (1926). *In Savage Australia*. London: Allen.

Dalrymple, G. (1874). *Narrative and Reports of the Queensland North–East Coast Expedition, 1873*. Brisbane: Government Printer.

Davidson, D. S. (1948). Disposal of the dead in Western Australia. In *Proceedings of the American Philosophical Society* 93 (1): 78–79.

Davies, N. (1981). *Human Sacrifice.* New York: William Morrow.

Dornstreich, M. D., & Morren, G. E. D. (1974). Does cannibalism have nutritional value? *Human Ecology* 2: 1–12.

Evans-Pritchard, E. E. (1960). Zande cannibalism. *Journal of the Royal Anthropological Institute* 90: 238–258.

Eyre, E. J. (1845). *Journals of Expeditions of Discovery into Central Australia.* London: T & W Boone. Facsimile edition, Adelaide: Libraries Board of South Australia, 1964.

Farb, P., & Amelagos, G. (1980). *Consuming Passions: The Anthropology of Eating.* Boston, MA: Houghton Mifflin.

Forrest, F. (1876). On the natives of central and western Australia. *Royal Anthropological Institute Journal 5* (31): 6–322.

Frazer, J. G. (1899). Preface. In W. B. Spencer & F. J. Gillen, *The Native Tribes of Central Australia.* London: Macmillan.

Freud, S. (1913 [1950]). *Totem and Taboo.* New York: W. W. Norton.

Gillison, G. (1983). Cannibalism among women in the Eastern Highlands of Papua New Guinea. In D. Tuzin & P. Brown (eds.), *The Ethnography of Cannibalism.* Washington, DC: Society for Psychological Anthropology.

Gregory, A. C., & Gregory F. T. (1884). *Journals of Australian Explorations.* Brisbane: Government Printer. Reprinted Adelaide: Libraries Board of South Australia, 1969.

Hankey, Sir F. (1838). Letter cited in M. Cannon, *1983 Historical Records of Victoria: Volume 2b: Aborigines and Protectors 1838–1839* (pp. 371–372). Melbourne: Victorian Government Printing Office.

Hanson, P. (1996). *Pauline Hanson—The Truth.* Ipswich, QLD: P. Hanson.

Harris, M. (1977). *Cannibals and Kings.* New York: Random House.

Heap, E. G. (1967). Some notes on cannibalism among Queensland aborigines 1824–1900. *Queensland Heritage* 1 (7): 27–29.

Helms, R. (1893) Anthropology. In Report of the Elder Scientific Expedition, 1891. *Transactions of the Royal Society of South Australia* 16 (3): 237–332.

Helmuth, H. (1973). Cannibalism in Palaeoanthropology and Ethnology. In A. Montague (ed.), *Man and Aggression.* New York: Oxford University Press.

Hiatt, L. R. (1975). Introduction. In L. R. Hiatt (ed.), *Australian Aboriginal Mythology.* Canberra: Australian Institute of Aboriginal Studies.

Hobhouse, L. T., Wheeler, G. C., & Ginsberg, M. (1915 [1965]). *The Material Culture and Social Institutions of the Simpler Peoples: An Essay in Correlation.* London: Routledge, Kegan Paul.

Hogg, G. (1962). *Cannibalism and Human Sacrifice.* London: Pan.

Horne, G., & Aiston, G. (1924). *Savage life in Central Australia.* London: Macmillan.

Howie-Willis, I. (1994). Cannibalism. In David Horton (ed.), *Encyclopaedia of Aboriginal Australia.* Canberra: Aboriginal Studies Press.

Howitt, A. W. (1904). *The Native Tribes of South-East Australia.* London: Macmillan.

Howitt, W. (1854). *A Boy's Adventures in the Wilds of Australia: Or Herbert's Note-Book.* London: Routledge.

Jardine, F. L., & Jardine, J. (1867). *Narrative of the Overland Expedition of the*

Messrs. Jardine from Rockhampton to Cape York, North Queensland: Compiled from the Journals (ed. F. J. Byerley). Brisbane: Buxton.

Keppel, H. (1853). *A Visit to the Indian Archipelago, in H. M. Ship Meander.* London: Bentley.

Kilgour, M. (1990). *From Communion to Cannibalism: An Anatomy of Metaphors of Incorporation.* Princeton, NJ: Princeton University Press.

Lakic, M., & Wrench, R. (1994). *Through Their Eyes: An Historical Record of Aboriginal People of Victoria As Documented by the Officials of the Port Phillip Protectorate 1839–1841.* Melbourne: Museum of Victoria.

Lang, G. D. (1861). Cannibalism at Wide Bay. In J. D. Lang, *Cooksland in North-Eastern Australia.* London: Longmans Green.

Layton, R. (1995). Relating to the country in the western desert. In E. Hirsch & M. O'Hanlon, *The Anthropology of Landscape: Perspectives on Place and Space* (pp. 210–231). Oxford: Clarendon Press.

Le Souef, A. A. C. (1878). Notes on the Natives of Australia. In R. B. Smyth, *The Aborigines of Victoria.* Melbourne: Government Printer.

Leigh, E. (1839). *Reconnoitering Voyages, Travels and Adventures in the New Colonies of South Australia etc.* London: Smith and Elder.

Levi-Strauss, C. (1966). The culinary triangle. *Partisan Review* 33: 586–595.

Lindenbaum, S. (1983). Cannibalism: Symbolic production and consumption. In D. Tuzin & P. Brown (eds.), *The Ethnography of Cannibalism.* Society for Psychological Anthropology, Special Publication 1, USA: 94–105.

Loos, N. A. (1978). The pragmatic racism of the frontier. In H. Reynolds (ed.), *Race Relations in North Queensland* (pp. 279–301). Townsville, QLD: History Department, James Cook University.

Love, J. R. B. (1922). *Our Australian Blacks.* Melbourne: PWMU.

MacCormack, C. P. (1983). Human leopards and crocodiles: Political meaning of categorical analysis. In D. Tuzin & P. Brown (eds.), *The Ethnography of Cannibalism.* Society for Psychological Anthropology, Special Publication 1, USA: 51–60.

Mackenzie, D. (1852). *Ten Years in Australia.* London: Orr.

Maddock, K. (1982). *The Australian Aborigines: A Portrait of Their Society* (second edition). Victoria: Penguin.

Massola, A. (1968). *Bunjil's Cave: Myths, Legends and Superstitions of the Aborigines of South-East Australia.* Melbourne: Lansdowne Press.

McDonald, A. (1873). Mode of preparing the dead among the natives of the upper Mary River, Queensland. *Journal of the Royal Anthropological Institute* 2: 176–179.

McDonald, A. (1872). Extract of a letter to W. Boyd Dawkins. *Journal of the Royal Anthropological Institute* 1: 214–219.

McKenzie, K. (1980). *Waiting for Harry* (Film and Video). Canberra: Australian Institute of Aboriginal Studies.

Meehan, B. (1971). *The Form, Distribution and Antiquity of Australian Mortuary Practices.* M.A. Thesis, University of Sydney.

Meggitt, M. J. (1962). *Desert People.* Chicago, IL: University of Chicago Press.

Meston, E. A. (1924). Entertained by cannibals: An ancient custom. *World News* 8: 11.

Meston, E. A. (1955). Mestonian flashes. *Cummins and Campbell's Monthly Magazine* (Aug. 1954, June 1956, Aug. 1956).

Mowbray, H. M. (1886). Granite range: Close to the head of the Mitchell River and east of the Hodgkinson Goldfields. In Edward Curr (ed.), *The Australian Race* (pp. 402–407). Melbourne: Ferres.

Murray, H. (1898). Letter to C. J. LaTrobe, Colac. 18 August. In T. F. Bride (ed.), *Letters from Victorian Pioneers* (pp. 3–5). Melbourne: Government Printer.

Palmerstone, C. (1883). The explorer: From Mourilya Harbour to Herberton. *Queenslander* 24: 477–478, 518–519, 557–558.

Parliamentary Papers (1839). *Copies of Extracts of Despatches Relative to the Massacre of Various Aborigines of Australia, in the Year 1838, and Respecting the Trial of Their Murderers.* London: Colonial Office, House of Commons.

Peterson, N. (1976). Mortuary customs of north-east Arnhem Land: An account compiled from Donald Thomson's field notes. *Memoirs of the National Museum of Victoria* 37: 97–108.

Petrie C. C. (1899–1902). Correspondence. Letters to A. W. Howitt. Murrumba, North Queensland 28 Aug. 1899 and 23 Nov. 1902. Howitt Papers, Box 1, Folder 6, Museum of Victoria.

Petrie, C. C. (1904). *Tom Petrie's Reminiscences of Early Queensland.* Brisbane: Watson. Reprinted Melbourne: Currey O'Neil, 1980.

Petrie, C. C. (1902a). Tom Petrie's reminiscences. *The Queenslander Illustrated Supplement* (10 May): 1021–1022.

Petrie, C. C. (1902b). Tom Petrie's reminiscences of the aborigines of Queensland. *Science of Man* 5 (1): 15–16; (2): 29–30; (3): 47–48.

Pickering, M. (1985). *Cannibalism amongst Aborigines? A Critical Review of the Literary Evidence.* Lit.B. Thesis, Australian National University, Canberra.

Pickering, M. (1989). Food for thought: An alternative to "Cannibalism in the Neolithic." *Australian Archaeology* 28: 35–39.

Pickering, M. (1995a). Cannibalism? *The Skeptic* 15 (1): 58–59.

Pickering, M. (1995b). A reply to Blake on Sievwright. *The Skeptic* 15 (3): 48–49.

Poole, F. J. P. (1983). Cannibals, Trickster and witches: Anthropophagic images among the Bimin-Kuskusmin. In D. Tuzin & P. Brown (eds.), *The Ethnography of Cannibalism.* Society for Psychological Anthropology, Special Publication 1, USA: 6–32.

Rae-Ellis, V. (1988). *Black Robinson: Protector of Aborigines.* Melbourne: Melbourne University Press.

Robinson, G. A. (1839). Letter. In M. Cannon, *Historical Records of Victoria: Volume 2b: Aborigines and Protectors 1838–1839* (p. 445). Melbourne: Victorian Government Printing Office, 1983.

Robinson, G. A. (1841a). Cited in I. D. Clark, "In quest of the tribes: G. A. Robinson's unabridged report of his 1841 expedition among western Victorian Aboriginal tribes: Kenyon's 'Condensation' reconsidered." In *Memoirs of the Museum of Victoria* 1 (1, 1990): 97–130.

Robinson, G. A. (1841b). Cited in G. Presland (ed.), "Journals of George Augustus Robinson: March–May 1841." *Records of the Victoria Archaeological Survey* (6, 1977). 24–25, 30, 32–35, 46, 64.

Roheim, G. (1974). *Children of the Desert.* New York: Basic Books.

Rose, D. B. (1984). *Dingo Makes Us Human: Being a Purpose in Australian Aboriginal Culture.* Ph.D Thesis, Bryn Mawr College, Bryn Mawr, PA.

Roth, W. E. (1901). Food: Its search, capture and preparation. *North Queensland Ethnography Bulletin No. 3.* Brisbane: Government Printer.

Roth, W. E. (1907). Burial ceremonies and disposal of the dead. *Australian Museum Records* 6 (5): 365–403.

Sagan, E. (1974). *Cannibalism: Human Aggression and Cultural Form.* New York: Harper & Row.

Sahlins, M. (1983). Raw women, cooked men, and other "Great Things" of the Fiji Islands. In D. Tuzin & P. Brown (eds.), *The Ethnography of Cannibalism.* Society for Psychological Anthropology, Special Publication 1, USA: 72–93.

Salvado, D. D. (1851). *The Salvado Memoirs* (ed. & trans. E. J. Storman). Perth: University of Western Australia Press, 1977. (Originally published as *Memorie Storiche Dell'Australie.* Society for the Propagation of the Faith, Rome.)

Sanday, P. R. (1988). *Divine Hunger: Cannibalism as a Cultural System.* New York: Cambridge University Press.

Searcy, A. (1912). *By Flood and Field, Adventures Ashore and Afloat in North Australia.* London: Bell.

Searcy, A. (1909). *In Australian tropics.* London: Robertson.

Shankman, P. (1969). Le roti et le boulli: Levi Strauss' theory of cannibalism. *American Anthropologist* 71 (1): 54–69.

Sievwright, C. W. (1844). Report dated 25 April 1841 In *British Parliamentary Papers Accounts and Papers* (3). Colonies Session 1 February–5 September, Volume 34: 240–242.

Simpson, A. W. B. (1984). *Cannibalism and the Common Law: The Story of the Tragic Last Voyage of the Mignonette and the Strange Legal Proceedings to Which It Gave Rise.* Chicago, IL: University of Chicago Press.

Smyth, R. B. (1876). *The Aborigines of Victoria.* Melbourne: Government Printer.

Spencer, W. B. (1914). *Native Tribes of the Northern Territory of Australia.* London: Macmillan.

Spencer, W. B., & Gillen, F. J. (1899). *The Native Tribes of Central Australia.* London: Macmillan.

Spencer, W. B., & Gillen, F. J. (1927). *The Northern Tribes of Central Australia.* London: Macmillan.

Stanner, W. E. H. (1969). *After the Dreaming.* Sydney: Australian Broadcasting Commission (reprinted 1974).

Strachan, A. (1870). *The Life of the Rev. Samuel Leigh, Missionary to the Settlers and Savages of Australia and New Zealand.* London: Wesleyan Mission House.

Street, B. V. (1975). *The Savage in Literature.* London: Routledge and Kegan Paul.

Sturt, C. (1833). *Two Expeditions into the Interior of Southern Australia.* London: Smith and Elder.

Tannahill, R. (1975). *Flesh and Blood: A History of the Cannibal Complex.* New York: Stein & Day.

Taplin, G. (1879). *The Folklore, Manners, Customs and Languages of the South Australian Aborigines.* Adelaide: Government Printer.

Tonkinson, R. (1978). *The Mardudjara Aborigines*. New York: Holt Rinehart and Winston.

Tuzin, D. (1983). Cannibalism and Arapesh Cosmology: A wartime incident with the Japanese. In D. Tuzin & P. Brown (eds.), *The Ethnography of Cannibalism*. Society for Psychological Anthropology, Special Publication 1, USA: 61–71.

Tuzin, D., & Brown, P. (eds.) (1983). *The Ethnography of Cannibalism*. Society for Psychological Anthropology, Special Publication 1, USA.

Westgarth, W. (1848). *Australia Felix*. Edinburgh: Oliver and Boyd.

4

Anasazi Mutilation and Cannibalism in the American Southwest

John Kantner

INTRODUCTION

"It would therefore seem that these . . . Indians, either through stress of hunger or for religious reasons, had occasionally resorted to the eating of human flesh" (Pepper 1920:378): thus concluded George Pepper's discussion of the turn-of-the-century excavations at Pueblo Bonito in northwestern New Mexico. His evidence was the highly fragmented and charred skeletal remains, which were decidedly different from typical Anasazi burials. Since then, almost 100 years of archaeological research has resulted in the identification of at least 40 similar cases of reputed Anasazi cannibalism, resulting in a spate of articles in the popular media, some of which have gone so far as to claim that "cannibalism was widely practiced by American Indians" (Nelson 1997:64). However, not all scholars have agreed that cannibalism ever occurred. In a recent news article, archaeologist Kurt Dongoske is paraphrased as noting that dismembered remains do not actually prove that human flesh was consumed (Associated Press 1997), a position shared by a number of others (e.g., Arens 1979; Bullock 1991).

Fortunately, the meticulous research by scholars such as Christy and Jacqueline Turner and Tim White has created a rapidly growing database of information on suspected cases of Anasazi cannibalism. These researchers have made significant advances both in collecting the raw data on skeletal trauma and in creating the models used to interpret this osteoarchaeological evidence. However, their research has also been necessarily tied up in the complex history of research on reputed cannibalistic activity in the American Southwest, and subsequently some of the behavioral models can be criticized as being somewhat narrowly conceived, a point emphasized by scholars such as Dongoske and Bullock. This chapter hopes to make a modest contribution to the debate by reviewing the history of research on Anasazi cannibalism, investigating possible behavioral analogues needed for interpreting the osteoarchaeological research, and then examining the data from mutilated skeletal remains identified in the American Southwest.

HISTORY OF RESEARCH ON ANASAZI CANNIBALISM

Even before the turn of the century, archaeologists working in the northern Southwest noted the occasional discovery of disarticulated, charred, and fragmented human remains. Although often labeled as "mass burials," these deposits were clearly different from other Anasazi burials, which typically consist of a single individual formally situated in a predictable interment location and often accompanied by burial goods. Interpretations of these unique assemblages quickly gravitated to propositions of cannibalism. For example, George Pepper noted in his report on the 1890s excavations of Pueblo Bonito that "the finding of cracked and calcined human bones in some rooms brings up the question of the eating of human flesh by the people of this pueblo" (Pepper 1920:378). Similarly, in his 1926 excavations of the Small House site in Chaco Canyon, F. H. H. Roberts Jr. discovered a "charnel pit" containing mutilated human remains that he, too, concluded might have been the result of cannibalism or human sacrifice (Turner 1993:424; see also Turner & Turner 1992a). However, despite these intriguing cases early in the history of Southwestern archaeology, research on prehistoric cannibalism was not rigorously pursued during the first half of this century, and in a 1948 article Erik Reed concluded that the evidence for this behavior having occurred at all was unconvincing.

In the 1960s, the topic of Anasazi cannibalism reemerged. In 1961, physical anthropologist Christy Turner suggested that some unusual skeletal remains that he examined from the Pueblo III site of Coombs might be the result of cannibalism (Turner 1961). A few years later, the topic became more widely discussed when at least 30 highly fragmented individuals radiocarbon-dated to A.D. 1580 were excavated from Polacca Wash (Olson 1966). An analysis of these skeletal remains initiated by Turner convincingly indicated that the individuals had been intentionally disarticulated, including decapitation using stone knives, and the bones had then been crushed using stone choppers (Turner & Morris 1970). The researchers concluded that the remains were evidence "not only of a slaughter of unprecedented magnitude in the Southwest but also cannibalism of a sort seemingly out of character for Western Pueblo Indians" (Turner & Morris 1970:330).

The 1970 Polacca Wash article was controversial, for, as Turner himself has recently noted (in Gibbons 1997:635), "in the 1960s, the new paradigm about Indians was that they were all peaceful and happy. So, to find something like this was the antithesis of the new way we were supposed to be thinking about Indians." Nevertheless, led by the prolific Turner and his wife, more and more suspected cases of Anasazi cannibalism began to be reported. In a 1983 article, Turner discussed 10 sites with purported evidence of cannibalistic activity. He also directly responded to the then recently published book by William Arens (1979) in which the historical and ethnographic record of cannibalism was challenged:

> The recent book by W. Arens . . . argues that since no anthropologist ever witnessed cannibalism, it therefore probably doesn't exist. . . . The flaw in this sort of tree-falling-in-the-forest-noiselessly argument is obvious. No earth scientist saw the planet formed, yet none doubts that it had a beginning. Similarly, no Southwest anthropologist ever witnessed an Indian mass burial, yet a pattern of mass human burial has emerged. . . . [Turner 1983:219]

In the same article, Turner presented a series of "taphonomic indicators" that could be used by researchers to identify evidence of prehistoric cannibalism from skeletal remains. Although at the time he did not propose why this behavior occurred, a few years later he was characterizing Anasazi cannibalism as relatively rare, "pathological" behavior (Turner 1989).

Cannibalism continues to be a prominent topic in Southwestern archaeology, inspired by a several recent articles by Christy Turner and the publication of Tim White's 1992 study of the site of Mancos Wash. The latter is the only full-length book yet to come out on the subject, and it is extremely thorough and well-illustrated. The 29 disarticulated, fragmented, and burned individuals at Mancos Wash were first described in a 1975 article by Paul Nickens, and his suggestion that cannibalism occurred is corroborated by White's research (1992). Both scholars conclude that the human remains, probably deposited in the middle A.D. 1100s, were the result of starvation cannibalism precipitated by climatic degradation and subsistence stress. In contrast, Turner's articles have taken a different angle:

> We doubt that famine or drought was the sole cause of the Southwest cannibalism. Likewise, social pathology loses some of its explanatory appeal. . . . Violent social control, possibly initiated by socially pathological individuals, is an increasingly attractive idea. . . . [Turner & Turner 1995:13]

Turner further proposes that the introduction of a Mesoamerican cult into the Southwest promoted cannibalism in certain Anasazi populations (Turner & Turner 1995:13–14). This is in accordance with his view that institutionalized violence required that "the Anasazi had evolved, borrowed, or had imposed upon them from Mesoamerica, complex social organization with ranked individuals and specialized organizations, including quasi-military war societies" (Turner 1993:434). Christy Turner (1999) has just finished a new book that expands upon these propositions as well as extensively reviewing all of the skeletal evidence of mutilation and cannibalism in the American Southwest.

Not all scholars have accepted the contention that the severe perimortem trauma found in some skeletal assemblages can be attributed to cannibalism. A brief exchange between Peter Bullock (1991, 1992) and the Turners (1992b) has taken place in the journal *Kiva*. Bullock decries the fact that little research has been initiated to determine whether other behaviors could have produced the mutilation that Turner and others are arguing is evidence of cannibalism. According to Bullock (1991:9–12), other activities related to warfare or to burial practices could have also produced the patterns of trauma found on the skeletal remains, and he presents several ethnographic examples of severe mutilation not associated with cannibalistic behavior. Turner and Turner (1992b:189) counter that Bullock has failed to look at "taphonomic bone damage evidence in its totality or *gestalt*" but, rather, has focused on discrediting each indicator, one at a time. They conclude that "episodic events of mass human death are complex multivariate phenomena, and in the end, all variables and context have to be considered simultaneously" (Turner & Turner 1992b:190).

The debate between Bullock and the Turners illustrates the three major issues that surround the study of prehistoric Anasazi cannibalism. The first issue concerns the actual identification of cannibalism, which involves the demonstration that conspecific consumption actually occurred. This is an extraordinarily difficult question to address, as archaeologists and osteologists have no foolproof ways of demonstrating that human flesh was actually eaten. For all archaeologists, bridging the gap between the static remains that we discover and the dynamic behaviors that created them is always a challenge, and certainly osteoarchaeologists are not immune from it. Similarly, the second issue concerns the identification of the general behaviors that included the alleged acts of severe mutilation and cannibalism. Were the assailants starving, or were they merely out for revenge? Or was the activity part of a burial ritual? And if the skeletal trauma was merely the result of severe mutilation and not cannibalism, why did this occur? Finally, the third issue involves explaining why the behaviors occurred when they did. Even a cursory examination of the database of skeletal trauma shows that it was temporally and spatially restricted. In other words, not all Anasazi engaged at all times in whatever behaviors were responsible for creating these unusual assemblages. Therefore, why did these behaviors emerge when they did?

IDENTIFYING THE BEHAVIORS RESPONSIBLE FOR ANASAZI PERIMORTEM MUTILATION

Early research on mutilated Anasazi skeletal remains concluded that cannibalistic activity had occurred, based on the severity of disarticulation and fragmentation of the remains. For example, in a 1902 story on the Canyon Butte assemblage, Hough pointed to the "shattered bones" and the "marks of implements" and concluded that "without doubt this ossuary is the record of a cannibal feast" (Hough 1902:901). Similarly, the tendency for most researchers up to the late 1980s was to underscore the severity of damage to the bones and allude to cannibalism as the only reasonable explanation for the patterns.

In his landmark 1983 article, Turner (1983:233–234) summarized the data from 10 mutilated assemblages and developed a list of 14 characteristics common to these skeletal remains:

1. A single short-term depositional episode. . . .
2. Bone preservation is good to excellent. . . .
3. Total whole bone and bone fragment count ranges between 400 to 3500 elements in a given episode. . . .
4. All or most body segments are disarticulated.
5. Vertebrae are usually missing.
6. Massive perimortem breakage occurs in 40 to 100% of the skeletal elements.
7. Breakage is by percussion hammering against some form of anvil. . . .
8. Head, face, and long bone breakage is almost universal.
9. Burning after butchering and breakage is evident in 2 to 35% of all elements.
10. Butchering and skinning cutmarks occur on 1 to 5% of all whole and fragmentary elements. . . .
11. Possible animal gnawing and chewing occurs on only a small percentage of all elements. . . .
12. Bone and body reconstruction shows that the damage sequence was mainly cutting, breaking, and burning, or if evident, gnawing.
13. Only one piece out of more than 10,500 can be considered a tool. . . .
14. The ratio of human and other alteration to these bone lots is: perimortem breakage, 95; burning, 20; cutmarks, 3; possible gnawing, 2. . . .

An important point to recognize is that this list was only a description of the osteoarchaeological patterns from the mutilated assemblages that were suspected to have been cannibalized. But even within the same article, Turner (1983:233) was claiming that these were "the taphonomic characteristics of human butchering and cannibalism," revealing a potential circularity in the definition of the criteria.

Over the past two decades, Turner has reduced his list of criteria of cannibalism to consist of five major characteristics. These include the presence of intentional bone breakage, cutmarks, burning, and anvil abrasions, and the absence or crushing of vertebrae (Turner 1993:422; Turner & Turner 1992a:663). The rationales behind most of these criteria are fairly obvious. Cutmarks are argued to be produced during dismemberment and defleshing, while anvil abrasions are caused when bones that have already been stripped of flesh are fractured to obtain marrow. The frequency of missing vertebrae, which was originally a mystery (Turner 1983:232), is now believed to be attributable to their use in the processing of oils and marrow (Turner 1993:422–426). Based on experimental studies using deer bones and replica ceramic pottery, White (1992) has added a sixth criterion, pot polish, which allegedly forms when bone fragments are rubbed against the sides of a ceramic pot during cooking. Proponents of this final list of six criteria have further noted that any single attribute is not a sufficient indicator of cannibalism, instead emphasizing the need for multiple criteria and a consideration of the totality of evidence (Turner & Turner 1992b). The tendency, however, is for the criteria to be examined on a presence–absence basis, and if all (or at least most) are present, cannibalism is assumed to have taken place, even though the amount of variability in the actual frequencies of skeletal trauma is intriguingly high (e.g., Turner & Turner 1995:8–11).

   With the exception of pot polish, none of the criteria was developed through experimental testing or the direct observation of cannibalism. This is partly attributable to the accretional nature of osteological research on Anasazi canni-balism, which has taken place over a long time. And in their various articles, both the Turners and White have presented compelling arguments as to why these criteria should be considered valid indicators of prehistoric cannibalism, including comparisons with nonhuman faunal assemblages (White 1992). How-ever, the fact remains that they were derived primarily by describing the com-mon characteristics of assemblages that were presumed to have been cannibalized due to the severity of skeletal trauma. Part of the problem is that there is, of course, no way of directly observing cannibalism or the immediate material remains of cannibalistic activity and then develop the taphonomic crite-ria. However, as Bullock points out (1991, 1992), innumerable ethnographic examples do exist that demonstrate that human behaviors other than cannibalism can also produce some or all of the six taphonomic indicators. Despite this promising source of comparative material, however, Turner and Turner (1992b:196) acknowledge that they "have specifically chosen to avoid cross-cultural analogies. . . . We have always maintained that what we are interpreting as cannibalism has been done so by exclusion." To address this apparent defi-ciency in comparative modeling, this study examines examples of other behaviors that could produce highly mutilated human remains. These compara-tive examples are then used for developing models that are compared with the skeletal evidence for mutilation and cannibalism.

BEHAVIORAL ANALOGUES OF PERIMORTEM MUTILATION

   To develop models for interpreting Anasazi perimortem mutilation, a total of 35 examples of behaviors that could produce severe trauma to a person either before or immediately after death were assembled. These ethnographic, ethno-historic, and archaeological cases, which are described in greater detail in

Kantner (1999), are listed in Table 4.1. The examples suggest that three general behaviors can produce mutilated skeletal remains:

1. preparation of the deceased;
2. emergency or starvation cannibalism;
3. warfare and social control.

The evidence suggests that cannibalism of varying intensities can be associated with all of these behaviors.

Ten of the 35 cases examined in this study prepared their dead in ways that produced perimortem mutilation. Endocannibalism is associated with these preparations among only four of the groups, while six societies engaged in non-cannibalistic mortuary practices that resulted in severe damage to the bodies of the deceased. In general, the ethnographic cases indicate that methods of preparing the dead, whether or not cannibalism is involved, would be likely to produce some or all of the following characteristics:

1. disarticulated skeletons;
2. cutmarked bones;
3. burning;
4. the removal of skeletal parts, especially the crania;
5. high bone fragmentation;
6. burial in pots, pits, or other formalized loci.

The context of the activity would also be distinctive:

1. burials would not be expected to be intermingled with nonhuman faunal remains;
2. the burials would be likely to receive formal mortuary treatment;
3. the manner of preparation would be expected to be a standardized pattern characteristic of most burials.

Only two examples examined in this study—the Japanese in New Guinea and the Donner Party in California—demonstrate cannibalism occurring in emergency or starvation situations. The cannibalistic activities are not well recorded in these examples, but in both cases the victims were consumed far from populated areas, suggesting that archaeologists will not normally encounter examples of emergency cannibalism. However, starvation cannibalism can also occur in other more visible contexts, such as within communities during periods of extreme nutritional stress. In such circumstances, the following skeletal characteristics would be expected:

1. disarticulated skeletons;

Table 4.1. Ethnographic, Ethnohistoric, and Archaeological Examples of Behaviors Producing Severe Perimortem Skeletal Trauma

Society/Geographical Area	References
Alabama	Bridges 1996
Alaska	Melbye & Fairgrieve 1994
Asmat, New Guinea	Zegwaard 1959
Australia	Hiatt 1969; Pickering 1989; Roth 1907
Aztecs	Harner 1977
Bavenda, Africa	Stayt 1968
Bimin-Kuskusmin, New Guinea	Poole & Porter 1983; White & Toth 1991
Busama, New Guinea	Hogbin 1951
California Donner Party	Grayson 1990; Hardesty 1997
Caribs	Tannahill 1975; Whitehead 1984, 1990
Europe, Prehistoric	Villa 1992; Villa et al. 1986
Europe, Historic	Abler 1992; Villa 1992
Fiji	Carneiro 1990; Sahlins 1983; Spennemann 1987
Gimi, New Guinea	Gillison 1983
Hawaii	Snow 1974; White 1992
Hopi	Parsons 1936; Titiev 1944
Iroquios and Huron	Abler 1992; Abler & Logan 1988; Tuck 1974
Japanese in New Guinea	Tuzin 1983
Maori, New Zealand	Barber 1992; Bowden 1984; Sahlins 1983
Marquesas	Kirch 1984
North & South Dakota	Malville 1989
Pacific Northwest	Krantz 1979
Plains Indians	Quaife 1950; Snow & Fitzpatrick 1989
Rossel Island, New Guinea	Armstrong 1928
Samoa	Davidson 1979; Tannahill 1975
Sea Dyaks	Gomes 1911
South Africa	Klapwijk 1989
Teotihuacan	White 1992
Tibet	Malville 1989
Trobriand Islanders	Lewis 1983
Tupinamba, Brazil	Forsyth 1983, 1985
Wari, Brazil	Conklin 1995
Woodland, U.S.	White 1992
Wuxuan, Guangxi, China	Sutton 1995
Yaqui	Kelley 1989

2. cutmarked bones;
3. burning and other evidence of cooking;
4. the fracturing of bones to obtain marrow.

Furthermore, the context of the deposits would be important:

1. the bones would be likely to be deposited with other food residues, such as nonhuman faunal remains, rather than being interred in a typical burial context;
2. the victims would be likely to be weaker individuals, such as the young or old;
3. the remains probably would not receive formal mortuary treatment, especially if the victims were not related to the cannibals (e.g., Grayson 1990:239);
4. the environmental conditions would be expected to be extremely poor, and related indicators of nutritional stress should therefore be present.

In 23 of the 35 comparative examples, acts of cannibalism occurred within the context of aggression and violence, while 5 other societies engaged in activities that produced perimortem mutilation without the inclusion of any cannibalistic behavior. Cannibalism was often a component of intergroup warfare, while some groups also used cannibalism as a form of social control over individuals or groups within their own society. Notions of intimidation or revenge played a role in most of these cases, with torture, mutilation, and other indignities often accompanying the cannibalism. In most examples, both the cannibalism and excessive mutilations were used to terrify enemies or to control subordinates and potential political rivals. In general, whether or not cannibalism occurred, skeletal mutilation associated with warfare and social control would be likely to produce deposits with the following characteristics:

1. disarticulated skeletons;
2. bones exhibiting cutmarks from the removal of limbs or flesh;
3. burning;
4. the removal of skeletal parts, especially hands, feet, and heads, for trophies;
5. scalping;
6. violent trauma to the long bones and skull, but not in a manner necessarily consistent with the extraction of marrow or brains (which would be more consistent with the expectations for starvation cannibalism).

Several contextual circumstances would also be expected in these cases of violent mutilation:

1. burial would be unlikely, especially if the site was destroyed or abandoned when the deaths occurred;

2. a greater number of males might be present, especially in cases of warfare;
3. the bones would not be consistently deposited with nonhuman faunal remains.

Determining whether warfare and social control included cannibalistic activity or whether severe mutilation produced the trauma is difficult to determine since the process of violent mutilation often produces a comparable osteoarchaeological pattern. In contrast to torture or corpse mutilation, cannibalism might be expected to result in higher levels of bone processing as well as direct evidence of cooking. For example, marrow extraction is often associated with cannibalism, and this can produce a higher degree of fragmentation, as well as distinctive anvil abrasions that are not found as frequently on remains affected by violent but non-cannibalistic mutilation (Turner 1993:426; White 1992:150–151). The victims of violent torture or postmortem mutilation might also be expected to be more completely articulated than in cases where cannibalism also occurred. Other contextual information will also be important for determining whether cannibalism accompanied warfare or social control.

The comparative examples indicate that positively identifying cannibalism is exceedingly difficult. A variety of behaviors, such as those associated with violent warfare or the preparation of the deceased, could have produced most of the criteria that are used to identify cannibalism in the Southwest. The only criterion that appears as if it could only be produced in the context of conspecific consumption is pot polish; none of the comparative cases indicates that other behaviors would produce human remains that were cooked but not eaten. However, pot polish is also a relatively new taphonomic feature that has not yet been extensively evaluated; as Turner comments (1993:427), it "is difficult to identify because it usually occurs on a very small surface area, usually less than 0.25 mm^2." The possibility that postdepositional processes could cause similar polishing has also not been ruled out. The conclusion, therefore, is that none of the taphonomic criteria constitutes definitively convincing evidence for the occurrence of cannibalism. However, as Turner and Turner (1992b) emphasize, the analysis of mutilated human remains should consider all osteological variables while also acknowledging other contextual factors that contributed to the formation of mutilated skeletal assemblages.

AN EXAMINATION OF ANASAZI PERIMORTEM MUTILATION

Given the behavioral analogues derived from the exploration of ethnographic, ethnohistoric, and archaeological data, can Turner's and White's claims that cannibalism occurred be substantiated? And, perhaps more importantly, what general behaviors were responsible for causing such trauma to the Anasazi remains? To address these issues, a comparison of the behavioral models discussed above can be made with the actual data from the northern Southwest. For this analysis, information from Anasazi sites with skeletal remains exhibiting severe perimortem trauma were assembled (Figure 4.1). Summarized in Tables 4.2 and 4.3, the list of variables examined includes the six taphonomic criteria thought to constitute indicators of cannibalism (Malville 1989; Turner 1983, 1993; Turner & Turner 1990, 1995; White 1992).

Acknowledging that human mutilation is a multivariate phenomenon, this study employed factor analysis, a technique designed to identify important variables and to distill them into fewer variables, or "factors," that represent the original data. This analysis was conducted on a sample of 29 sites with relatively complete information. The following variables were selected due to the completeness and comparability of the available information: frequencies of missing vertebrae, bone fragmentation, anvil abrasions, cutmarks, and burning. Because the ranges of these variables were quite different, the data were first normalized

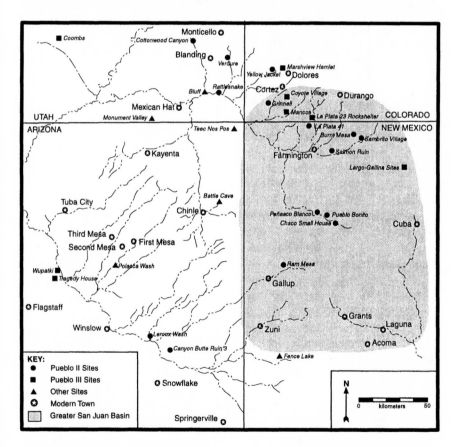

Figure 4.1. Map of the Four Corners area of the northern American Southwest, illustrating locations where evidence of perimortem trauma has been identified.

Table 4.2. Contextual and Demographic Data for Skeletal Assemblages Used in This Study

	CONTEXT			DEMOGRAPHY		
SITE	Occupation Dates	Location of Remains	W/Faunal Remains	Total MNI	% Adults	% of Adults = Males
Ash Creek	1360	Floor of pueblo	yes	5	80.0	
Battle Cave	unknown	Pit in rock shelter		13		
Bluff (St. Chris.)	1200?	On old ground level	no	4	25.0	
Burnt Mesa	900–950	Floor of pithouse		11	63.6	57.1
Canyon Butte Ruin 3	1100	Cemetery of pueblo	no	4	50.0	50.0
Chaco Small House	950–1050	Pit in floor of pueblo		8	25.0	
Coombs	1100–1200	Floor of pueblo		14		
Cottonwood Canyon	890–920	Pit in fill of pueblo	no	4	50.0	50.0
Cowboy Wash	1125–1150	Floors of pithouses and pueblos	no?	24	50.0	25.0
Coyote Village	1100–1200	In midden		1		
Fence Lake	unknown	Fragments in firepit	no	5	80.0	50.0
Grinnell	1050–1150	Cist and floor of kiva	no	7	57.1	50.0
Hansen Pueblo	1134	Floors of kiva and pueblo		2		
La Plata 23RS	1100–1300	Firepit and jar in shelter		2	50.0	100.0
La Plata 41	1100	Pits in floor of pueblo		6	66.7	100.0
La Plata Hwy/LA37592	1100–1200	Fill and floor of pithouse		7		
La Plata Hwy/LA37593	1000–1100	Fill and floor of pithouse		5		
La Plata Hwy/LA65030	1100–1200	Fill and floor of pithouse		6		

Site	Date	Context		n	%	%
Largo-Gallina Bg2	1100–1300	Floor of pithouse	no	17	88.2	46.7
Largo-Gallina Bg3	1100–1300	Floor of pueblo	no	11	63.6	57.1
Largo-Gallina Bg20	1100–1300	Floor of pithouse	no	13	92.3	66.7
Largo-Gallina Bg51	1100–1300	Floor of tower	no	3	100.0	33.3
Largo-Gallina Bg88B	1100–1300	Floor of pithouse	no	11	90.9	100.0
Leroux Wash	1000–1100	Pit near pueblo		35		
Mancos Canyon	1100–1175	Floors of pueblo and kiva	yes	29	51.7	
Marshview Hamlet	1150	Fill of pithouse	no	6	50.0	33.3
Monument Valley	unknown	Isolated slab pit	no	7	42.9	66.7
Peñasco Blanco	900–1140	Room of pueblo		2		
Polacca Wash	1600–1700	Pit near Awatobi	no	30	60.0	5.6
Pueblo Bonito	900–1140	Floor of pueblo	yes	11		
Ram Mesa/423-124	1000–1120	Floor of kiva	no	12	41.7	40.0
Ram Mesa/423-131	700?	Fill of pithouse	no	1	100.0	0.0
Rattlesnake Ruin	1050–1100	Pit near pueblo		20	45.0	22.2
Salmon Ruin	1210–1263	Tower kiva	no	35	5.7	50.0
Sambrito Village	900–950	Floors of pithouses		14	42.9	
San Juan/NA7166	1250–1300	Floor of room		2		
Teec Nos Pos	700–900?	Floor of pueblo	no	2	50.0	100.0
Tragedy House	1100–1300	Floors of pueblo and kiva	no	4	75.0	66.7
Verdure Canyon	900–1100	In cliff crevice		1	100.0	100.0
Wupatki Pueblo	1100–1200	Floor of pueblo	no	19	26.3	80.0
Yellow Jacket 5MT1	950–1025	Pit in floor of pueblo	yes	4		
Yellow Jacket 5MT3	1025–1050	Floor of kiva	no	10	60.0	33.3

Table 4.3: Osteological Data and References for Skeletal Assemblages Used in This Study

Site	Fragmentation	Missing Vertebrae	Anvil Abrasions	Cutmarks	Burning	Pot Polish	Scalping	References
Ash Creek	97.6	98.1	–	3.3	25.9	–	–	Turner 1983; White 1992
Battle Cave	5.5	84.0	1.7	0.5	0.0	–	–	Turner & Turner 1995
Bluff (St. Chris.)	67.4	89.6	4.1	5.8	0.0	–	–	Turner & Turner 1995; White 1992
Burnt Mesa	98.0	73.9	yes	2.8	35.4	yes	yes	Flinn, Turner, & Brew 1976; Turner 1983; White 1992
Canyon Butte Ruin 3	87.5	92.7	2.4	4.0	4.4	41.1	yes	Turner & Turner 1992a
Chaco Small House	58.5	97.9	6.6	7.9	3.9	–	–	Turner 1993
Coombs	yes	–	yes	yes	–	yes	–	Turner 1961; Turner & Turner 1995
Cottonwood Canyon	90.0?	87.5	0.3	0.3	4.9	–	–	White 1991, 1992
Cowboy Wash	high	yes	yes?	yes	yes	–	no	Billman 1997; Lambert 1997
Coyote Village	yes	–	yes	yes	yes?	–	–	Turner & Turner 1995
Fence Lake	99.9	yes	yes	0.2	0.5	yes	yes?	Grant 1989; Turner 1993; White 1992
Grinnell	97.9	96.8	–	1.0	10.8	–	–	Leubben 1983; Leubben & Nickens 1982
Hansen Pueblo	91.4	85.4	5.0	2.9	45.7	–	–	Turner & Turner 1995
La Plata 23RS	–	97.0	–	yes	yes	–	–	Turner & Turner 1995
La Plata 41	high	–	–	–	yes	–	–	Turner & Turner 1995; White 1992
La Plata Hwy/LA37592	64.3	89.3	1.0	2.1	5.5	–	–	Turner & Turner 1995
La Plata Hwy/LA37593	28.4	98.2	1.7	1.7	1.3	–	–	Turner & Turner 1995
La Plata Hwy/LA65030	30.2	95.8	5.9	4.0	0.0	–	–	Turner & Turner 1995
Largo-Gallina Bg2	94.8	32.0	0.0	0.0	86.5	no	no	Mackey & Green 1979; Turner, Turner, & Green 1993

Site								Reference
Largo-Gallina Bg3	6.3	86.0	1.0	0.3	0.0	no	no	Mackey & Green 1979; Turner et al. 1993
Largo-Gallina Bg20	47.6	39.7	0.3	1.0	0.0	no	–	Mackey & Green 1979; Turner et al. 1993
Largo-Gallina Bg51	98.6	95.8	0.0	0.0	98.6	no	no	Mackey & Green 1979; Turner et al. 1993
Largo-Gallina Bg88B	49.6	0.0	0.0	0.0	0.0	no	no	Mackey & Green 1979; Turner et al. 1993
Leroux Wash	99.7	91.4	yes	2.6	1.7	yes	yes	Turner 1983; White 1992
Mancos Canyon	98.4	80.5	18.5	11.7	21.5	6.0	yes	Nickens 1975; White 1992
Marshview Hamlet	99.9	94.5	yes	2.6	30.7	yes	yes?	Turner 1988; Wiener 1988; Wilshusen 1988
Monument Valley	80.1	97.6	–	0.9	12.6	5.0	–	Nass & Bellantoni 1982; White 1992
Peñasco Blanco	95.3	91.7	8.1	5.2	1.8	yes	–	Pepper 1920; Turner & Turner 1995
Polacca Wash	90.0	93.2	yes	no	36.0	no	no	Olson 1966; Turner & Morris 1970
Pueblo Bonito	high	–	yes	–	–	–	no	Pepper 1920; Turner & Turner 1995
Ram Mesa/423-124	99.4	78.8	yes	0.3	18.7	yes	yes	Herrmann et al. 1993; Sullivan & Phippen 1994
Ram Mesa/423-131	100.0	75.0	0.0	1.2	0.6	–	–	Herrmann et al. 1993; Wellman 1994
Rattlesnake Ruin	92.3	68.3	yes	3.7	3.0	–	–	Turner 1993; Turner & Turner 1995
Salmon Ruin	yes	–	yes	yes	yes	yes	–	Shipman 1980; Turner & Turner 1995
Sambrito Village	93.4	87.1	2.5	2.8	16.9	–	–	Dittert, Eddy, & Dickey 1966; Turner & Turner 1995
San Juan/NA7166	28.7	79.2	2.6	1.7	10.4	–	–	Turner & Turner 1995
Teec Nos Pos	5.4	83.3	0.0	10.7	1.8	–	–	Turner 1989; Turner 1993
Tragedy House	11.3	yes	1.6	1.6	1.6	–	–	Smith 1952; Turner & Turner 1990
Verdure Canyon	high	–	–	yes	yes	–	–	White 1992
Wupatki Pueblo	11.0	66.1	0.0	0.0	0.0	no	no	Turner & Turner 1990
Yellow Jacket 5MT1	limited	50.0	–	8.6	2.6	–	yes	Malville 1989; White 1992
Yellow Jacket 5MT3	88.0	88.8	yes	2.1	10.9	–	yes	Malville 1989; Turner 1993; White 1992

The Anthropology of Cannibalism

and standardized. The factor analysis, which employed varimax rotation, identified two major factors that explain 70% of the variance in the data. The first factor represents three variables: anvil abrasions (with a loading of 0.87), cutmarks (0.85), and missing vertebrae (0.62). The loadings, which indicate the variance of each variable represented in each factor, are interesting, since these three taphonomic characteristics are considered to be important for demonstrating the actual processing of bodies for consumption. The second factor has high loadings of the bone fragmentation (0.89) and burning (0.88) variables. These variables may, in fact, be related, since burning often results in the fracturing of bones (Turner et al. 1993:90). However, because the two variables only exhibit a correlation of .44, both were included in the analysis.

A plot of the two factor scores for the 29 sites reveals three different clusters and one isolated case (Figures 4.2 and 4.3). The first cluster, found on the left

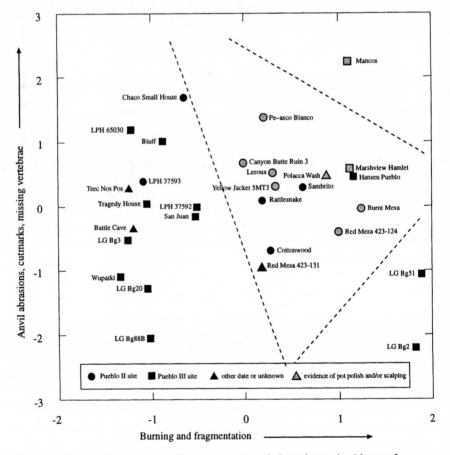

Figure 4.2 Plot of factor scores illustrating temporal clustering and evidence of pot polish and scalping.

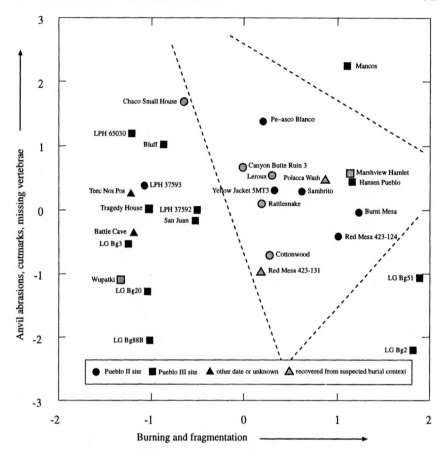

Figure 4.3. Plot of factor scores illustrating temporal clustering and indicating those sites where mutilated skeletal remains were recovered from suspected burial contexts.

side of the plots, includes those sites with relatively low degrees of skeletal trauma and low frequencies of burning and fragmentation. Several variables not used in the factor analysis support the integrity of this group. Almost all of these sites date to Pueblo III, none of the skeletal elements exhibit pot polish or scalping (Figure 4.2), and no faunal remains were associated with the human skeletal material. The few assemblages dominated by males are all found in this Pueblo III group, and only two of the skeletal collections were recovered from contexts indicating that they were intentionally buried (Figure 4.3); most of the remains were, instead, found scattered indiscriminately on the floors of pueblo rooms or pit structures. In general, the pattern of skeletal trauma in this cluster is consistent with ethnographic descriptions of warfare accompanied by torture or corpse mutilation. For example, at Bg88B (Mackey & Green 1979:147), the

The Anthropology of Cannibalism

mostly articulated and primarily male individuals were found in a heap on the floor of a pithouse. Their remains exhibited perimortem fractures and embedded arrow points, and, apparently to further damage the victims, rocks had been thrown down on the bodies from above. Overall, the sites in this cluster do not exhibit extensive perimortem mutilation, and there is no evidence that decisively demonstrates that cannibalism occurred. This conclusion is consistent with one that the Turners and White might make, for pot polish is not found at these sites and the other five taphonomic criteria are for the most part poorly represented.

The next cluster illustrated in Figures 4.2 and 4.3 consists of skeletal assemblages that generally exhibit a higher degree of intentional trauma. Most of the sites in this cluster date to Pueblo II, and many of the remains exhibit scalping and pot polish; in fact, all but one of the sites in the entire analysis with these two attributes fall into this group, even though these variables were not considered in the factor analysis. Almost all skeletal assemblages that appear to have been intentionally buried are also found in this cluster (Figure 4.3), and the demographic profiles are not dominated by a single sex or age group. This cluster is of particular interest because some of these skeletal assemblages have been interpreted as representing cannibalism induced by starvation (Malville 1989; White 1992:361–363). At least three lines of evidence, however, cast doubt on this explanation. (a) None of the skeletal assemblages was in clear association with nonhuman faunal remains. (b) In those cases where adequate demographic data are reported, each case appears to represent an entire nuclear or extended family that was killed in a single event; the victims were not only the weak, the young, or the old, and the quantities of people in these assemblages are inconsistent with the attrition that characterizes historical examples of starvation cannibalism (Askenasy 1994; Hardesty 1997). (c) Almost all of the sites in this group are from a period in which the environmental conditions on the Colorado Plateau were relatively benign, and presumably starvation would therefore have been a relatively less frequent problem, at least compared with other periods (Plog et al. 1988:235).

Because starvation was apparently not a motivating factor for the Pueblo II skeletal mutilations, the next task is to compare the evidence with the other behavioral models. Warfare or social control involving extremely violent perimortem mutilation and perhaps even cannibalism seems a more likely explanation. This hypothesis is supported by a variety of evidence. The degree of violence to the corpses is especially revealing, for it includes scalping and severe facial and cranial trauma of such severity that Turner and Turner (1992a:677) note that the damage "does not register well with simple straightforward emergency cannibalism." Much of the evidence tends to favor the conclusion that the mutilation was the result of violent social control rather than of warfare. For example, if these assemblages had been the result of warfare, the inhabitants of the sites would probably have been driven away and the sites abandoned (Ferguson 1990:32–33; Wilcox & Haas 1994:215, 234–236), as appears to have happened to sites in the Pueblo III group. However, many of the Pueblo II remains were actually buried in pits, and the sites continued to be occupied. This pattern may be more characteristic of violence stimulated by revenge, punishment, or intimidation. Other anecdotal evidence supporting the contention that this group represents violent social control is provided by Polacca Wash, a site included in the Pueblo II cluster. Some scholars argue that the 30 individuals found at Polacca Wash were the victims of an A.D. 1700 massacre in which other Hopi villages attacked, captured, tortured, killed, and perhaps cannibalized people living in the village of Awatobi due to their alliance with Spanish authorities (Turner 1993:435; Turner & Turner 1992a:676–677). Historical evidence suggests that the massacre was initiated by an aspiring leader who wanted to enhance his own political position by appealing to other village leaders whose traditional authority was threatened by Spanish colonization (Rushforth & Upham 1992: 103–106).

If the Pueblo II assemblages analyzed in this study were the result of violent social control, were the victims also cannibalized? The intensity of mutilation exhibited by the assemblages in this cluster does suggest something beyond simple torture or corpse mutilation. The presence of pot polish in this group also provides compelling evidence suggesting that cannibalism occurred, perhaps in an attempt to cause extraordinary insult to the deceased, humiliate kin, and terrify others. Overall, the convergence of taphonomic and contextual factors indicates that cannibalism is a likely explanation for at least some of the Pueblo II sites, but severe perimortem mutilation without any accompanying cannibalism could still conceivably explain the patterns. Perhaps only human proteins or skeletal material preserved in fecal remains will provide sufficiently convincing evidence of cannibalism. Nevertheless, whether or not conspecific consumption actually occurred, certainly extremely violent behavior resulting in severe perimortem trauma did occur at these Pueblo II sites.

In addition to the two large clusters of Pueblo II and Pueblo III sites, the plot of factor scores shows an additional small group and an isolated case (Figures 4.2 and 4.3). The small cluster, which includes Pueblo III sites Bg2 and Bg51, exhibits patterns very similar to those found in the larger Pueblo III cluster, although the smaller group includes very high frequencies of bone fragmentation and burning. Based on this evidence, this small cluster is likely to represent behaviors similar to those described above for the larger group. Finally, in the upper right-hand corner of the plot is Mancos. This site, which dates to the middle A.D. 1100s, exhibits extraordinarily high frequencies of all skeletal attributes analyzed in this study. Mancos is alleged to provide the best evidence for cannibalism induced by hunger (White 1992), and its isolation in the plot is therefore intriguing.

The comparison between the factor analysis and the behavioral models suggests that two different sets of behaviors resulted in Anasazi perimortem skeletal mutilation. The evidence indicates that the Pueblo II assemblages were probably produced by acts of extreme violence, possibly accompanied by cannibalism. The resulting osteoarchaeological patterns are most similar to ethnographic examples of extremely violent social control that is often precipitated by factional competition or the maintenance of sociopolitical asymmetries. The second set of behaviors, exhibited primarily by the Pueblo III sites, is associated with relatively minimal evidence of mutilation and probably no cannibalistic activity. The patterns suggest, instead, that activities associated with intergroup warfare resulted in the severe trauma in these assemblages that is sometimes mistaken to be evidence of cannibalism (e.g., the La Plata Highway sites, Bluff, and Tragedy House).

EXPLAINING THE EMERGENCE OF PERIMORTEM MUTILATION AMONG THE ANASAZI

Relatively little attention has been dedicated to explaining why the behaviors responsible for Anasazi perimortem trauma emerged when they did. This is partly because most research has focused on identifying whether or not the actual acts of cannibalism occurred. Researchers have also yet to acknowledge that, as the factor analysis has suggested, two or more different kinds of behaviors could be responsible for the variation in the data on skeletal trauma. Subsequently, some theories have tended to regard mutilation and cannibalism as aberrant cases of pathological behavior inspired by hunger (e.g., Flinn et al. 1976). Other scholars have suggested that the behavior may be punishment for witchcraft that the deceased were accused of practicing (e.g., Nass & Bellantoni 1982). None of these suggestions have considered the interesting temporal and spatial patterning that seems to be represented by the data.

More recently, however, a few researchers have begun to recognize that the evidence for Anasazi mutilation is spatiotemporally clustered. Turner and Turner (1995:15) suggest that:

> the concentration of these sites in and relatively near Chaco Great Houses and outliers leads to the hypothesis that part of the explanation for Anasazi cannibalism is tied to whatever is finally worked out for the development of the Chaco . . . sociopolitical system.

Similarly, in another publication in which the temporal patterning in the skeletal data was first discussed (Kantner 1999), I employed a game-theoretical analysis that demonstrated that Pueblo II would have represented a period ripe for the emergence of unusually violent sociopolitical behavior. These studies suggest a scenario that may explain why severe mutilation and cannibalism emerged during Pueblo II and why this behavior changed during Pueblo III.

Most Basketmaker (before A.D. 750) and Pueblo I (A.D. 750–900) Anasazi groups were relatively small and widely dispersed in piñon–juniper woodlands over a large area. Communities seem to have consisted primarily of closely related individuals, and many were probably occupied on a seasonal basis, especially prior to the A.D. 700s (Gilman 1987; Wills 1991; Wills & Windes

1989). Basic resources such as arable land were relatively easy to obtain since populations were small and mobile (Dean et al. 1994; Gumerman & Gell-Mann 1994), and the archaeological evidence suggests that personal property was not formally delineated, at least until very late in Pueblo I (e.g., Kohler 1992; Sebastian 1992:27–29). Sociopolitical differentiation appears to have been very ephemeral, with little evidence for leadership or unequal access to basic necessities (e.g., Lightfoot & Feinman 1982; Mathien 1993:43–43; Sebastian 1992:103–105; Tainter & Gillio 1980:79–83). Within this general context, there would have been little incentive to engage in violence, since competition for social and physical resources was comparatively low. The skeletal evidence is consistent with this conclusion, for very few examples of perimortem trauma used in this study date to these early periods in Anasazi prehistory. Of course, specific contexts may have promoted unique instances of violent behavior, evidence for which is not represented by the skeletal assemblages analyzed in this study (e.g., Farmer 1997; LeBlanc 1997; Wilcox & Haas 1994:226–230), but in general people were probably able to avoid violent encounters with one another.

The transition from Pueblo I to Pueblo II (A.D. 900–1100) is associated with changing environmental conditions and sociopolitical contexts in the northern Southwest. This includes a proliferation of sedentary Anasazi communities (Dean et al. 1994), and some scholars suggest that new groups immigrated into the region (Berry 1982; Judge 1989:220–221). Associated with the growing population was a related reduction in the availability of necessary resources. Arable land would have been an especially valuable commodity, and this may explain the appearance of fieldhouses as people became increasingly concerned with protecting their fields (Kohler 1992). Finally, Pueblo II mortuary practices (Akins 1986), architecture (Kantner 1996), access to prestige items (Mathien 1993), and even skeletal indicators of health (Akins 1986; Martin 1994:102) indicate that sociopolitical and economic inequality was emerging, perhaps due in part to disparities in the productivity of resources held by different people (e.g., Kantner 1996). This is also a time when multivillage systems such as the Chaco Anasazi and Mimbres were emerging (e.g., Cordell et al. 1994; Gumerman & Gell-Mann 1994; Sebastian 1992). In general, the Pueblo II context is one in which competition for resources was increasing at the same time as sociopolitical differentiation was developing.

The inequalities that appear in Pueblo II were probably maintained through a variety of economic and social means. The comparative ethnographic material demonstrates that the use of violence and intimidation is one way to promote and maintain inequities. People in a wide variety of societies have used extremely violent behavior to intimidate their enemies (see also Turner 1993:434–435; Wilcox & Haas 1994). The intention is not just to kill one's enemy and obtain or defend the contested sociopolitical or economic resource, but also to engage in extraordinary violence. Such violence does not just kill someone; it also disgraces the deceased and shames surviving relatives and compatriots while enhancing the credibility of threats in future interactions. In this context, canni-

96 The Anthropology of Cannibalism

balism is often seen as the most odious kind of perimortem violence. For example, among the Busama of New Guinea, "the bodies of the slain were carried back and treated with great indignity . . . the underlying notion [of cannibalism] seems to have been . . . a determination to humiliate him to the greatest possible degree" (Hogbin 1951:147). In the Chinese county of Wuxuan, the Cultural Revolution of 1968 was associated with interfactional cannibalism, for "to chop up, cook, and masticate was a . . . complete way of offending bodily integrity, depriving the enemy of humanity by reducing him to the status of a comestible" (Sutton 1995:146; see also MacCormack 1983:59).

Powerful individuals and factions in Pueblo II Anasazi communities could have used threats of torture, corpse mutilation, and cannibalism to intimidate opponents. Through threats of such violence, potential competitors seeking sociopolitical or material resources could be deterred, resulting in the maintenance of prevailing inequalities. By occasionally following through with this behavior, the validity of the threats would be maintained. The evidence from Pueblo II supports this scenario, for the severity of the trauma from this period indicates that the perpetrators of the violence wanted to do more than just kill someone. The relative rarity of such extreme violence and the absence of other archaeological indicators of warfare in Pueblo II (e.g., Haas 1990; LeBlanc 1997; Wilcox & Haas 1994) further indicates that this strategy was successful at shaping sociopolitical behavior.

The different form of violence that characterizes the Pueblo III (A.D. 1100–1300) skeletal assemblages indicates, however, that competitive behavior changed after Pueblo II. Archaeologists believe that the multivillage systems that had developed earlier collapsed during Pueblo III, stimulated by changing environmental conditions that disrupted fragile alliances (Gumerman & Gell-Mann 1994; Plog et al. 1988). This collapse resulted in the breakup of large groups, reducing the economic and social inequities that characterized Pueblo II and that produced clear evidence of differentiation in the archaeological record (e.g., Akins 1986; Mathien 1993). Without these asymmetries, strategies of intimidation would have been difficult to maintain, since threats of physical mutilation and cannibalism would not have had the support of differential physical or economic power. In other words, as individuals and factions became more equal, such threats would have become less credible and more difficult to actualize. At the same time, however, the overall high population levels and the relatively poor environmental conditions would have further increased the value of necessary resources. Within this context, competition would have been just as fierce as ever and would probably have resulted in hostile confrontations directed at obtaining key resources. The skeletal data support this expectation, for most Pueblo III perimortem trauma is consistent with damage caused by warfare rather than the by exaggerated violence exhibited by the Pueblo II skeletal assemblages. Changes in architecture, settlement patterns, and other cultural material also demonstrate that the frequency of warfare increased during Pueblo III (Haas 1990; LeBlanc 1997; Wilcox & Haas 1994).

SUMMARY AND CONCLUSIONS

Did cannibalism occur among the Anasazi of the American Southwest? This study suggests that the answer to this question is "rarely." Of the more than 40 reported cases of highly mutilated skeletal remains in the northern Southwest, probably fewer than half exhibit compelling evidence that cannibalism occurred. Ultimately, critics such as archaeologist Kurt Dongoske are correct in noting that there is no definitive evidence proving that human flesh was actually consumed. The pot polish taphonomic criterion is especially promising, and hopefully further research will confirm that no other processes could produce similar polishing on buried human bones. Of particular interest will be the results of recent attempts to identify human myoglobin, a protein common in muscle cells, in Anasazi fecal matter (Associated Press 1998).

Whether or not cannibalism actually occurred, the evidence indicates that extremely violent mutilation did occur among the Anasazi. The distribution of these cases through time reveals that the clear majority took place during Pueblo II, a period during which socioeconomic inequality and political differentiation appear to have emerged. Given the comparison of the evidence with behavioral models derived from ethnographic, ethnohistoric, and archaeological examples, the co-occurrence of exceptionally violent behavior and sociopolitical competition was probably not coincidental. This study proposes that violent mutilations and perhaps cannibalism were calculated behaviors intended both to eliminate enemies and to intimidate potential competitors. Given this conclusion, the rarity of skeletal assemblages exhibiting this kind of trauma is not surprising, as the use of such extreme forms of intimidation was probably resorted to only in exceptional circumstances. On the other hand, it would also not be surprising if many more cases of severe mutilation and cannibalism were to be identified as archaeologists become more aware of research on the subject.

Evidence for extraordinarily violent mutilation and cannibalism, if it existed, appears to be less common at sites dating to Pueblo III, a period characterized by environmental instability and sociopolitical dissolution. The factor analysis conducted in this study clearly separates Pueblo III perimortem trauma from the more severe mutilations of Pueblo II, suggesting that a different behavioral pattern was responsible for the damage seen in the later skeletal assemblages. Because a wide variety of evidence confirms that this was a period of upheaval (Euler 1988; Gumerman & Gell-Mann 1994; LeBlanc 1997; Plog et al. 1988), this chapter proposes that trauma experienced during warfare is represented by the lesser degree of damage seen at Pueblo III.

The patterns identified in this analysis are, of course, generalizations derived from what is a complex dataset spanning a wide range of time. Other modeling techniques, such as the game theoretical approach employed in Kantner (1999), will be needed to accommodate the complex contextual factors that shaped Anasazi behavior in the American Southwest. Despite this caveat, however, this study does confirm that the unusual cases of Anasazi perimortem mutilation were almost certainly the result of violent human behavior that was the likely result of a variety of motivations. Whether cannibalism also occurred is an unresolved issue, but the preponderance of evidence indicates that at least some of the reputed cases are valid. The development of more precise tools for reconstructing specific episodes of consumption, such as protein analysis, will hopefully bring us closer to confirming or rejecting claims of prehistoric cannibalism. In the meantime, we are still dependent on less accurate analytical techniques that, although compelling, will never be irrefutable.

REFERENCES

Abler, T. S. (1992). Scalping, torture, cannibalism and rape: An ethnohistoric analysis of cultural values in war. *Anthropologica* 34: 3–20.
Abler, T. S., & Logan, M. H. (1988). The florescence and demise of Iroquoian Cannibalism: Human sacrifice and Malinowski's hypothesis. *Man in the Northeast* 35: 1–26.
Akins, N. J. (1986). *A Biocultural Approach to Human Burials from Chaco Canyon, New Mexico.* Reports of the Chaco Center No. 9. Santa Fe, NM: Branch of Cultural Research, National Park Service.
Arens, W. (1979). *The Man-Eating Myth: Anthropology & Anthropophagy.* Oxford: Oxford University Press.
Armstrong, W. E. (1928). *Rossel Island: An Ethnological Study.* Cambridge: Cambridge University Press.
Askenasy, H. (1994). *Cannibalism: From Sacrifice to Survival.* Amherst, NY: Prometheus Books.
Associated Press (1997). Evidence found of cannibalism in early Southwest. *Boulder Daily Camera* (4 Mar.).
Associated Press (1998). Colorado microbiologist may answer question of Anasazi cannibalism. *Boulder Daily Camera* (2 Sept.).
Barber, Ian (1992). Archaeology, ethnography, and the record of Maori cannibalism before 1815: A critical review. *Journal of the Polynesian Society* 101 (3): 241–292.
Berry, M. S. (1982). *Time, Space, and Transition in Anasazi Prehistory.* Salt Lake City, UT: University of Utah Press.
Billman, B. (1997). *Cannibalism in Cowboy Wash Part 3: The Colorado Plateau in the Twelfth Century A.D.* Paper presented at the 1997 Annual Meetings of the Society for American Archaeology, Nashville, TN.
Bowden, R. (1984). Maori cannibalism: An interpretation. *Oceania* 55 (2): 81–99.
Bridges, P. S. (1996). Warfare and mortality at Koger's Island, Alabama. *International Journal of Osteoarchaeology* 6: 66–75.
Bullock, P. Y. (1991). Reappraisal of Anasazi cannibalism. *Kiva* 57 (1): 5–16.
Bullock, P. Y. (1992). Return to the question of cannibalism. *Kiva* 58 (2): 203–205.
Carneiro, R. (1990). Chiefdom-level warfare as exemplified in Fiji and the Cauca Valley. In Jonathan Haas (ed.), *The Anthropology of War* (pp. 190–211). Cambridge: Cambridge University Press.
Conklin, B. A. (1995). Thus are our bodies, thus was our custom: Mortuary cannibalism in an Amazonian Society. *American Ethnologist* 22 (1): 75–101.

Cordell, L. S., Doyel, D. E., & Kintigh, K. W. (1994). Processes of aggregation in the prehistoric Southwest. In G. J. Gumerman (ed.), *Themes in Southwest Prehistory* (pp. 109–135). Santa Fe, NM: School of American Research Press.

Davidson, J. M. (1979). Samoa and Tonga. In J. Jennings (ed.), *The Prehistory of Polynesia* (pp. 82–109). Cambridge: Harvard University Press.

Dean, J. S., Doelle, W. H., & Orcutt, J. D. (1994). Adaptive stress: Environment and demography. In G. J. Gumerman (ed.), *Themes in Southwest Prehistory* (pp. 53–86). Santa Fe, NM: School of American Research.

Dittert, A. E. Jr., Eddy, F. W., & Dickey, B. L. (1966). LA 4195: Sambrito Village. In F. W. Eddy (ed.), *Prehistory in the Navajo Reservoir District, Northwestern New Mexico*. Papers in Anthropology No. 15 (pp. 230–254). Santa Fe, NM: Museum of New Mexico.

Euler, R. C. (1988). Demography and cultural dynamics on the Colorado Plateau. In G. J. Gumerman (ed.), *The Anasazi in a Changing Environment* (pp. 192–229). Cambridge: Cambridge University Press.

Farmer, J. D. (1997). Iconographic evidence of basketmaker warfare and human sacrifice: A contextual approach to early Anasazi art. *Kiva* 62 (4): 391–420.

Ferguson, R. B. (1990). Explaining war. In Jonathan Haas (ed.), *The Anthropology of War* (pp. 26–55). Cambridge: Cambridge University Press.

Flinn, L., Turner, C. G. II, & Brew, A. (1976). Additional evidence for cannibalism in the Southwest: The case of LA 4528. *American Antiquity* 41 (3): 308–318.

Forsyth, D. W. (1983). The beginnings of Brazilian anthropology: Jesuits and Tupinamba cannibalism. *Journal of Anthropological Research* 39 (2): 147–178.

Forsyth, D. W. (1985). Three cheers for Hans Staden: The case for Brazilian cannibalism. *Ethnohistory* 32 (1): 17–36.

Gibbons, A. (1997). Archaeologists rediscover cannibals. *Science* 277: 635–637.

Gillison, G. (1983). Cannibalism among women in the Eastern Highlands of Papua New Guinea. In P. Brown & D. Tuzin. (eds.), *The Ethnography of Cannibalism* (pp. 33–50). Washington, DC: Society for Psychological Anthropology.

Gilman, P. A. (1987). Architecture as artifact: Pit structures and pueblos in the American Southwest. *American Antiquity* 52: 538–564.

Gomes, E. H. (1911). *Seventeen Years among the Sea Dyaks of Borneo*. London: Seeley.

Grant, S. S. (1989). Secondary burial or cannibalism? An example from New Mexico. *American Journal of Physical Anthropology* 78: 230–231.

Grayson, D. K. (1990). Donner party deaths: A demographic assessment. *Journal of Anthropological Research* 46 (3): 223–242.

Gumerman, G. J., & Gell-Mann, M. (1994). Cultural evolution and the prehistoric Southwest. In G. J. Gumerman (ed.), *Themes in Southwest Prehistory* (pp. 11–32). Santa Fe, NM: School of American Research Press.

Haas, J. (1990). Warfare and evolution of tribal polities in the Prehistoric Southwest. In Jonathan Haas (ed.), *The Anthropology of War* (pp. 171–189). Cambridge: Cambridge University Press.

Hardesty, D. L. (1997). *The Archaeology of the Donner Party*. Reno, NV: University of Nevada Press.

100 The Anthropology of Cannibalism

Harner, M. (1977). The ecological basis for Aztec sacrifice. *American Ethnologist* 4: 117–135.

Herrmann, N. P., Ogilvie, M. D., Hilton, C. E., & Brown, K. L. (1993). *Human Remains and Burial Goods. Across the Colorado Plateau: Anthropological Studies for the Transwestern Pipeline Expansion Project Vol. XVIII.* Albuquerque: Office of Contract Archaeology and Maxwell Museum of Anthropology.

Hiatt, B. (1969). Cremation in Aboriginal Australia. *Mankind* 7: 104–119.

Hogbin, H. I. (1951). *Transformation Scene: The Changing Culture of a New Guinea Village.* London: Routledge and Kegan Paul.

Hough, W. (1902). Ancient people of the Petrified Forest of Arizona. *Harper's Monthly Magazine* 105: 897–901.

Judge, W. J. (1989). Chaco Canyon–San Juan Basin. In L. S. Cordell & G. J. Gumerman (eds.), *Dynamics of Southwest Prehistory* (pp. 209–262). Washington, DC: Smithsonian Institute Press.

Kantner, J. (1996). Political competition among the Chaco Anasazi of the American Southwest. *Journal of Anthropological Archaeology* 15: 41–105.

Kantner, J. (1999). Survival cannibalism or sociopolitical intimidation? Explaining perimortem mutilation in the American Southwest. *Human Nature 10* (1): 1–50.

Kelley, J. H. (1989). "Law-talk," mobilization procedures, and dispute management in Yaqui society. *Kiva* 54 (2): 79–104.

Kirch, P. V. (1984). *The Evolution of the Polynesian Chiefdoms.* Cambridge: Cambridge University Press.

Klapwijk, M. (1989). Pot- and pit-burials from the Northeastern Transvaal, South Africa. *South African Archaeological Bulletin* 31: 75–98.

Kohler, T. A. (1992). Field houses, villages, and the tragedy of the commons in the early Northern Southwest. *American Antiquity* 57 (4): 617–634.

Krantz, G. S. (1979). Oldest human remains from the Marmes site. *Northwest Anthropological Research Notes* 13: 159–174.

Lambert, P. M. (1997). *Cannibalism in Cowboy Wash, Part II: The Osteological Evidence.* Paper presented at the 1997 Annual Meetings of the Society for American Archaeology, Nashville, TN.

LeBlanc, S. A. (1997). Modeling warfare in Southwestern prehistory. *North American Archaeologist* 18 (3): 235–276.

Leubben, R. A. (1983). The grinnell site: A small ceremonial center near Yucca House, Colorado. *Journal of Intermountain Archaeology* 2: 1–26.

Leubben, R. A., & Nickens, P. R. (1982). Mass internment in an early pueblo III Kiva in Southwestern Colorado. *Journal of Intermountain Archaeology* 1: 66–79.

Lewis, I. M. (1983). *Religion in Context: Cults and Charisma.* Cambridge: Cambridge University Press.

Lightfoot, K. G., & Feinman, G. M. (1982). Social differentiation and leadership development in early pithouse villages in the Mogollon region of the American Southwest. *American Antiquity* 47 (1): 64–86.

MacCormack, C. P. (1983). Human leopards and crocodiles: Political meanings of categorical anomalies. In P. Brown and D. Tuzin (eds.), *The Ethnography of Cannibalism* (pp. 51–60). Washington, DC: Society for Psychological Anthropology.

Mackey, J., & Green, R. C. (1979). Largo-Gallina towers: An explanation. *American Antiquity* 44 (1): 144–154.

Malville, N. (1989). Two fragmented human bone assemblages from Yellow Jacket, Southwestern Colorado. *Kiva* 55 (1): 3–22.

Martin, D. L. (1994). Patterns of health and disease: Stress profiles for the prehistoric Southwest. In G. J. Gumerman (ed.), *Themes in Southwest Prehistory* (pp. 87–108). Santa Fe, NM: School of American Research Press.

Mathien, F. J. (1993). Exchange systems and social stratification among the Chaco Anasazi. In J. E. Ericson and T. G. Baugh (eds.), *The American Southwest and Mesoamerica: Systems of Prehistoric Exchange* (pp. 27–64). New York: Plenum Press.

Melbye, J., & Fairgrieve, S. I. (1994). Massacre and possible cannibalism in the Canadian Arctic: New evidence from the Saunaktuk Site (NgTn-1). *Arctic Anthropology* 31 (2): 57–77.

Nass, G. G., & Bellantoni, N. F. (1982). Prehistoric multiple burial from Monument Valley evidencing trauma and possible cannibalism. *Kiva* 47 (4): 257–271.

Nelson, R. H. (1997). Cannibals in Eden. *Forbes Magazine* 160 (6): 64.

Nickens, P. R. (1975). Prehistoric cannibalism in the Mancos Canyon, Southwestern Colorado. *The Kiva* 40 (4): 283–293.

Olson, A. P. (1966). Mass secondary burial from Northern Arizona. *American Antiquity* 31 (6): 822–826.

Parsons, E. C. (ed.) (1936). *Hopi Journal of Alexander M. Stephens*. New York: Columbia University Press.

Pepper, G. H. (1920). *Pueblo Bonito*. Anthropological papers of the American Museum of Natural History Vol. 27. New York: American Museum of Natural History.

Pickering, M. P. (1989). Food for thought: An alternative to "Cannibalism in the Neolithic." *Australian Archaeology* 28: 35–39.

Plog, F., Gumerman, G. J., Euler, R. C., Dean, J. S., Hevly, R. H., & Karlstrom, T. N. V. (1988). Anasazi adaptive strategies: The model, predictions, and results. In G. J. Gumerman (ed.), *The Anasazi in a Changing Environment* (pp. 230–276). Cambridge: Cambridge University Press.

Poole, F., & Porter, J. (1983). Cannibals, tricksters, and witches: Anthropophagic images among Bimin-Kuskusmin. In P. Brown & D. Tuzin (eds.), *The Ethnography of Cannibalism* (pp. 6–32). Washington, DC: Society for Psychological Anthropology.

Quaife, M. M. (1950). *Absaraka, Home of the Crows*. Chicago, IL: Lakeside Press.

Reed, E. K. (1948). *Fractional Burials, Trophy Skulls, and Cannibalism*. Region 3 Anthropology Notes 79. Santa Fe, NM: National Park Service.

Roth, W. E. (1907). Burial ceremonies and disposal of the dead. *Records of the Australian Museum* 6 (5): 365–403.

Rushforth, S., & Steadman, U. (1992). *Hopi Social History*. Austin, TX: University of Texas Press.

Sahlins, M. (1983). Raw women, cooked men, and other "great things" of the Fiji

Islands. In P. Brown & D. Tuzin (eds.), *The Ethnography of Cannibalism* (pp. 72–93). Washington, DC: Society for Psychological Anthropology.

Sebastian, L. (1992). *The Chaco Anasazi: Sociopolitical Evolution in the Prehistoric Southwest.* Cambridge: Cambridge University Press.

Shipman, J. H. (1980). Human skeletal remains from the Salmon ruin (LA 8846). In C. Irwin-Williams & P. H. Shelley (eds.), *Investigations at the Salmon Site: The Structure of Chacoan Society in the Northern Southwest,* Vol. 4 (pp. 47–60). Portales, NM: Eastern New Mexico University Printing Services.

Smith, W. (1952). *Excavations in Big Hawk Valley, Wupatki National Monument, Arizona.* Bulletin 24. Flagstaff, AZ: Museum of Northern Arizona.

Snow, C. E. (1974). *Early Hawaiians: An Initial Study of Skeletal Remains from Mokapu, Oahu.* Lexington, KY: University of Kentucky Press.

Snow, C. C., & Fitzpatrick, J. (1989). Human osteological remains from the Battle of Little Big Horn. In D. Scott, R. A. Fox Jr., M. A. Conner, & D. Harmon (eds.), *Archaeological Perspectives on the Battle of the Little Big Horn* (pp. 243–282). Norman, OK: University of Oklahoma Press.

Spennemann, D. H. R. (1987). Cannibalism in Fiji: The analysis of butchering marks on human bones and the historical record. *Domodomo* 2: 29–46.

Stayt, H. A. (1968). *The Bavenda.* London: Frank Cass.

Sullivan, R. B., & Phippen, G. R. (1994). Ram Mesa community site excavations, Site 423–124. In R. B. Sullivan (ed.), *Excavations at Anasazi Sites in the Upper Puerco River Valley* (pp. 306–391). Across the Colorado Plateau: Anthropological Studies for the Transwestern Pipeline Expansion Project Vol. X. Albuquerque, NM: Office of Contract Archaeology and Maxwell Museum of Anthropology.

Sutton, D. S. (1995). Consuming counterrevolution: The ritual and culture of cannibalism in Wuxuan, Guangxi, China, May to July (1968). *Society for Comparative Study of Society and History* 37 (1): 136–172.

Tainter, J. A., & Gillio, D. (1980). *Culture Resources Overview, Mt. Taylor Area, New Mexico.* Manuscript produced for United States Department of Agriculture, Forest Service, Southwestern Region, Albuquerque, New Mexico.

Tannahill, R. (1975). *Flesh and Blood: A History of the Cannibal Complex.* New York: Stein and Day.

Titiev, M. (1944). *Old Oraibi: A Study of the Hopi Indians of Third Mesa.* Papers of the Peabody Museum of American Archaeology and Ethnology, Vol. 22. Cambridge: Harvard University.

Tuck, J. A. (1974). The Iroquois Confederacy. In: E. B. W. Zubrow (ed.), *New World Archaeology* (pp. 190–200). San Francisco, CA: W. H. Freeman.

Turner, C. G., II (1961). Human skeletons from the Coombs Site: Skeletal and dental aspects. In R. H. & F. C. Lister (eds.), *The Coombs Site, Part III, Summary and Conclusions* (pp. 117–136). Anthropological Papers No. 41. Salt Lake City, UT: University of Utah.

Turner, C. G., II (1983). Taphonomic reconstructions of human violence and cannibalism based on mass burials in the American Southwest. In G. M. LeMoine & A. S. MacEachern (eds.), *Carnivores, Human Scavengers & Predators: A Question of Bone Technology* (pp. 219–240). Calgary: University of Calgary.

Turner, C. G., II (1988). Another prehistoric Southwest mass human burial suggesting violence and cannibalism: Marshview Hamlet, Colorado. In G. T. Gross & A. E. Kane (eds.), *Dolores Archaeological Program: Aceramic and Late Occupations at Dolores* (pp. 81–83). Denver, CO: Department of the Interior, Bureau of Reclamation.

Turner, C. G., II (1989). Teec Nos Pos: More possible cannibalism in Northeastern Arizona. *Kiva* 54 (2): 147–152.

Turner, C. G., II (1993). Cannibalism in Chaco Canyon: The charnel pit excavated in 1926 at small house ruin by Frank H. H. Roberts, Jr. *American Journal of Physical Anthropology* 91: 421–439.

Turner, C. G. II, & Morris, N. T. (1970). Massacre at Hopi. *American Antiquity* 35 (3): 320–331.

Turner, C. G. II, & Turner, J. A. (1990). Perimortem damage to human skeletal remains from Wupatki National Monument, Northern Arizona. *Kiva* 55 (3): 187–212.

Turner, C. G. II, & Turner, J. A. (1992a). The first claim for cannibalism in the southwest: Walter Hough's 1901 Discovery at Canyon Butte Ruin 3, Northeastern Arizona. *American Antiquity* 57 (4): 661–682.

Turner, C. G. II, & Turner, J. A. (1992b). On Peter Y. Bullock's "A Reappraisal of Anasazi Cannibalism." *Kiva* 58 (2): 189–201.

Turner, C. G. II, & Turner, J. A. (1995). Cannibalism in the prehistoric American Southwest: Occurrence, taphonomy, explanation, and suggestions for standardized world definition. *Anthropological Science* 103 (1): 1–22.

Turner, C. G. II, & Turner, J. A. (1999). *Man Corn: Cannibalism and Violence in the American Southwest and Mexico.* Salt Lake City, UT: University of Utah Press.

Turner, C. G. II, Turner, J. A., & Green, R. C. (1993). Taphonomic analysis of Anasazi skeletal remains from Largo-Gallina sites in Northwestern New Mexico. *Journal of Anthropological Research* 49 (2): 83–110.

Tuzin, D. (1983). Cannibalism and Arapesh cosmology: A wartime incident with the Japanese. In P. Brown & D. Tuzin (eds.), *The Ethnography of Cannibalism* (pp. 61–71). Washington, DC: Society for Psychological Anthropology.

Villa, P. (1992). Cannibalism in prehistoric Europe. *Evolutionary Anthropology* 1 (3): 93–104.

Villa, P., Courtin, J., Helmer, D., Shipman, P., Bouville, C., & Mahieu, E. (1986). Cannibalism in the Neolithic. *Science* 233: 431–436.

Wellman, K. D. (1994). Ram Mesa community site excavations, Site 423–131. In R. B. Sullivan (ed.), *Excavations at Anasazi Sites in the Upper Puerco River Valley* (pp. 226–243). Across the Colorado Plateau: Anthropological studies for the Transwestern Pipeline Expansion Project Vol. X. Albuquerque, NM: Office of Contract Archaeology and Maxwell Museum of Anthropology.

White, T. D. (1991). *Human Osteology.* New York: Academic Press.

White, T. D. (1992). *Prehistoric Cannibalism at Mancos 5MTUMR–2346.* Princeton, NJ: Princeton University Press.

White, T. D., & Toth, N. (1991). The question of ritual cannibalism at Grotto Guattari. *Current Anthropology* 32 (2): 118–124.

Whitehead, N. L. (1984). Carib cannibalism: The historical evidence. *Journal–Societé des Americanistes* 70: 69–87.

Whitehead, N. L. (1990). The snake warriors—Sons of the Tiger's Teeth: A descriptive analysis of Carib Warfare, Ca. 1500–1820. In Jonathan Haas (ed.), *The Anthropology of War* (pp. 146–170). Cambridge: Cambridge University Press.

Wiener, A. L. (1988). Human remains from Marshview Hamlet. In G. T. Gross & A. E. Kane (eds.), *Dolores Archaeological Program: Aceramic and Late Occupations at Dolores* (pp. 71–72). Denver, CO: U.S. Department of the Interior, Bureau of Reclamation, Engineering and Research Center.

Wilcox, D. R., & Haas, J. (1994). The scream and the butterfly: Competition and conflict in the Prehistoric Southwest. In G. J. Gumerman (ed.), *Themes in Southwest Prehistory* (pp. 211–239). Santa Fe, NM: School of American Research Press.

Wills, W. H. (1991). Organizational strategies and the emergence of prehistoric villages in the American Southwest. In S. A. Gregg (ed.), *Between Bands and States* (pp. 161–180). Center for Archaeological Investigations Occasional Paper No. 9. Carbondale, IL: Southern Illinois University.

Wills, W. H., & Windes, T. C. (1989). Evidence for population aggregation and dispersal during the Basketmaker III Period in Chaco Canyon, NM. *American Antiquity* 54: 347–369.

Wilshusen, R. H. (1988). Excavations at Marshview Hamlet (Site 5MT2235), a Pueblo III Habitation Site. In G. T. Gross and A. E. Kane (eds.), *Dolores Archaeological Program: Aceramic and Late Occupations at Dolores* (pp. 17–53). Denver, CO: U.S. Department of the Interior, Bureau of Reclamation, Engineering and Research Center.

Zegwaard, G. (1959). Headhunting practices of the Asmat of Netherlands New Guinea. *American Anthropologist* 61: 1020–1041.

5

The White Man as Cannibal in the New Guinea Highlands

Alan Rumsey

INTRODUCTION

It is a commonplace in anthropology that cannibalism is often imputed to other people beyond one's cultural horizon, the implication being that they are less than fully human (Arens 1979; Farb & Amelagos 1980:135). This form of "othering" has been most fully explored in its Western manifestations, as an aspect of the legitimating ideology of colonialism, missionization, and other forms of cultural imperialism. Though Arens (1979) is no doubt wrong to claim that there is no reliable evidence for cannibalism ever have been regularly practiced anywhere (Brown & Tuzin 1983; Sahlins 1979; Sanday 1986), and his argument may inadvertently concede much of the ethical ground he seeks to defend (Gardner, chapter 2, this volume), he was no doubt right about the important part that imputations of cannibalism have played in Western constructions of the savage "other" beyond the frontiers of civilization.

With but few exceptions (e.g., Fallers 1969:38; Middleton 1970:14; Wormsley 1993), far less attention has been paid to the imputation of cannibalism to Europeans by others. Here I will try to redress that imbalance by adducing some examples of the discourse of cannibalism among the Ku Waru people of Highland New Guinea. Before doing that, I turn first to some general considerations regarding cannibalism in New Guinea and how it has been interpreted by anthropologists.

Though New Guinea has a special place in the European imagination as an island of cannibals (or as having formerly been one), the ethnographic record shows wide variation in its incidence and in people's attitudes to it across the island. Across a large part of the central and western highlands it seems seldom if ever to have occurred over the reliably reconstructable past and is feared and abhorred (see, e.g., Strathern 1982:112). In the mountain Ok region to the west it was routinely practiced by the Mianmin on their neighbors, and not hedged about with any ritual sanctions (Dornstreich & Morren 1974; Gardner, chapter 2, this volume), while the nearby Bimin-Kuskusmin normally practiced it only in certain ritualized forms and regarded the Mianmin's more casual indulgence in it with horror and disgust (Poole 1983:7). The Arapesh people of the East Sepik region do not seem to have practiced cannibalism, but rather than being horrified by its putative practice elsewhere, according to Tuzin they display "an amused, faintly condescending interest that is morally neutral in tone. Extreme cultural relativists, my informants find nothing provocative in such faraway customs, and often dismiss the whole matter by pronouncing that those Sepiks are 'another kind of man'; if they chose to eat each other, that is their business" (Tuzin 1983:62).

In an attempt to account for some of these kinds of variations, Andrew Strathern has pointed out some apparent correlations between these and other variables (cf. Tuzin 1983). Comparing a number of societies in the central highlands and "fringe Southern Highlands," he notes that:

the societies in which cannibalism definitely appears to have been practiced share another characteristic: they were all ones in which very small-scale local groups, of just a few individuals, engaged in marriage patterns which were variants of sister-exchange, appearing often in its "delayed" form of patrilateral cross-cousin marriage.

... it is notable that cannibalism is not stigmatized in these societies in the same way as in my "type-cases" of larger, central Highland societies, the Melpa, Kuma, and Chimbu. I suggest that this is because of two factors: (1) the idea of "turning back" or of repeating marriages is not seen as wrong; (2) in the Fringe societies herds of domestic pigs, which could be used as substitutes for the exchange and consumption of persons, are less prominent. . . .

It is possible that I am forcing the argument onto a comparative scale here, when in fact it was developed originally to fit the Melpa themselves. For them it is clear that there are elaborate rules against marrying kin, against repeating marriages between small groups, and against direct sister-exchange. And these elaborate prohibitions also go with an obvious stress on proliferating exchange ties, on facing outwards to an expanding network, and cn continuous substitution of wealth items, pork and shell valuables (or nowadays cash), for the person. In this context cannibalism stands for an unacceptable "turning back" and is thus symbolically associated with incest. Further it represents greed for consumption, a tendency which must be held in check in favour of a stress on production, conservation and exchange, according to the big man. [Strathern 1982:127–128]

Strathern supports these propositions not only with evidence from "traditional" aspects of Melpa social practice, such as their idioms for talking about incest and homicide compensation, but also with reference to the Melpa reaction to the rise of the cash economy in the 1970s. As opposed to the previously dominant Melpa emphasis on production for exchange, there was at around this time an exponential increase in the home consumption of newly available market goods such as beef, tinned fish, and beer, bought with earnings from home-grown coffee. There was considerable anxiety about this new form of "turned-back" consumptive activity and, at around the same time, an epidemic of rumors about the rise of cannibalism among the Melpa, supposedly being practiced in secret by people who had become "converts" to it after inadvertently being exposed to the taste of human flesh, bits of which were purportedly being put into the water supply by previous converts in order to gain new ones. Strathern argues that these two developments were related in that the rumor "coincided with [the] increase in the introduction of consumer goods in the particular local clan areas where the rumor spread most strongly" (Strathern 1982:15).[1]

Strathern's remarks about the Melpa in all the above respects are highly relevant for the Ku Waru case because Ku Waru and Melpa are near neighbors and virtually identical with respect to all the features adduced by Strathern for his comparison with the "Fringe southern Highlands people." Indeed, in most respects the Nebilyer Valley (in which the Ku Waru region lies) and the neighboring Melpa region are similar enough to be considered a single culture-area, as indeed they have been by Strathern, who refers to the people of both areas as "Hageners" (1971:4–8), a usage I will follow here.

In the rest of this chapter I am not concerned with Strathern's comparison between the "central" and "fringe" highlands as such, or with trying to account for differences across New Guinea in "traditional" attitudes to cannibalism. Rather, I explore the ways in which Hageners have taken a set of ideas that they and their forebears had already worked out about cannibalism in relation to other groups on their intercultural horizon (such as the ones dealt with in Strathern's comparison) and applied them to their encounter with Euro-Australians. In order to address that question, I now turn to some specific details of the Ku Waru language and examples of discourse about Europeans and cannibalism.

FOREIGNER AS CANNIBAL IN KU WARU

The Ku Waru expressions for "foreigner" and "cannibal" are almost synonymous. There is a word *kewa*[2] which can be glossed as "foreign," "alien," "exogenous," which contrasts with *bo* ["indigenous," "autochthonous"]. The usual expression for "cannibal" is *kewa nuyl*, the word *nuyl* (sometimes also *nui*) being an agent noun based on the verb root *no-* "to eat." So the expression literally means something like "foreign eater," or "one who eats in the foreign manner." A less often used but more explicit expression for it is *kewa yab nuyl*. *Yab* means "human," "people," so that expression can be glossed "foreign human-eater." It is with some care that I place a hyphen between the last two words of this gloss but not the first two, because it is by no means assumed that cannibals eat only people who are foreign *to them*, as we shall see in one of the stories below. The implication is, rather, that cannibalism is foreign to *us* Ku Waru people and our ilk.[3] The converse, that foreigners are likely to be cannibals, is also strongly implied.

This is an assumption that Ku Waru people say they made about Europeans when they arrived on the scene in the Western Highlands beginning in 1933 (regarding the Melpa, see Connolly & Anderson 1989, and Strathern 1979:134–135, 1982:112). To exemplify this and to see how this assumption might be related to other aspects of their understanding of the Euro-Australians with whom they came into contact, I now present a translation of an account given to me and Francesca Merlan in Ku Waru in 1998 by Kopia Noma, a man now probably about 80 years old, who recalls his first experiences with "red" men [*kuduyl yabu*] as a young man:

"When the red men first arrived we thought they must be ghosts—our own ancestors coming back. I was a boy, or young man. . . . Dan Leahy came and stayed at Kiluwa. Then a plane came and circled around and we wondered what this creature was that was coming. We dug a hole and jumped in for cover. But it just kept buzzing around up there and didn't land. We kept looking, and said 'Boy! What's making that noise!' We cut a hole in the wall of the house to look out. It kept buzzing around until we finally heard it die down. We kept wondering what it had been. Dan Leahy knew, of course, and he started building an airstrip. We wondered what he was doing.

"Then the plane landed, and we wondered what it could possibly be. We felt sure they were going to kill us. People spread the news that these were ghosts. But actually they were Australians. They were wearing what looked to us like women's aprons, so we thought they must be female ghosts. We thought: 'These foreigners [*kewa yab*] that have come, they must be cannibals [*kewa nui yabayl*], people who eat other people. They must have come around here in order to kill us and eat us.' People said not to go walking around at night.

"They had brought shells to trade for pigs and other supplies, but people still thought they had really come to eat us up. We gave them lots of food in exchange for shells, matches, and things like that. Then we learned some words from their language, such as *i kam, i go*. But we still thought they must be ancestral ghosts. We were amazed and went around telling everybody about it. But some people didn't listen to us, and shot arrows at them. . . . We thought, 'These people who are said to be cannibals [*kewa yab nuyl*] must be our own relatives who have died. That's who it is that has come.'

"One day one of our men stole a handkerchief that had been washed and hung out to dry. They chased him, but he got away. They came to an area they had fenced off around where Hagen market is now, with their guns and dogs. Some men tried to fight them, and we saw two of our men get killed. We had said the red men were going to eat us, and now it looked as if they were going to do just that. We thought about the men we had seen get killed and didn't know what to make of it. The plane had turned out to be a different sort of thing than we imagined. But as for the red men, we had said they were cannibals, and now they had indeed started killing people. We thought surely they would now carry them off on stretchers to cook and eat. We watched and watched, but, lo and behold, they didn't take them! People said 'Hey! These guys were supposed to be cannibals, so what is it that they eat?'

"Then they killed a pig, and we watched with interest. They didn't leave it there! Instead, they boiled some water, skinned and gutted it, then cooked and ate it. Seeing this, we said 'Let's keep an eye on them and see what else other sorts of things they do.' Well, pretty soon a company came and set itself up here, then a mission. Then the government came and set itself up at Kiluwa. More planes came. We expected more people would be killed like those other two, but it didn't happen. We asked the red men why they had killed us. By then they had thrown the handkerchief away. 'You think we are thieves, but we are not.' They felt ashamed and asked themselves why they had killed those two. By then the government had come, and we were glad it had.

"You see, when we had thought they were ghosts, we hadn't really observed them closely, so I think we formed a mistaken impression. Actually it was the steel axes that had first given us that idea. Those and steel knives had reached us first, before the people themselves, and we thought they had come from down in the land of the dead, so we called them 'ghost axes' and 'ghost knives.' Now that we have seen a lot more of them, we know better. In the same way, we thought the red people were cannibals who were going to eat us, and so we were afraid of them. But then they didn't eat any of us."

Noma then goes on to recount some of his own experiences with various kinds of red folks, including missionaries, with whom he didn't get along, and patrol officers, for whose work he showed a good deal more enthusiasm, becoming their assistant and later a local government councillor. He closes his account as follows:

"When [the Australians] first came it wasn't only I who thought they were ghosts. Everyone did. . . . And everyone thought they were cannibals. But now we think differently. We said 'They're going to kill and eat us, so we'd better be quiet.' That's what really settled us down. That's what I say."

As Noma suggests, Ku Waru people nowadays no longer generally speak of Europeans as cannibals—to adults, anyway. But they do so, in a more or less playful way, to children, often with the idea of trying to frighten them into behaving themselves: "You'd better stop crying, or the red man will come and take you away for his dinner" (compare Noma's remark above about how people were settled down by the fear of being eaten). It is not clear whether this actually chastens the children, but it does succeed in making the younger ones very frightened of Europeans. During our fieldwork at Kailge, for example, it was not unusual for toddlers whom we met on the path to shriek in terror and have to have their eyes covered by their mothers to get past. Other "red" people told us of similar experiences.

We were visited at Kailge in 1982 by a pair of Belgian art buyers from the Museum of Brussels, who were unaware of these beliefs about Europeans and cannibalism. We were horrified when one of them, who happened to be a very large man both in height and in girth, tried to drive away the curious children who had crowded around him by telling them that he ate children. We shuddered to think what our fate would have been if a child from somewhere in the area had gone missing at around that time.

The staying-power of such suspicions is underwritten by a lively tradition of *kewa nui kange* [cannibal stories] (see Merlan 1995), which often tell of women or children who get lost or stranded in the forest and are then taken in by a strange figure who turns out to be a cannibal. In some of these stories, the cannibal figure is a European. The following example is a story told to us in 1982 by Ab Noma (no relation to the Kansil Noma above), a woman at that time in her late twenties, with three young sons, to whom she often told such stories.

"There were these two red people (Euro-Australians) who had two children. They were really poor, and went around eating rubbish food. They looked around all day for food and brought it back home. The two children finished it all off, and they got angry with them. The red couple slept, and in the morning they went to some other red people's house, got some of the garbage they had thrown away, brought it back, and ate it. They slept, and next morning they went around doing the same thing again. Again the two children ate up all the food. The red couple said to each other, 'They're eating all our food. What are we going to do? We'll have to take these children to the cooking shed and leave them there.'

"The children heard this and thought 'We're going to be abandoned.' The boy had some money that he had earned a little at a time by working for another European. He kept it in a tobacco tin, which he had buried in a hole. When he thought they were about be abandoned, he took that money, went to a store, and bought some bread, tinned meat, a knife, new clothes for himself and his sister, and a backpack. He put the things in it and went back home. He and the girl hid the backpack outside and went into the house. The red man said, 'Today we're all going to the forest to gather flowers for decorating the house.' The boy wrapped up the backpack in some of his old clothes to conceal it and set out with his father. The father said 'You go first.' They went a long way, until they came to an unfamiliar forest. Then the red man said 'Now let's pick flowers. You two stay here and pick them and I'll go over there and then come back.' The red man went away, and those two children stayed and stayed, but their father did not come back. It got dark. They came running back on the path, all the way back to the house. When the red couple saw them they said 'Hey, the children have come back! We left them in the forest and came back, and now they've come following behind!' They ate and went to bed without giving those children any food.

"Next morning he took those two again, to another forest much further away—deep into the jungle. He went away, saying 'You stay here and pick flowers and I'll come back.' They followed after him, but they got lost in the forest. They got onto a different path. A heavy rain started to fall. They didn't know where to go. The boy shouldered his backpack and they went and slept under a little tree trunk. He cut them each four slices of bread and meat, they ate it, put the rest back in the backpack and went to sleep. Next morning they got up and went a long way, until they saw a path at the head of a river. . . . Then the two boys [sic]⁴ came to a drinking place, and a washing place at end of the path. They bathed and washed their dirty clothes, then set off along the path. They heard somebody plodding along. They saw a boy and girl with big ears, sunken eyes, and stubby noses. They were coming to get water. When they saw the two boys, they ran back to their mother, who also had big, flat ears, and told her they were coming. She asked 'Where? Where?' Then she saw them coming. She greeted them, and they said hello. The older boy was really frightened. He hid his younger brother from the woman. The woman liked the look of them and wanted to eat them.

"They could hear the sound of wood being chopped, and something being thrown down with a thud. They saw the father with his two children, bringing the corpse of a red [European] man that he had killed. Then they knew that they had come to a cannibal place. The older brother came outside to play with the boy and girl. He took out some of the tinned meat, bread, and tomato sauce, made a sandwich, and secretly ate it. He and his little brother stayed there until it got dark. The cannibals butchered the corpse and went to sleep while the cooking stones heated up in the fire. When they had cooked the meat, they took it out of the roasting pit and gave some to the boys. The little boy wanted to eat it. The big boy took out some more bread and tomato sauce, made him a sandwich, and said 'You eat this and be quiet.' The cannibals thought the boys were eating the human flesh that they had given them. The boys huddled in the corner, staying as far away as they could. The older brother was afraid the two of them were going to be eaten. He hugged his little brother as hard as he could. Two boys like Lucas and Maki [the narrator's sons; see note 4].

"When it got dark, the parents put down a sleeping mat in the bedroom and said 'Let the older boy sleep on one side and the younger boy on the other. Our two children will sleep in the middle,' They did as they were told. But the older boy knew what was going to happen and was frightened. He took off their nice new clothes and put them on the cannibal children, and dressed himself and his brother in the cannibal children's clothes. Then he and his brother shifted to the centre of the bed and moved the cannibal children to the sides. Not having seen this, the cannibal man and his wife then came in with the knife they used for killing people and stabbed the one they thought was the older brother in the heart. He gave out with a dying groan and then they stabbed the other one. Not wanting to waste the blood by letting it flow down onto the mat, they put down a layer of edible greens to soak it up. Then they went back to bed. Terrified, the older boy broke a hole in the doorway, threw his little brother out, and climbed out after him. They slipped off quietly into the dense forest. Carrying his little brother piggy-back, he walked for miles and miles, till after daybreak.

"Come morning, those red cannibals saw that they had killed their own children and that the other two boys had escaped. The man went running after them. He ran and ran, from river to river, from ridge to ridge, till he had nearly caught up with them. He shouted out, 'You two can keep going, but now that I've seen you I am sure to catch up with you, kill you and eat you. Where can you possibly go?' But they ran and ran, across the Nebilyer River, up the embankment, and down the ridge till they reached Tega. By the time he got there, they had reached Waibip.[5] By the time he got there, they had reached to Pulapuka Gardens. By the time he got there, they had come right into Mt. Hagen. By now they were all drenched with sweat. The two boys ran into the police station panting. The police asked 'What happened to you?'

"The red couple who had abandoned those children had been afraid of getting caught and charged for it, so they had gone to the police with a story about how the children had disappeared and how they had looked all over and been unable to find them. Realizing that these were the missing children, the police asked them what had happened. They said 'Our parents said we had eaten up all their food, so they took us to the dense forest and left us there. On our way back, at a cannibal place they were going to eat us. The man has chased us all the way here, saying he is going to kill us. Here he comes now!'

"So the police got their rifles and headed down the road. There he was, face covered with blood, panting and smacking his lips. He came staggering down the middle of the road, not even thinking about the danger of being hit by a car. When they saw him, they shot him dead. Then they asked the boys to tell their story. When they told it again, the police sent for their red parents. They asked them, 'Do you recognize these boys?' The parents looked at the ground in embarrassed silence. The policemen asked, 'Why did you abandon them?'

"'Let's jail them,' they said. They tied them up, shot them and lit a fire. They were amazed by how the boy had out-smarted the cannibals and escaped from them: 'Let this boy be made the boss and protector of everyone, European and New Guinean alike. And let the little brother be put in charge in the army.' And because the boys had won out against the cannibals, that's just what happened to them. That's the end of my story."

CANNIBALISM, CONSUMPTION, AND KU WARU DISCOURSE GENRES

In light of this story and the preceding narrative by Kansil Noma, let us now return to the questions raised above about the relationship between Ku Waru people's apprehensions of Europeans and their traditionally rooted [*bo*] ideas about cannibalism. Both of these stories would seem to provide evidence to support Andrew Strathern's perception that Hageners' stance toward cannibalism is tied up with a particular set of ideas about consumption and exchange.

Turning first to Kansil Noma's story, consider the criteria according to which Noma says Europeans were assessed. At first the default assumption about foreigners was applied to them—that they were cannibals. The first thing the strangers did that seemed to cast doubt on this assumption was to present items for exchange (gold-lipped pearl shells, no less—the exchange item *par excellence* in local terms). But maybe this was just a ruse. Noma suggests he believed otherwise, but his attempts to convince others were undercut by the strangers' actions when they killed two men, surely in order to eat them. But no, they killed and ate a pig instead. And when they then did not appear to eat any people, that was generally taken to lay the matter to rest.

Or was it? That question will have to be raised again in connection with the second story, by Ab Noma, in a somewhat different way because that text is a more patently "fictional" one. But before moving on to that text, it is important to note that Kansil Noma's disquisition, too, is a carefully crafted performance and not simply to be taken as a transparent window on the past, or on what people thought at the time. Although now an old man, Noma has a continuing reputation at Kailge as a masterful user of language, in several genres, including oratory (Merlan & Rumsey 1991:147–152), chanted epic tales (Rumsey 1995, and forthcoming), song, and storytelling. Though the present text invokes themes that are standard in western highlanders' accounts of their initial reactions to the arrival of Europeans, it does so in a way that evinces a remarkable control of what post-Bakhtinian students of discourse (Bakhtin 1981; Hill 1986) would call "voicing" (a concept that bears an interesting family resemblance to what Ku Waru people call *nuimka* [neck]). Over the course of his narrative, delivered to a mixed audience of younger Ku Waru people (none of whom were alive during the events he recounts) and anthropologist Francesca Merlan, to whose query he was responding, Kansil Noma speaks in such a way as to intermingle at least two distinct voices: (1) that of his present persona, the respected local government councillor who has the benefit of hindsight over the events he is narrating; and (2) that of a stereotypical awe-struck onlooker who is situated in the time and place of the narrated events. Noma does this by his choice of wording, by intonation (as I try to reflect in my punctuation and choice of wording in the translation), facial expression, and vocal gestures (more difficult to reflect this medium). A good example occurs at the point in the story when Noma juxtaposes the two observed events, in which he and his companions first see the Europeans kill the men without eating them, and then kill a pig and eat it. By the parallelism he sets up in the two lines "They didn't take them!" [the two corpses] and "They didn't leave it there! [the slaughtered pig]" he creates an exaggerated sense of surprise that simultaneously mimics that of the onlookers and distances himself from them as the *kewa*-worldly-wise commentator in the here and now of 1998.

But the exaggeration here works in two directions at once. On the one hand, it would probably be overliteral of us to assume (as Strathern's comparative framework might lead us to) that central highlanders ever saw the traffic in pork as *simply* a surrogate for cannibalism. But it would be equally mistaken to assume that the absence of direct evidence that Europeans ever actually ate anyone should have completely disabused highlanders of their idea that there was something cannibalistic about them. At the very least, this idea remains "good to think," as shown by the second story, told by Ab Noma. Before discussing that story in particular, I will first say a little about some relevant features of Ku Waru story genres.

Ku Waru make a broad distinction between two kinds of stories, which they call *kange* and *temani.* The two genres differ in a number of subtle ways (for details, see Merlan 1995), but in general *kange* are somewhat more like European "fairy tales" in that they tell of characters and events in a world that is more explicitly set off from everyday reality, whereas *temani,* though sometimes set in the distant past, tell of a world which is more continuous with the here and now. While *kange* differ from European fairly tales in not being set off in time (as in "Once upon a time . . ."), they are *spatialized* in distinctive ways, typically playing on an ethically loaded contrast between the normal everyday order of cleared, cultivated spaces [*kulyi*] and the "wild" space of the deep forest [*taina*], the latter inhabited by ghosts, cannibals, and other weird beings (cf. Goldman 1998). Another, related kind of spatial contrast that figures in these stories is between known territory and unknown, the latter sometimes explicitly placed beyond certain conventionally identified limits of the known world such as *no jimi*, the Jimi River, at the northern edge of the central highlands.

Consonant with the spatial dislocation of the events narrated in them, the narrative *form* of *kange* tends to be more distinctively marked off from everyday speech than that of *temani,* both by characteristic turns of phrase and in the way the *kange* performance is often explicitly introduced as such (*na kange tobu tekir* [I going to tell a *kange*] or the like), and ended with stock expressions such *konta mong rltup rltap* [There the ball stops].

Somewhat paradoxically, the hiatus between the fantasy world of *kange* and the quotidian world is at the same time marked out and partially effaced by the use within this genre of certain conventional devices, which Merlan (1995) has called "techniques of verisimilitude." These include the drawing of explicit parallels between characters in the stories and real people known to the narrator and his/her audience—often his/her own children. Another standard device of this kind is the use of fulsome visual descriptions of central characters and/or their dwellings, with great attention to details of dress, decoration, and overall appearance.

To a much greater extent than *temani, kange* stories make use of a standard set of plots, motifs, and characters, such as Ab Waipi, "The face-paint woman," *pim payl,* a person without orifices, and, of course, *kewa yabu nuyl,* cannibals.

Several of these genre features of *kange* are displayed by Ab Noma's story above: her identification of the central characters with her own sons, the movements between home ground and *taina* ["deep forest"] where cannibals are encountered, and the visually explicit description of their weird physiognomy. For all that the plot resembles the Hansel and Gretel story, many of the motifs in it are standard *kange* ones, including the attempt to lose someone in the forest, the ruse of going there to get flowers, the encounter with cannibals there, and the subterfuge used to escape them. But in other respects it is more *temani*-like. For example, it does not include the explicit framing devices mentioned above. Even more unusually for a *kange,* at the end it brings the action into a kind of quasi–here-and-now world (of places along the highlands highway in Mt. Hagen).

In other words, the story is in some respects intermediate in genre between *kange* and *temani.* In this regard it follows a general tendency, pointed out by Merlan (1995), for the *kewa* stories dealing with European characters to be of this intermediate variety, in which the degree and manner of distantiation between the storyteller's world and that of story is rather more indeterminate than in either *kange* or *temani.*

Indeed, a curious feature of this particular story is that the identity of the cannibals themselves is not strongly established as between European and New Guinean. They are said at one point in the story to be *kuduyl* "red"/"European" cannibals, but nothing that is said about their abode or lifestyle would be taken to identify them that way. Their appearance is that of the standard cannibal figure, with big ears and beastly visage; they live in the deep forest, sleep on mats, cook their food in traditional-style earth ovens, place greens under the freshly killed children just as Ku Waru people do when slaughtering a pig, etc. All of this is not to say that they are strongly identified as *bo* "local" people, as opposed to Europeans. Rather, that particular opposition fades into the background in relation to the one that is here more sharply in focus—namely, the difference between cannibals and noncannibals. Insofar as the cannibal family are identified as "red/European cannibals" [*kuduyl kewa nui*], we are invited to think of these as creatures of the same sort that is already known from the established genre of cannibal stories [*kewa nui kange*].

The European identity of the other family in the story, or at least of the parents, is rather more sharply in focus. The word *kuduyl* ["red"/"European"] is used of them nine times in the story and also in reference to the people whose garbage they ate, and the man for whom the boy had worked. And unlike the cannibal figures in the story, these Europeans *are* identified with a life-way that is thought of as European, at least in origin—namely, the money-based consumer economy. Like typical Europeans, they apparently have no gardens from which to feed themselves, but unlike most they have no money either (except for the boy) and so are forced to go around looking for others' scraps and refuse. It is this fact about them (rather than a wicked stepmother) that establishes the initial problematic of the story, insofar as they are unable to provide for the children and respond by resolving to abandon them.

But even these characters in the story—the ones who abandon their children— are not placed entirely on the *kewa* side of the *bo/kewa* opposition. They live somewhere near the edge of the forest, presumably in the Nebilyer Valley (from where the final chase starts out) or closer to Mt. Hagen (where they are known to the police). And they go into the forest in *bo* fashion to collect flowers for decorating their house.

Nor do Ku Waru folks think of the *bo/kewa* distinction as one in which *people* are placed entirely on one side or the other. For it is equally a difference between ways of doing things (Merlan & Rumsey 1991:28–30), a difference that is nowadays regularly confounded in the course of Ku Waru people's everyday lives. One of the ways in which it is confounded is in people's increasing reliance on money in order to feed themselves: money and the market economy may be *kewa* in origin, but by the time Ab Noma told her story in 1982, they had become firmly established as dimensions of *bo* people's existence. Ku Waru people's engagement with the cash economy has been a source of great exhilaration for them, but also of great anxiety, just as Strathern reports for the northern Melpa region in the late 1970s. On the one hand, there is the perceived threat to the Hagen *bo* ethic of production-for-exchange, which is posed by the possibility of escalating home consumption, as discussed by Strathern. On the other hand—or, we might say, at the opposite end of the scale of possibilities—there is the perceived threat of pauperization that may result from the abandonment of home food-production.

In addition to being a rattling good yarn, Ab Noma's story can be taken as, among other things, a meditation on this threat. In casting the cannibals and their near-victims as Europeans, she is commenting on or speculating not only about the nature of Europeans but about the entailments of *bo* people's own engagement with the *kewa*. And she does it in good Hagen fashion, drawing on the complex symbolic associations brought out by Strathern between cannibalism and other sorts of inward-directed consumption.

If so, then Ab Noma's tale cannot be taken to come down entirely on the side of the *bo*, because the children's victory over the cannibals depends in part on the older brother's success in earning and saving money, hiding it from his parents, and using it to buy just the right items that will be needed to survive: ready-to-eat foods, new clothes with which to trick the cannibals, and a backpack to carry it all. In this he contrasts with his parents in their inability to raise and handle money, but he resembles them in his refusal to share with them, as they refuse to share with him. (He does, however, share with his younger sibling, and is able to save his life partly because he has *not* given the money to his parents).

CONCLUSIONS

Notwithstanding the difference of genre, Ab Noma's story bears some notable resemblances to Kansil Noma's in the way it positions Europeans and local [*bo*] people with respect to each other, and both with respect to cannibalism. And in both texts the relationship between cannibalism and otherness is construed very differently from the way it tends to have been on the European side of the encounter with the "other." William Arens has claimed that the idea of "'others' as cannibals . . . is [a] universal phenomenon" (Arens 1979:139), a kind of "collective prejudice," which is "not a uniquely western failing [but] finds expression wherever there are two human groups in contact. . . . part of the attempt by every society to create a conceptual order based on differences in a universe of often competing neighboring communities. In other words, one group can appreciate its own existence more meaningfully by conjuring up others as categorical opposites" (Arens 1979:145). But here things work rather differently. In the New Guinea Highlands, as illustrated by these two texts and a wealth of other evidence (see, e.g., Connolly & Anderson 1989; Schieffelin & Crittenden 1991), people did not and do not construe Europeans as "categorical opposites" of themselves, but rather as intimately related to themselves.

At first contact, and for a long time after,[6] highlanders commonly took the Europeans to be their own ancestors returning from the dead, as recounted by Kansil Noma.[7] So when they speculated about whether these Europeans were cannibals, they were not thereby construing them as opposite to themselves, but speculating about a potential within themselves.[8] Similarly, to the extent that the rumors of cannibalism that circulated among the Northern Melpa can be linked to anxieties about spiraling consumption, this was not perceived as an "external" threat but one that was based on the inherent human potential for *kum* ["greed"]. The actualization of that potential may have been set off by the new access to European-derived money and consumer goods, but the resulting epidemic of purported cannibalism was seen by the Northern Melpa as something that was developing from within their own community.

Ab Noma's story differs from those rumors in being—as she told me in 1998—"just a story" [*kange midi*]. But within the fantasy world she conjures in it, the relation she sets up between the *bo* and the *kewa* is similar to that which is presupposed by the rumors, and in Kansil Noma's account of what his people had thought of real Europeans. In all three cases the other, the *kewa*, is construed not as the mere negative or categorical opposite of "us" but as an *alternative version* of "us": a spectre that is capable of revealing latent possibilities within ourselves, for better or worse. Just as Arens would expect, the imputation of cannibalism figures strongly in these construals of the "other," but not in the *way* he expects.

For here the effect is not to exaggerate the difference between "us" and "them" but, rather, to obviate it within a schema of possibilities that are taken to be common to both.

Insofar as that schema is concerned with questions of escalating inward-directed consumption, it does indeed provide a basis for addressing some truly horrendous possibilities that have been opened up by the very processes of global-economic intensification that first brought Europeans into contact with New Guinea Highlanders. Consider, for example, the recent finding by the World Conservation Monitoring Centre at Cambridge University that "Humans have destroyed more than 30% of the natural world since 1970, with serious depletion of the forests, fresh water and marine systems on which life depends. Consumption pressure has doubled in the past 25 years and continues to accelerate . . ." (*Sydney Morning Herald*, 3 Oct. 1998, p. 15). This is self-consumption raised to a higher power than has ever been imaginable even by the Hageners—not because of any exponential increase in our collective *kum* ["greed"], but because advancing technology and the expanding world economy have placed us in a common clearing [*kulyi*] and impelled us to eat so far into the previously surrounding *taina* [forest] that the process has become, as the Hageners say, "turned back," and we are now all in serious danger of eating ourselves. For its total effect on the human life world, the impact of all the necrophagy that has ever been committed pales into insignificance beside that of these recent more intensive forms of environmental cannibalism. As an ethical basis for addressing these issues, Hagen ways of thinking about cannibalism and consumption have much to recommend them. For not only do they alert us to the perils of "turned back" consumption, they also compel us to recognize that *we* and *they* are not *categorical opposites* with respect to this process, but mutually implicated in it.

On a more specifically anthropological note, I hope the Ku Waru texts I have presented and discussed here will help dispel another form of *collective prejudice* apart from the imputation of cannibalism to *others*—namely, a tendency to assume that *their* ways of coping with radically new historical contingencies are fully and straightforwardly determined by existing cultural schemas. For while it is clear that the Hageners did have a cultural schema that they brought to bear on the encounter with Europeans, it should also be clear that this did not result in a single definitive interpretation of it. Both through complexities of voicing and through explicit representation of conflicting views about the Europeans, Kansil Noma conveys a sense of Ku Waru people's radical openness to the new and to the possibility that their established forms of understanding may be undermined or transformed by the encounter with it (cf. Merlan & Rumsey 1991:224–242). And, as I have discussed above with respect to both texts, what is taken to be at issue for those forms of understanding is not just the other (the *kewa*), but *we bo* as well. In other words, Hageners have long recognized what to some anthropologists has seemed like a distinctly *modern* or *postmodern* discovery, that our accounts of the other are inherently relational. But unlike in some forms of postmodernism, they do not take this to mean that there is *nothing outside the text*—no hard-edged empirical reality by which the interpretions must be constrained. On the contrary, as Kansil Noma makes clear (cf. Connolly & Anderson 1989; Schieffelin & Crittenden 1991), highlanders based their understandings about the nature of Europeans on close observation of their appearance and behavior, took a keen interest in it, and treated those understandings as provisional and ever subject to revision in light of it. This healthy combination of relational-perspectivism and empirical rigor is one from which contemporary anthropology has much to learn.

NOTES

To Ku Waru associates and friends who have discussed the themes of this paper during many conversations since 1981, and especially to Kansil Noma and Ab Noma for their stories, *na aima age anumuyl nyikir*. For funding of the fieldwork with Ku Waru people on which this chapter is based, I would like to thank the (U.S.) National Science Foundation, the Australian Research Council, the University of Sydney, and the Research School of Pacific and Asian Studies, Australian National University. For their helpful comments on earlier drafts of this paper I would like to thank Laurence Goldman, Diana McCarthy, Francesca Merlan, Anthony Redmond, and James Rumsey-Merlan. My conversations with them, as well as my earlier ones with Ku Waru people, provided many of the leads on which my argument is based and many others that I lacked the space or the competence to take up. I fully realize that my discussion of Kansil Noma's and Ab Noma's stories has only scratched the surface of what could be said about them, and I would be delighted if others would take advantage of my translations to continue the conversation about them. For my part, I would be glad to take their comments back to the storytellers and see what happens from there.

1. Compare Stewart and Strathern (1997 and forthcoming), where this same case is discussed and the argument is made more explicit about the nature of the connection, phased in the quote above as "coincidence," between the rumors and the changes in consumption patterns. In the more recent publications, following Sperber (1985), this is framed as an "epidemiological" relation, where the political–economic conditions have created certain pathways that are conducive to the spread of certain kinds of belief, "expression," or "representation," in this case about the secret practice of cannibalism.

2. Laurence Goldman (personal communication 10/98) points out that the term *kewa* or *hewa* is widely used across the Kutubu-Kikori region of the Southern Highlands and Gulf Province for "other people," usually "southerly" and foreign.

3. In this respect Ku Waru ideas resemble those of the Arapesh, who, Tuzin says, think of their culture as "an island of civilization surrounded on all sides by more-or-less constantly menacing man eaters" (Tuzin 1983:68).

4. At this point in the story Noma changes these two characters from brother and sister to elder brother and younger brother, perhaps to make them more comparable to her own sons, Lucas and Maki—a comparison that she explicitly makes further in her telling of the story (Noma has no daughters).

5. These two named places, and the next one, are places along the Highlands Highway, on the way from the Southern Highlands to the Western Highlands provincial center (and biggest town in the Highlands) Mt. Hagen.

6. In 1981, when Francesca Merlan and I first settled at Kailge, our field site in the Western Highlands, we were taken in by a man of Kansil Noma's generation, who told us with utter

conviction that, try as we might to deny it, he knew we were his own parents returned from the dead.

7. This belief was, of course, not confined to the New Guinea Highlands but common across much of Melanesia, where it figured as an underlying premise of the so-called cargo cults.

8. In the nearby Southern Highlands, the Huli people explicitly posit a period in the past when they were preceded by a race of cannibals (Goldman 1998:214–215), as do many other peoples around the world. (Arens 1979). As far as I know, the Ku Waru and Melpa people do not.

REFERENCES

Arens, W. A. (1979). *The Man-Eating Myth: Anthropology and Anthropophagy.* New York: Oxford University Press.

Bakhtin, M. (1981). *The Dialogic Imagination.* Austin, TX: University of Texas Press.

Brown, P., & Tuzin, D. (eds.) (1983). *The Ethnography of Cannibalism.* Washington, DC: Society for Psychological Anthropology.

Connolly, B., & Anderson, R. (1989). *First Contact: New Guinea's Highlanders Encounter the Outside World.* New York: Viking Penguin.

Dornstreich, M., & Morren, G. (1974). Does New Guinea cannibalism have nutritional value? *Human Ecology* 2: 1–12.

Fallers, L. (1969). *Law without Precedent.* Chicago, IL: University of Chicago Press.

Farb, P., & Amelagos, G. (1980). *Consuming Passions: The Anthropology of Eating.* Boston, MA: Houghton Mifflin.

Goldman, L. (1998). *Child's Play: Myth, Mimesis and Make-Believe.* Oxford: Berg.

Hill, J. (1986). The refiguration of the anthropology of language. *Cultural Anthropology* 1: 89–102.

Merlan, F. (1995). Indigenous narrative genres in the Highlands of Papua New Guinea. In P. Silberman & J. Loftlin (eds.), *SALSA 2: Proceedings of the Second Annual Symposium about Language and Society Austin* (pp. 87–98). Austin, TX: University of Texas (*Texas Linguistic Forum* 34).

Merlan, F., & Rumsey, A. (1991). *Ku Waru: Language and Segmentary Politics in the Western Nebilyer Valley.* Cambridge: Cambridge University Press.

Middleton, J. (1970). *The Study of the Lugbara.* New York: Holt, Rinehart and Winston.

Poole, F. J. P. (1983). Cannibals, tricksters and witches: Anthropophagic images among the Bimin-Kuskusim. In P. Brown & D. Tuzin (eds.), *The Ethnography of Cannibalism* (pp. 6–32). Washington, DC: Society for Psychological Anthropology

Rumsey, A. (1995). Pairing and parallelism in the New Guinea Highlands. In P. Silberman & J. Loftlin (eds.), *SALSA 2: Proceedings of the Second Annual Symposium about Language and Society Austin* (pp 108–118). Austin, TX: University of Texas (*Texas Linguistic Forum* 34).

Rumsey, A. (forthcoming). Aspects of Ku Waru ethnosyntax and social life. To appear in N. Enfield (ed.), *Ethnosyntax.*

Sahlins, M. (1979). Reply. *New York Review of Books* 26: 46–47.

Sanday, P. (1986). *Divine Hunger: Cannibalism as a Cultural System.* Cambridge: Cambridge University Press.

Schieffelin, E., & Crittenden, R. (1991). *Like People You See in a Dream: First Contact in Six Papuan Societies.* Stanford, CA: Stanford University Press.

Sperber, D. (1985). Anthropology and psychology: Towards an epidemiology of representations. *Man* (n.s.), 21: 73–89.

Stewart, P., & Strathern, A. (1997). Sorcery and sickness: Spatial and temporal movements in Papua New Guinea and Australia. *James Cook University Centre for Pacific Studies Discussion Papers Series* 1: 1–27.

Stewart, P., & Strathern, A. (forthcoming). Invasions, dismemberments, consumptions: "Feasting on my enemy." To appear in A. Rumsey & J. Weiner (eds.), *Emplaced Myth: The Spatial and Narrative Dimensions of Knowledge in Australian and Papua New Guinea Societies.*

Strathern, A. (1971). *The Rope of Moka: Big Men and Ceremonial Exchange in Mt. Hagen, New Guinea.* Cambridge: Cambridge University Press.

Strathern, A. (1979). *Ongka: A Self-Account by a New Guinea Big-Man.* London: Duckworth.

Strathern, A. (1982). Witchcraft, greed, cannibalism and death. In M. Bloch & J. Perry (eds.), *Death and the Regeneration of Life* (pp. 111–133). Cambridge: Cambridge University Press.

Tuzin, D. (1983). Cannibalism and Arapesh cosmology. In P. Brown & D. Tuzin (eds.), *The Ethnography of Cannibalism* (pp. 61–71). Washington, DC: Society for Psychological Anthropology.

Wormsley, W. (1993). *The White Man Will Eat You! An Anthropologist among the Imbonggu of New Guinea.* Fort Worth, TX: Harcourt Brace.

6

Asmat Cosmology
and the Practice of Cannibalism

Kerry M. Zubrinich

INTRODUCTION

In 1959, Fr. G. Zegwaard published the seminal article on Asmat headhunting. The article is an eclectic consideration of aspects of Asmat culture as they impinge upon the headhunt and initiation ritual he is describing. He collected the information while establishing a Catholic mission among the central Asmat. Zegwaard's paper has as its focal point an exegesis on headhunting practice and ritual by Warsekomen, an Asmat fight leader. The exegesis involves both an elaboration of the myths surrounding the headhunt and cannibalism and a description of headhunting raids and male initiation rites. The combination of myths and descriptive material is in part derived from the narrative style of Warsekomen who according to Zegwaard "unconsciously shifts from myth into reality" (1959:1021). Such a combination of what are considered different narrative forms is not unusual in published collected versions of Asmat stories (see, particularly, Voorhoeve 1965).

This mixture of narrative forms draws attention to the way in which myth is part and parcel of lived experiences in particular cultures. Kapferer points out, in another context, that

the myths have broad thematic structures through which the experiential possibilities and the import or meanings of particular contexts of action can be constructed. The myths are not so much structures of meaning in themselves as instruments through which dimensions of human actualities are enframed and grasped. [1998:62]

The myth of the first act of decapitation and cannibalism, together with the male initiation ritual, provides a set of circumstances that allows just such possibilities in an examination of the Asmat social world. Through their actions, the Asmat were able to elaborate upon the myth and their existence, and in the process they ensured the creation and maintenance of the social world.

The fact that ritual "does something" makes it an ideal phenomenon for the examination of crucial concepts of any cosmology. Headhunting, as it occurred among the Asmat, was tied up with initiation and was itself a form of ritual practice. As the social world emerges in the examination of the ritual and myths surrounding headhunting and cannibalism, significant understandings of what it is to be Asmat emerge. Therefore it is important to examine what the ritual is doing and to remember:

the world is not immune to culture, nor does it sustain culture on its surface as an overlay which can be lifted to reveal a stratum of pure nature without the imprint of a human body. [Dillon 1997:196]

Considering cannibalism as a phenomenon embedded in Asmat existence reveals a concern with the very characteristics of what it meant to be Asmat. In particular, it reveals meanings constituted in and by the human body in its experience of the world.

The following reanalysis of Zegwaard's material focuses upon the centrality of cannibalism to Asmat cosmology, for in Asmat cosmology headhunting and cannibalism were inextricably linked. It should be noted here that I am not arguing, as did Lévi-Strauss (1984), that headhunting and cannibalism are logically the same thing. For example, an examination of the analyses of headhunting without cannibalism in southeast Asia indicates not merely a difference in the perspectives developed by the anthropologists, but very different meanings for the people involved (Freeman 1979; McKinley 1976; Rosaldo 1980).[1] For the central Asmat, the two were inextricably bound together, and an examination of the myths, ritual, and other practices surrounding them reveals that cannibalism must be considered more than a mere interlude in the ritual cycle of headhunting. My project is to explore specific characteristics of Asmat cosmology evident in the headhunt and cannibalism, paying special attention to what it means for the Asmat to have eaten people.

The Asmat inhabit large stretches of swampy plains on the south coast of the island of New Guinea in the former colony of Dutch New Guinea. The central Asmat occupy the region around Flamingo Bay. As the colonial project of the Dutch paved the way for the absorption of West Papua into Indonesia, the Asmat are now considered citizens of Irian Jaya. They have, into the 1990s, maintained subsistence activities that are based on the production of sago, hunting, collecting, and fishing (Smidt 1993). These continuing activities as they affect the analysis are discussed further on, as they are relevant to the analysis of the earlier practices of headhunting and cannibalism.

HEADHUNTING AND CANNIBALISM

Central to European images of the Asmat throughout the early part of this century were the practice of decapitation and the ingestion of flesh as part of the ritual cycle. Lévi-Strauss (1984:111) and Castro (1992) have both remarked upon the reluctance of anthropologists to deal with cannibalism.[2] Lévi-Strauss considered this reluctance a mere gustatory sensitivity. Castro's explanation is more subtle and interesting with respect to this, because it relates both Western anthropological and Tupi (the South American people he is describing) concepts regarding cannibalism by considering incest as the common ingredient in the different cosmologies:

Anthropophagy, emblem of the Tupi in the Western imagination since Montaigne, has always posed a certain enigma for anthropology—due less, I believe, to phagic reasons than a sort of logical repugnance. After all, cannibalism is, like incest, impossible: impossible in the sense of making bodies and signs, persons and names coincide. [Castro 1992:269]

The bodies and signs that the Asmat tried to keep apart are significantly different from those that the anthropologists wish to separate. Simultaneously incorporating others while making them different is at the very basis of Asmat cosmology. While other forms of violence were evident among the Asmat, it is headhunting and cannibalism that enable us to understand the way that the Asmat conceive themselves in relation to other people and from which understandings of sociality may be drawn.

Zegwaard rightly relates headhunting to the construction of Asmat sociality, yet he sees cannibalism as a byproduct of the headhunt, viewing it as the most unsavory aspect of the killings. He maintains that:

It may be mentioned in passing that the Asmat have associated headhunting with cannibalism. I had many an opportunity to observe this, but this exposition may make it clear that cannibalism is not the objective of headhunting (as far as the Asmat are concerned), but only a subsidiary part of it. [Zegwaard 1959: 1020]

An examination of the operations and the myths surrounding headhunting and the eating of flesh, however, shows that cannibalism, far from being ancillary, is central to the headhunt in Zegwaard's description.

The need to exact revenge for a death is said to have driven the continuing search for heads among the Asmat people. But additionally the impetus toward the headhunt and cannibalism may be viewed as an aspect of the continuing battle for equilibrium among the living and has origins in the necessity of maintaining relationships with the dead. For the Asmat, the connection with their ancestors was always precarious. For example, the exploits of the living were used to drive ancestral spirits from the places the living wish to go, and such actions need to impress the spirits both with the ferocity of the living people and with their ability to exist successfully in the chosen environment.

One example of this relationship with the spirits was a characteristic of a powerful male's relationship with the world of the spirits, the *dewan atakam* [enumeration of achievements]. The *dewan atakam* involved a warrior listing his ability to take heads and defeat enemies, thus not needing the spirits to protect him. This recital took place in both ritual and everyday settings and was also a device whereby the warrior sought to scare off the ancestral spirits in order to ensure the safety of the task at hand (Zegwaard 1959:1040). The ancestors and other spirits were at once being appeased and driven from the places of the living. In the headhunt that accompanies initiation, the newer generation of Asmat men was being constituted and links between sociopolitical groups established.

While marriage is the primary connector between groups among the Asmat and polygamy denotes a man's prestige, it was not a primary factor in the creation of maleness. Although a man could marry without taking heads, in order for a man to achieve prestige, indeed to get a soul, among the central Asmat it was necessary for him to take heads. The married man who had taken no heads had no authority in the political life of the village,

When his wife wants to hurt him, she calls him *nas minu*, piece of meat; she declares that he is only meat, that he has no soul, no courage. [Zegwaard 1959:1041]

Prestigious links with other groups and individuals emerged from the constitutive element of headhunting and cannibalism, whereby the man became more than meat by killing and eating others.

CONSIDERING VIOLENCE AND THE ASMAT

Most recorded early Western encounters with the Asmat resulted in violence. Yet, despite the superior firepower of the intruders, it was the Asmat who were always construed as violent. The violence described within the Asmat ethnography has its origins in two different sources, each of which have ramifications for the location of people as well as being constitutive of them. The construction of Asmat by the invaders is an issue in colonial situations, because a regime of colonial violence affects the local practices the colonial regime itself considers violent and abhorrent. But violence also arises from indigenous beliefs and practices, and it is an aspect of such violence that I am concerned with here. Although recorded by the colonizers and used for their own purposes, analyzing aspects of indigenous violence among the Asmat is important because it reveals fundamental aspects of Asmat cosmology.[3]

There are two points to be considered with respect to Asmat headhunting and everyday life. (a) This form of violence did not alienate the victim or the perpetrators. The headhunt was important in the making of people for the victorious group in two ways. First, the act of taking a head established a man's prowess, and the skull itself was integral to initiation. Second, by virtue of a relationship to the victim, the initiate became a member of the victim's group. Also, the prestige certain individuals gain through their prowess as a warrior or as a woman who takes heads ensures a more significant position for that person within a group.[4] The victim was bodily incorporated and became part of the social world of the victorious group. (b) At a mundane level, the time taken by everyone for the ceremonial cycles that require heads could not be considered dissociation from ordinary life. The ongoing nature of the cycles and their preparation through subsistence activities means that they were part of ordinary social life. The taking of heads was part and parcel of the ritual corpus and daily life in the situation described by commentators at the midpoint of the twentieth century. It was also part of the political life of the Asmat, and it defined boundaries, expanded victorious villages, and depleted (or totally destroyed) the losing groups. Every village was potentially at war with every other village, with no mechanism for creating an overarching state-like structure.

A perspective—which resonates with such an understanding of Asmat warfare—is found in Deleuze and Guattari's paper on nomadology (1987). For Deleuze and Guattari, the war machine exists in the interstices between state and nonstate formations and does not become a part of state apparatus. In terms of human involvement, it is at the moment of the war machine's destruction that the following question arises:

> Could it be that it is at the moment the war machine ceases to exist, conquered by the State, that it displays to the utmost its irreducibility, that it scatters into thinking, loving, dying machines that have at their disposal vital or revolutionary powers capable of challenging the conquering State. [1987:356]

In other words, at the point of the destruction of the war machine humanity is constituted. For the Asmat, the act of destruction in terms of outside villages continually constituted the victor. Simultaneously, the vanquished are merged and constituted in the acts of cannibalism and the taking on of names. At the same time, the distillation of a situation where a high priest or despot reigned was prevented by the proximity of competing war machines in the region.

Nevertheless, Deleuze and Guattari's analysis cannot be pushed too far, because their analysis relies on an ever-present state form. Cannibalism becomes a reaction to that state form, and "Every time they eat a dead man, they can say: one more the State won't get" (1987:118). However, war machines also exist in the interstices of social systems, which, while the inexorable character of the State apparatus has inevitably impinged upon them, are able to provide in indigenous terms meanings for headhunting and cannibalism that are far more complex than the withholding of bodies from the state.

The political life of the Asmat must be located in an exploration of the cosmological underpinnings of Asmat culture. This applies to all aspects of their political world. The politics of Asmat interaction with the state and global capital are informed by the same cosmology as the politics of the village. Then one may see how the Asmat conceive of violence and the necessity for it. While violence as an aspect of social control is an important problem explored in anthropological literature (see Gluckman 1963; Meggitt 1977; Taussig 1986), in the Asmat ethnography social control appears as only a small part of the indigenous understandings surrounding violence. The Asmat situation, especially before the increase in colonial activity in the 1950s, is akin to that described by Castro for the Arawete:

> Rather than a judicial system based on a restorative vendetta, it was a war of ontological predation, formulated in the idiom of vengeance—the idiom of the social relationship of reciprocity. [1992:278]

Enmeshed with these constitutive elements of violence and the ways in which Asmat men were continually being made and renewed through the headhunt and cannibalism is an understanding of the relational and gendered characteristic of Asmat social life.

RELATIONSHIPS AND KILLING

In the Asmat ethnography there are two ways of getting heads described. The first is the opportunistic killing of people: people were killed because a group from another village happened upon them. Also, people who found themselves in a village for whatever reason and considered that they had some protection in the form of connections through marriage, trade, or previous warfare may have been murdered.[5] In these cases, like the end of the headhunting raid I describe further along, social relationships were an important aspect of the killings.

Eyde relates the case of a woman who was murdered in response to a previous killing, whereby a man belonging to the Awok group in the village of Amannamkai had ensured his own death by arming and placing himself provocatively outside the village of Jacsiw. Some time later:

> A woman who had been born in the Namkaj men's group, but who had married a man of the Ac men's house group came to visit her relatives in Aman-namkaj. The female relatives of the Awok man who had been killed gathered around the house in which she was visiting, peering in at the door and through the thatching, their tongues lolling out of their mouths saying things like *"us normomo,"* "I love your flesh." Finally, a crowd of Awok people broke into the house and carried the struggling woman away to the other side of the Kampong river, where she was killed. [1967:77–78]

The host family in this case was not strong enough to prevent the killing. When such killings occured, it caused argument, and those offended may even have moved from the village (Zegwaard 1959:1027, 1032). Nevertheless, while her relatives were unable to protect the woman in the above case, her relationship to the village stopped her body being decapitated and eaten. According to Eyde:

"Some of the men wished to take her head and to eat her, but the elders of the group intervened, saying that she was, after all, from their own village" (1967: 78–79).

All killings, whether opportunistic or planned as part of a raid, encoded understandings about relatedness as a key factor in the direction in which people kill, as the following incident from the Sawa people reveals. In a description of the relationship between Pam Pyamnebis, a warrior and leader among the Sawa people, and the Weo people collected by the Walker group in 1974, the expectations of hospitality are included in understandings of particular ties. The story concerns the adoption of the son of the war leader, Sibir, by Pam through capture in battle. According to the notes, Pam's wife had asked him to bring back a son, and he did so after the following exchange with Sibir:

Sibir: Pam, will you keep my son Are and grow him up, or will you kill him?

Pam: I won't kill him. My wife requested me when we left the village if I find a boy in this fight I should take that boy back to her because she likes to grow up a boy.

Sibir: If you just like to grow him up, that is ok, but my only request is that if in the future you people will make a war against us please take the boy with you.

Pam: Fair enough. And now I will leave this place.

While Pam said that, he moved into his prau, but Sibir said, "Wait a minute, Pam." Sibir grabbed the arrows of his fellows, made a big bunch of them, and carried them to the praw of Pam. After he put the bunch of arrows in the praw he helped to push the prau of Pam to the other side of the river. Then Sibir rolled himself in the mud and cried for his son Are, who should go to Sawa. The rest of Weo cried also for their deaths and also for the little boy. [Walker n.d.: collected 19 May 1974]

Pam took Are back to Sawa, passing on the arrows when he matured and giving him another name, Kase Pyamnebis. Kase became a renowned hunter who married within Sawa and died in February 1974. Although the Weo people remained unfriendly to the villages of Sawa and Er, Erma and Sona, Pam was protected from harm by his good treatment of the boy and was not harmed even during wartime when he met Weo people on the river.[6] Both of these killings involved the recognition of social ties. In the one case the further degradation of the victim's body was stopped, while in the other a specific tie was established between the successful headhunter and the vanquished group. Like all ideologies, that of relatedness does not need to be taken up in all of its aspect at all times to provide an understanding of what should happen under particular circumstances. The killing under certain circumstances of people who were under protection does not obviate the positive aspect of relationships established in different domains. Bravado, as a personal characteristic, may be there, but the underlying understanding that marks specific relationships, if properly attended to (as Pam attended to his with Weo through his adoption of Are/Kase), gives protection.

THE HEADHUNTING RAID

The exchange between Pam and Sibir took place at the end of a headhunting raid where Pam's group were the aggressors and the victors. In the recordings of the Dutch colonial period, a dawn raid or an ambush planned in advance to avenge ancestors and simultaneously gain heads for ritual purposes was planned by the war leaders, and it is they who arranged where to attack and when (Eyde 1967:69; Sowada 1961:14; Zegwaard & Boelaars 1970:54). In the process a shaman may have been consulted in order to ascertain the success of the mission, and if there was time a swine hunt may have been held prior to the raid.

In the published material on the Asmat, political women are difficult to find, except as reactors.[7] This may be due to a number of factors, ranging from the bias of the ethnographers to the shyness of the women when faced with intruders. What does become obvious in the reading is that Wagner's point—that for the Daribi male contingency and female sufficiency is the most pervasive social obsession—holds true for the Asmat (1978:185). That this concern was general can be seen from the fact that central Asmat women were active participants in the violence of the headhunting and cannibalism and in the male initiation ritual described. Women played a significant part in the early part of the expedition: in its instigation and in the prior ritual (Zegwaard 1959:1035–1039). They spurred men on to take heads, thus taking initiative in the political life of the Asmat. Women who wished to gain prestige, and for their sons and husband to form proper relationships and to be more than "*nas minu,*" were able to have some say in the pattern of warfare. Relationships through women could also be used in strategies of warfare.

Ambush was one of the ways used to gain heads. In setting up an ambush, a specific group may have been lured to a location through the agency of a man who had access to the community being targeted, either through his mother and other relatives or because of relationships set up during previous warfare (Zegwaard 1959:1032). The lie [*nao piri*] told under such circumstances was aimed at luring an unsuspecting group to a place where the attacking villagers would be waiting in ambush. The importance of deception in maintaining life is a recurring motif in Asmat understandings of how to be in the world. Just as the spirits must be deceived with respect to the whereabouts of the child in naming practices (Zegwaard 1982; for further discussion see Zubrinich 1997, ch. 3), the warring groups must protect themselves by deceiving each other.

In describing Asmat warfare, some commentators have remarked upon the deceit and cunning that the Asmat deem necessary for engaging in warfare (Eyde 1967:69; Sowada 1961:14; Zegwaard & Boelaars 1970:54). They have seen this aspect of Asmat warfare as contrasting with Western warfare, which is ideologically considered open and declared confrontation. The constitution of warfare and the characteristics of courage are so obviously different cross-culturally that it probably requires no further exegesis at this point except to say that deceit and cunning play a different but still valued part in Western warfare. What is relevant is the processual nature of Asmat warfare, where every act of warfare not only constituted the aggressors but also sowed the seeds of revenge. It is at this point that the Asmat concerns in warfare differ from those evident in state forms where absolute domination in some aspect of social life is expected and stability is expected through such domination.

According to Zegwaard's account, the headhunting raid itself was a precarious undertaking because it may only have been the element of surprise that the aggressors had to their advantage. There were three groups of men involved in the raid: the leaders, the archers, and the in-close warriors. They arrived at the village about dawn and positioned themselves:

From one of the houses some man will call: "Who is that?" The answer is: "Your husband, Sjuru" (where Sjuru is the attacker). [Zegwaard 1959:1036]

The feminization reflected in this question-and-answer sequence wends its way through male relationships with each other. In affinal relationships, for example, the wife-givers make sexual jokes about wife-takers, while wife-takers treat their wife's brothers with deference (Eyde 1967:199–200). The joking relationships and the feminization of wife-takers are an example of the contextual nature of gender signification. In terms of the construction of gender, the contextuality of gender inscription emphasizes the way that gender characteristics are an aspect of all people and actions and are a constitutive rather than a taxonomic device.

The people of the target village were either killed or captured. If captured, to be killed later, they were treated cruelly on the way back to the aggressor's village. Female captives were sometimes taken as wives. There is a point of disagreement between Zegwaard and Eyde, as the former maintains that women captives were not raped and Eyde says they occasionally were (Eyde 1967:69; Zegwaard 1959:1036). Eyde goes on to say that if women were raped, they may not be killed (1967:69). This point of disagreement does not, in Asmat terms, constitute a contradiction, for in a raid women could be captured as wives. Their rape on the way home immediately affirmed them as wives. Zegwaard also points out that the warrior who wanted a wife or a child from the raid needed to make this apparent prior to the raid. In the excitement of the raid the accepted method of claiming a wife by saying: "Fathers, brothers, the women of our village never took any notice of me, I'll take this woman home" may not have been possible (Zegwaard 1959:1036). The killing took place at points along the way, or the captives were taken back and kept until such time as their captors needed heads and flesh as part of the ritual cycle.

The headhunt took place as part of important ritual cycles that could take some months to finish and could involve a relatively lengthy preparation. But, as I noted above, when there were opportunities to kill, the Asmat availed themselves of them. In the process of continuing warfare, the viability of groups was tested and their very existence was perpetually under threat.[8] The significance of the flesh in this process has much to do with its association with sago.

FLESH AND SAGO

There is no necessary division between the sacred and the mundane in the Asmat situation. The series of ritual and mythological links with other-worldly beings and the polity of "living people" are enmeshed. Each domain encodes elements of the sacred and the mundane, so that the struggle for territory and survival through warfare that is the organizing premise of Eyde's (1967) thesis is also the struggle to become men and overcome the spirit world. The representations of the ancestors in the carvings, the ordinary artifacts, as well as the awesome *bis* (ancestor) poles are at once symbols of the ancestors and necessary to sustain life.[9] Sago remains the staple food of the Asmat, and in the myths and activities surrounding the earlier headhunt and cannibalism the connections between flesh and sago can be traced out.

The eating of flesh combined with sago is physically and spiritually nurturing. In a myth about the origin of the songs to be sung at decapitation festivities, the male and female elements, necessary components of all aspects of Asmat cosmology, are also present. According to Zegwaard's published version, the myth begins with Biwiripitsj and his wife and children going to the river to pound sago. He fells a palm in full flower then lays his son on it, and he, or his wife, kill the boy with the sago pounder. The boy's head, which is decorated, flies into the *jimemtnul* tree, and blood drips from the head onto the trunk of that tree while the father (or the mother) pound the flesh and blood of the trunk into the sago pith. The merging of the boy's body with the sago changes the composition of the sago:

When the mother began to work the pith, it proved very easy to knead. She rejoiced and said: "before it was very hard to knead sago and wring it out, now it's extremely easy." The son, however, was not completely dead, for the head began to talk. He taught his father the songs that have to be sung at the decapitation festivities: the songs on the way home from a raid, at the arrival in the village, when shaking out the brains and so on. [Zegwaard 1959:1027–1028]

Maleness and femaleness are characterized in this myth by the tasks allotted in the actual production of the sago. Both the mother and the father are possible killers of the son, and the results of the slaying relate to both male and female domains.

The myth is tied to the nurturing projects of both men and women, with the two main features of Asmat food production being central to the myth.[10] The growth of Asmat males and their reproductive powers was also tied directly to the skull of the victim. Zegwaard points out that the relationship of the skull to the sago plant is one of regeneration derived from the loose head resembling fallen sago fruit. The latter, being the regenerative element of the sago plant, has an allegorical relationship to the skull, which, when placed between the legs of the initiate during the initiation ritual, ensures the rapid growth and reproductive capacity of Asmat men (Zegwaard 1959:1039).

All major rituals were accompanied by headhunting and cannibalism, and in the sections of the rituals that were celebrated once colonial intervention had become effective in lessening warfare, we find that sago and sago larvae remain fundamental to the ritual cycle. Eyde, in examining exchanges, wrote:

It should be made clear that both flesh and sago are exchanged in both directions between affines. A husband both gives and receives sago, for example, to and from his wife's brothers. But sago is not considered the true reciprocation for sago. The reciprocation for flesh is sago. [1967:202][11]

The connection between flesh and sago weaves through Asmat life and emerges particularly in ritual contexts and the exchanges between affines. What is important at this point is that the meanings encoded in the flesh-for-sago exchange are available even into the later colonial period through the association of sago and flesh. In the earlier period, when the headhunt took place sago was an integral part of the ritual cycle.

In the third quarter of this century headhunting and cannibalism ceased to all intents and purposes in the Asmat region. Lévi-Strauss noted:

One is also struck by the labile character of cannibalistic customs. In all the evidence available from the sixteenth century until the present, these customs emerge, spread and disappear in what is often a very short period of time. Doubtless this explains their frequent abandonment at the first contact with Whites, and even before the coercive measures could be deployed against the practitioners. It would be hard to understand how cannibalism could so frequently assume an unstable and subtly changeable form without recognizing an underlying schema wherein identification with the other plays a part. [1984:112; emphasis added]

In the Asmat context, the obliteration of the headhunt and cannibalism and the persistence of the underlying schema are best understood in terms of the interchangeability of flesh and sago.

MALE INITIATION

The taking of heads was fundamental to the male initiation ceremony of the central Asmat as described by Zegwaard (1959). The ceremony involved not only the eating of the flesh of the victim but also the initiate sitting in the men's house in front of the fire with the smoked skull between his legs, close to his genitals, for two to three days. During the ceremony he was attended by his mother's brothers, and in time he was taken to the river and toward the west (the direction of *Safan*).[12] When worn out, his life would be renewed, according to the myth, and he would become like a newborn babe, observing food taboos and learning quickly the things he had known before. Warsekomen told the myth to Zegwaard to explain the headhunting and cannibalism that went with initiation. The story begins with the assertion by Desoipitsj that the pig's head brought to him by his younger brother (another Biwiripitsj), while a fine gift, is not as good a presentation as a human head. Biwiripitsj demurs and asks where he could get a human head.[13] Desoipitsj insists and offers his own head. Biwiripitsj eventually kills his elder brother and cuts off his head (Zegwaard 1959:1021). Desoipitsj, apart from making the sacrifice, maintains his authority, because

The loose head, however, was able to speak and it gave instructions to Biwiripitsj, who obediently executed the orders given by it. [Zegwaard 1959]

In the beginning the older brother is already a man, but he will not survive. The younger, by decapitating the elder, gains another name (that of the elder brother) and survives. The younger brother is the initiate, and it is he who carries out the instructions of the older man and relays these instructions to the rest of the people. While the pig is a considerable coup, it is not enough to make men—the hunting of humans has more value than the hunting of pigs, although the techniques for slaying and the butchering are similar. The younger brother's slaying of his own brother involves both incest and the respect due to his brother as an older man.

There are five instructions for the treatment of the body. The first describes the butchering of the decapitated body, and the last finishes with the way the various portions are cooked. Of special interest is the fact that the flesh of the lower part of the body and the thighs was to be mixed with sago (Zegwaard 1959:1021). The sago and the body were once again merged. In this case it is the human body that is enhanced by the addition of sago—the inverse of the situation described in the story about the origin of the songs for the decapitation festivities.

Zegwaard's description then deals with the arrival back at the village of a victorious headhunting group. This is the point at which he mentions that not only Biwiripitsj actions are being described, but also those of Warsekomen and the men of Sjuru. The salient feature of the return is that it is a celebration of the successful killing, which is announced by the blowing of the hunting horn by the successful warriors. The hunters give the name(s) of those slain. It is also at this point that the initiate mother's eldest brother has to wash the head and take it to the bachelors' house, pinning it to the floor with a cassowary dagger, where the initiates had already assumed a pose of shame (Zegwaard 1959:1021–1022).

The previous set of instructions is obviously directed at headhunting raids in general, up to the point where it is the initiate mother's brother who takes the head. One of the important aspects of Asmat life is the concretization through naming, whether it be in terms of naming people in a village or the taking of the victim's in the headhunt. The victims are expected to ask the names of their attackers. Naming is what makes real and gives an object (be it a dish, a shield, a mask, etc.) or persons characteristics that locate it (or them) within the Asmat social world.

The initiate acted by Biriwiripitsj, received the name of his victim—that is of the elder brother Desoipitsj. The Asmat call this name the *nao juus* or decapitation name, often referred to as *owam juus* or bamboo name (after the bamboo breastplate that is later worn as a substitute of the hunted head). [Zegwaard 1959:1022]

The rest of Instruction 3 is concerned with the ritual identification and the adornment of the initiate. The initiate's relationship to the head is continually being strengthened during the ritual (myth), starting with the cleansing of the head by the mother's oldest brother and his preparation for the initiate. The mother's oldest brother is also charged with the preparation of the head and its assimilation to the initiate in the form of the smearing of a mixture of blood (collected on decapitation) and ash (from the victim's burnt hair over the initiate's head, shoulders, and body) (Zegwaard 1959:1022). Throughout the ritual, relatedness is the organizational principle; the location of the initiate in the Asmat social world is continually referred to by the performance of the actors.

Instruction 4 deals with the disposition of the head, which in the case of Desoipitsj and Biriwiripitsj is left until after the ceremony was completed. Again the mother's oldest brother is the person to prepare the head, which is to be roasted on the evening of the decapitation. The following morning all of the mother's brothers work on the skinning of the head and the removal of the jawbones (Zegwaard 1959:1024). In the process of the preparation of the skull, the human qualities of the victim, which are to be taken by the initiate, are recalled:

for example, while taking the skin off the mouth one would say: "yesterday this mouth ate fish on the bank of the river, today it is dead." [Zegwaard 1959:1023–1024]

In each part of the ceremony the concretization of the body in terms of its humanness, and thus its significance for the initiate, is prescribed, while his relationship to his mother's brothers is reinforced.

Zegwaard's account continues, and he describes the further preparation of the head, followed by the eating of the brains at around midnight by the old men. Once again the brains are mixed with sago. After the decoration of the head the initiate sits on the floor with the head against his groin and is supposed to contemplate it for the next two or three days. At the same time the women of the community collect sago and return each time sounding hunting horns (Zegwaard 1959:1024).

Instruction 5 has the young man journeying through life by making his way
slowly in a canoe with his mother's brother to the sea. He becomes revitalized in
the process. All of the villagers have to decorate themselves and their canoes and
participate in the boy's journey toward the sea. During this journey his demeanor
is described by Zegwaard as being "like an old man" (Zegwaard 1959:1024–
1025).

Zegwaard continues the description of the young man's journey to the west.
The young man becomes increasingly weaker, to the point of collapse onto the
shoulder of one of his mother's brothers. Another immersion takes place: this
time the youth, his decorations, and the skull are all immersed together. The
young man's ornaments are removed and put in the magic mat, and the skull is
taken from him and given to a woman who has received the privilege from the
owner–hunter. The skull is never alienated from the owner–hunter, to whom it
returns at the end of the ceremony (Zegwaard 1959:1025).

There are three matters worth mentioning here. In taking the head, the warri-
or's maleness is enhanced, and he gains soul, becoming more than "a piece of
meat." The skull itself is on a journey to its resting-place in the possession of the
killer. In effect, it is a part of the process not merely of making a man but of
making men: the headhunter and the initiate. The relationship of the skull to the
killer is differentiated through the mediation of the initiate, who is ultimately the
product of the relationships of both. The relational and contingent nature of
Asmat maleness is in effect laid out for contemplation in the headhunt and
initiation ritual.

The initiation ritual ends with the young man and his attendants returning
eastward and in the process hunting for crabs. During this time the initiate acts as
a newborn, and back in the village he goes to his family's house and is redeco-
rated: "Henceforth the initiate acted as a young man, full of vigor and admired by
all" (Zegwaard 1959:1025). He also gets to celebrate his newly created vigor.
Zegwaard describes another ritual (still a part of the initiation) a couple of days
later, carried out in the sago-woods, which culminates in yet another rite where
the initiate dances with the skull and the magic mat (1959:1026–1027).

THE BODY, THE UNIVERSE, AND MALENESS

The Asmat universe is dealt with in the headhunt and cannibalism and the
ceremonies surrounding them. Each element provides a set of meanings engaged
at particular times and is also part of other sets of meanings. The skull itself
contains the universe (Eyde 1967:76), while, according to Zegwaard,

> . . . the human body is associated with a tree: the legs compare to the plank roots, the
> trunk to the human body, the arms to the boughs, the head to the top (often with the
> fruit that sits in the top). [1959:1039]

The nurturing aspect of the male body is reflected in headhunting and cannibalism. The male body in the headhunt and cannibalism provides nurture for all.

The ingestion of flesh refracts the meanings of the male body, which in its association with trees provides a context for humans in the "natural" order. The view of particular bodies has ramifications for the position of people with respect to other people and the universe in general. In the process of the headhunt and cannibalism, the Asmat life world is continually threatened with extinction and, importantly, continually revitalized through the ingestion of flesh. The deaths of the victims precipitate the need to avenge their spirits and also tie the members of their families to the victor's line through the initiate. While the life world of the Asmat may indeed be unpredictable, it is not marginal in the sense that Western political economy would have it, because the very contingency and its continual renewal is stabilizing. Change, even destruction, can be righted through revenge and establishing relations. The bodies of the victims and the victors are integral to this process.

In the context of the initiation, for example, the victim's body is not only important symbolically but also constitutive of both the initiate and the Asmat social world. The victim's body is indeed constitutive of the group to which he belonged. The victim's body is *literally* assimilated to the initiate's, as his mother's oldest brother rubs ash from the victim's scorched hair mixed with blood from his head onto the head, shoulders, and body of the initiate (Zegwaard 1959:1023). The acts of submersion carried out during the initiation ritual indicate in the first instance the separate preparations of the two bodies involved. The second submersion, in which the skull is submerged with the young man, comes at the time when he has been rejuvenated through his close association with the skull.

The initiate's and his mother's brothers' trip westward is, as Zegwaard points out, in the direction both of the sun and of Safan. This journey westward, a liminal period, is one where the loss of vitality is restored through the social work of the mothers' brothers with existent ties being reinforced and new ones being established. The liminality is a time of potential danger (the young man could succumb to weakness) and of the reordering of the social world. In both of the myths relating to the headhunt and cannibalism and the initiation recorded above, the social world is made through the unthinkable. The incest taboo is broken when father (or mother) slays the son and uses his substance to prepare sago and also when brother slays brother to bring something that is better than killing and sharing a pig to the world of the Asmat. It is Asmat maleness that is being made through the rupture of the incest taboo, which is set right by the reconstitution of the social world through the meeting of social obligations to nurture and to avenge and provide protection from the ancestral spirits.

MALENESS THROUGH THE HEADHUNT AND CANNIBALISM

The characteristics associated with maleness are all evident in both the headhunt and the initiation ritual. The making of men entails an understanding of what a man is. Both in the headhunt and cannibalism and in the initiation we find that men needed to be made and that it requires the agency of both the mother's and the father's line. It is also the case that for a man to gain a soul he needed not only to be initiated but also to prove himself in warfare, thus providing for others as well as demonstrating his prowess. When a man was gaining personal worth, he was also protecting and maintaining the social world. He was reintegrating relationships that had already been set up in different ways with his affines, enemies, and bond friends.

In the course of getting these relationships, a man's body became the focus for an elaboration of the social world. The relationship of the body to the social world is one of the inscription of aspects of the cosmology upon the body. In Zegwaard's account, body adornment also shows a person's status in Asmat society. By wearing particular adornment, men show their wish to engage in hostilities (Zegwaard 1959:1033). The body is thus also a means of expressing intention.

The initiation ceremony as described by Warsekomen involved the making of Asmat men but did not complete the process. For the man to gain a soul, he needed to take a head, and further prestige was added as he continued to take heads. While the initiation ceremony is an important step in the making of one man, others are extending their manhood through the headhunt and the ingestion of flesh. While it is only the old men who ate the contents of the universe (the brains), the whole community took part in eating the distributed flesh. The ceremonies involved in the ritual cycle generally, and the initiation ritual as it was practiced by the central Asmat in particular, give a sense of the importance of the interrelationships of Asmat males. They also reveal the gendered nature of the Asmat world. If the way that women are seen to act in the myths and ritual of the headhunt and the initiation are examined, the nurturing and nurturant aspects of maleness of which I wrote above can also be seen as aspects of femaleness. The gendered horizon is one that makes both possibilities available to be precipitated in given political situations.

Furthermore, an understanding of Asmat cannibalism is necessary to any understanding of the way that the Asmat exist in the world. For the Asmat, eating people is about making both the individual male and the social world—complementary and inalienable processes in Melanesia, as Strathern (1988) so successfully pointed out. In the process of such examination the Asmat worldview is opened for consideration.

NOTES

This paper was written while I was a research visitor at the National Museum of Ethnology, Osaka. I am grateful for the support and facilities provided. Aletta Biersack and Stuart Kirsch provided useful comment on this material in another context. The general problems and issues surrounding cannibalism were discussed at different times with Shuji Yoshida, Jadran Mimica, and Thomas Ernst. All of these people provided useful comment, but the responsibility for the contents of the paper is mine.

The ethnographic sources used in my work on Asmat are all secondary (for a complete discussion of them see Zubrinich 1997). There are a number of sources, the quality of which varies greatly, which deal with cannibalism in Asmat. The material on cannibalism used in this paper comes mainly from the priest G. Zegwaard, m.s.c. Zegwaard was the first missionary to be based in the Asmat region and has a long familiarity and appreciation of Asmat social life and history. He was in the area at a time contemporary with the practices discussed here. The consistency of his approach, his direct and careful observation, and his unwillingness to place anthropophagy as central to his understanding of Asmat while not denying its historical actuality are among the reasons that I consider his reports, and others consistent with them, to be highly reliable.

1. Lorentz (1913:28) reported that his Dayak bearers considered the "New Guinean" peoples inhuman because of the practice of cannibalism.
2. For people with such skepticism and sensitivity, Himmelman's (1997) article about medical cannibalism and its antecedents in European history is recommended.
3. Warfare was a constant context for terror before colonization and continued among the Asmat well into the Dutch colonial period. Warfare was constituted differently by the Asmat and by the colonizing powers. Nevertheless, the element of terror remains a constant in both types of warfare. In the Asmat situation terror should be considered an aspect of the earlier social organization as well as part of the colonial situations. Walter (1969) provided a good functionalist framework for understanding terror in nonstate forms, which, while it has problems, certainly provides insight into the workings of systems of terror.
4. Women were sometimes given the privilege of severing the heads of captives (Eyde 1967:74).
5. I have described these two cases because they show how relationships can be used to mitigate circumstances even in situations where violence has taken place. The successful headhunting raid by the Sawa group established more relationships than those made through the adoption of Are through the taking of Weo heads.
6. It is worth noting the knowledge that the two men had about each other. Asmat warfare is conducted by groups who know each other and where understandings of the ramifications of such warfare is shared. Zegwaard points out that finding the name of the victim, which is necessary because the name is to be given to an initiate, is not a difficult matter in the Asmat situation (1959:1036; cf. Van Baal for the Marind Anim).
7. Sowada reported noticing that an old woman attended male meetings, and he was told that she reported back to the women of the village (1990:68).
8. The threat was very high in the period immediately after World War II until the early 1950s. About 6,000 Asmat were living to the west in Mimikan territory at this time to avoid the consequences of the efflorescence of headhunting among the Asmat that occurred after the Japanese and Australian occupations of West Papua (Trenkenschuh 1970:26).
9. Schneebaum argues that *Bis* poles are the most spectacular of Asmat carvings: "The poles are made from the trunk of one of the rhizophone species, with buttress root left intact. The trunk and root are carved with human and other designs, and the tree is turned upside down, so that the root projects from the groin of the uppermost figure. Several are made at the same time and stand in front of the men's house. They sometimes reach a height of 8 meters, and at least one had as many as twenty figures carved into it" (1990:42).
10. The myth of the creation of sago is one wherein the man searching for sago becomes, with his second wife, a sago palm (Voorhoeve 1965:182). The sago-as-man and sago-as-woman themes are woven throughout the available Asmat ethnography.
11. In the cases Eyde is discussing, pig flesh is being exchanged. The relationship of pig

140 _The Anthropology of Cannibalism_

flesh to the human body in the headhunt and cannibalism becomes obvious in the first instruction of the ritual described further along.

12. _Safan_ is the land of the dead.

13. Zegwaard points out that "the story presupposes that just the two brothers are around" (1959:1021).

REFERENCES

Baal, J. van (1966). _Dema: Description and Analysis of Marind Anim Culture._ The Hague: Martinus Nijhoff.

Castro, V. de (1992). _From the Enemies' Point of View._ Chicago, IL: University of Chicago Press.

Deleuze, G., & Guattari, F. (1987). Treatise on momadology: The war machine. In _A Thousand Plateaus: Capitalism and Schizophrenia_ (pp. 351–423). Minneapolis, MN: University of Minnesota Press.

Dillon, M. (1997). _Merleau-Ponty's Ontology._ Evanston, IL: Northwestern University Press.

Eyde, D. B. (1967). _Cultural Correlates of Warfare among the Asmat of South-West New Guinea._ Ph.D Dissertation, Ann Arbor, University Microfilms Inc.

Freeman, D. (1979). Severed heads that germinate. In R. H. Hook (ed.), _Fantasy and Symbol: Studies in Anthropological Interpretation_ (pp. 233–246). London: Academic Press.

Gerbrands C. (1967). The Asmat of New Guinea. _The Journal of Michael Clark Rockefeller._ New York: Museum of Art.

Gluckman, M. (1963). _Order and Rebellion in Tribal Africa._ London: Cohen and West.

Himmelman, P. K. (1997). The medicinal body: An analysis of medicinal cannibalism in Europe, 1300–1700. _Dialectical Anthropology_ 22: 183–203.

Kapferer, B. (1998). _The Feast of the Sorcerer: Practices of Consciousness and Power._ Chicago, IL: University of Chicago Press.

Lorentz, H. A. (1913). _Zwarte Mennschen—Witte Bergen._ Leiden: E. J. Brill.

Lévi-Strauss, C. (1984). Cannibalism and ritual transvestism. In _Anthropology and Myth: Lectures, 1951–1982_ (pp. 111–123; trans. Roy Willis). Oxford and New York: Basil Blackwell.

McKinley, R. (1976). Human and proud of it! A structural treatment of headhunting rites and the social definition of enemies. In G. N. Appell (ed.), _Studies in Borneo Societies: Social Process and Anthropological Explanation_, Special Report No. 12 (pp. 92–126). Chicago, IL: Center for Southeast Asian Studies, Northern Illinois University.

Meggitt, M. (1977). _Blood Is Their Argument: Warfare among the Mae-Enga Tribesmen of the New Guinea Highlands._ Palo Alto, CA: Mayfield.

Rosaldo, R. (1980). _Ilongot Headhunting: A Study in Society and History 1883–1974._ Stanford, CA: University of California Press.

Schneebaum, T. (ed.) (1990). _Embodied Spirits: Ritual Carvings of the Asmat._ Salem, MA: Peabody Museum of Salem.

Smidt, D. (ed.) (1993). _Asmat Art._ Amsterdam: Periplus Editions.

Sowada, A. (1961). *Socio-Economic Survey of the Asmat People of Southwestern New Guinea.* MA dissertation, Catholic University of America.

Sowada, A. (1990). Primary Asmat religious and philosophical concepts. In T. Schneebaum (ed.), *Embodied Spirits: Ritual Carvings of the Asmat* (pp. 65–70). Salem, MA: Peabody Museum of Salem.

Strathern, M. (1988). *The Gender of Gift: Problems with Women and Problems with Society in Melanesia.* Berkeley, CA: University of California Press.

Taussig, M. (1986). *Shamanism, Colonialism, and the Wild Man.* Chicago, IL: Chicago University Press.

Trenkenschuh, F. (1970). An outline of Asmat history in perspective, 1526–1970. In F. Trenkenschuh (ed.), *An Asmat Sketchbook No. 2* (pp. 25–38). Hastings, NE: Crosier Missions.

Voorhoeve, C. L. (1965). *The Flamingo Bay Dialect of the Asmat Language.* The Hague: H. L. Smits.

Wagner, R. (1972). *Lethal Speech: Daribi Myth as Symbolic Obviation.* Ithaca, NY: Cornell University Press.

Wagner, A. (1978). *Lethal Speech: Daribi Myth as Symbolic Obviation.* Ithaca, NY: Cornell University Press.

Walker, M. (ed.) (n.d). *Notes Taken during University of Cenderawasih Team Fieldwork Led by M. Walker,* Oct. 1973–June 1974.

Walter, E. V. (1969). *Terror and Resistance: A Study of Political Violence, with Case Studies of Some Primitive African Communities.* Oxford: Oxford University Press.

Zegwaard, G. (1959). Headhunting practices of Netherlands New Guinea. *American Anthropologist,* 61: 1020–1041.

Zegwaard, G. (1982). Name giving among the Asmat People (trans. F. Trenkenschuh & A. van de Wouw). In F. Trenkenschuh (ed.), *An Asmat Sketchbook No. 1* (pp. 39–44). Hastings, NE: Crosier Missions.

Zegwaard, G., & Boelaars, J. (1970). De Sociale Structuur van de Asmat Bevolking (trans. F. Trenkenschuh & A. van de Wouw). In F. Trenkenschuh (ed.), *An Asmat Sketchbook No. 1* (pp. 39–44). Hastings NE: Crosier Missions.

Zubrinich, K. (1997). *Cosmology and Colonisation: History and Culture of the Asmat of Irian Jaya.* PhD dissertation, Charles Sturt University.

7

Onabasulu Cannibalism and the Moral Agents of Misfortune

Thomas M. Ernst

The only valid question for the anthropologist is to know what
cannibalism is (in so far as it is anything at all), not in itself or for us,
but only for those who practise it. We shall not succeed in this by
artificially isolating the practise, but, contrariwise, by reintegrating it
into a larger semantic field containing other configurations which it
transforms and through which it is itself transformed.

Lévi-Strauss, 1987

When you eat a bird, can you fly?

Baliya Mataiya, 1970

INTRODUCTORY REMARKS

Cannibalism has always greatly exercised the imagination of European-derived
cultures. Since the sixteenth century, at least, the Western European image of the
"cannibal" was developed, honed, and utilized predominantly in its engagement
with the processes of European exploration, mercantile domination, and colonial
expansion. Its appropriateness as an image of depravity and savagery, and its
tabooed practice, stem from the ambiguities it exhibits in relation to desire and
revulsion. As Himmelman put it in his fascinating discussion of "medicinal
cannibalism" in Europe from the fourteenth through the seventeenth centuries,

Despite its apparently negative overtones, one can still detect the overtones of its
positive attraction. Its link to desire displays this ambiguity—the intimation that the
very reason for its taboo status stems from its allure, from the wish, as Freud would
have it, to orally incorporate the object of desire. [Himmelman 1997:183]

In this chapter I provide an analytic approach to cannibalism as previously practiced by the Onabasulu (and other groups of culturally related peoples) of the Strickland-Bosavi region of Papua New Guinea. Because of this ambiguity in the West's fascination with cannibalism and the role it has played in colonial ideology, such a task presents some special problems. Moreover, the historically recent reputation of the region in question creates some specific difficulties. For almost a decade, from the early 1960s to the early 1970s, the Strickland-Bosavi region gained a degree of notoriety in Papua New Guinea, in large part because of its reputed anthropophagic practices. A court case involving charges related to cannibalism and several popular written accounts helped the reputation gain a solidity. I present some of the bases of this reputation as well.

The chapter has two substantive parts. The first presents some nonanthropological perspectives on Strickland-Bosavi (and Onabasulu) cannibalism with comment. The second presents a contextual and analytic ethnography of historical Onabasulu cannibal practices. Throughout the chapter, attention is also focused more generally on some of the problems that cannibalism presents for contemporary anthropology. These are most specifically, if briefly, dealt with in the conclusions.

NONANTHROPOLOGICAL APPROACHES
TO STRICKLAND-BOSAVI CANNIBALISM

The Strickland-Bosavi region ethnographically comprises a number of linguistically and culturally related peoples living in inland Southern Papua New Guinea. The area stretches from the plains of the Strickland River in Papua New Guinea's Western Province to the northern slopes of Mt. Bosavi, bounded by the upper Kikori River (called the Hegigio above its junction with the Mubi River) in the Southern Highlands Province. We now have excellent ethnographic information on many of these component cultures (cf. Kelly 1993:27–51). In the recent past, these groups are all reported to have eaten the bodies of certain types of antagonists in specific circumstances.

In addition to the accounts of cannibalism scattered through the ethnographic accounts of peoples of the Strickland-Bosavi region, there are at least three commentaries in other genres. All are from the period around 1970, when Australian colonial administrative control was being consolidated and Christian mission activity initiated. Two of the accounts are from the area patrolled out of Nomad Patrol Post, a then relatively new administrative outpost in the Western Province (then the Western District). The area around Nomad captured the imagination of Western expatriates in Papua New Guinea as well as the population of Australia as the last example of the bringing of "civilization" to inhabitants of an "unknown wilderness." The third and earliest account deals with patrols in the Eastern part of the area—the Great Papuan Plateau between Mt. Bosavi and Mt. Sisa in the Southern Highlands Province (then District), where the Onabasulu—the people central to this chapter—are located.

RELATIVISM, LEGALITY, AND THE "ENLIGHTENED" APPROACH TO CANNIBALISM

In 1971–72 there was a celebrated legal case (*R v. Noboi-Bosai*) involving people arrested out of Nomad Patrol Post, who "were charged under §241(b) of the Code[1] with 'improperly or indecently interfering with, or offer[ing] any indignity to, any dead human body or human remains' after they cooked and ate parts of the corpse of a man from another village" (Weisbrot 1982:80). Weisbrot describes the results citing the judgment:

Prentice J (as he was then) acquitted the accused, holding that,

Concepts of decency and propriety (and obscenity) appear in many places of the ordinances and laws of Papua New Guinea. Having regard to the multifarious customs, languages, dress, beliefs, degrees of civilisation, and social organisation among the people who live in remote wildernesses, some where Europeans have walked only on a few occasions, one cannot conceive that the legislature would have intended to impose uniform blanket standards of decency and propriety, on all the peoples of the country. In assessing propriety and decency of behaviour in relation to corpses in the Gabusi area, I should endeavour to apply the standards, so far as I can ascertain them, of the reasonable primitive Gabusi Villager . . . in early 1971. . . . The funerary customs of the peoples of Papua New Guinea have been, and in many cases remain, bizarre in the extreme. These are matters of notoriety. Can it be said that the Government of Papua in 1902 by adoption of the Queensland Criminal Code, and in particular [this section], was intending to make so many varied pious, ritual, strength seeking practices, indecent or improper? I cannot find so (at 283–284, [PNGLR 271]).

Prentice J went on to find that in the circumstances the behaviour of the accused was "normal and reasonable." [Weisbrot 1982:80–81; see also Griffin 1972]

This was an interesting court case, but little emerged in the judgment that characterized the anthropophagic practices of the "Gabusi" men on trial in any way that resembled their practical or experiential "realities." Instead, what emerged was a set of general liberal understandings of cannibalism based on partial descriptions of its occurrence in a multitude of settings and infused with attitudes that have been expressed in Western thought since Montaigne published his essay "On the Cannibals in the 16th century" (Montaigne 1995).

THE "SAVAGE OTHER" AND THE CIVILIZING PROCESS

There are two other nonanthropological accounts of cannibalism in the Strickland-Bosavi region from the period around 1970. The first of these is a large-format book that is a collection of technically excellent dramatic black-and-white photographs entitled *Cannibal: A Photographic Audacity* by James Anderson (1970). It emphasizes the very male heroism of the photographer and Australian Administration officers he accompanied on a patrol from Nomad Patrol Post. There are remarkable photographs of the photographer himself, of men with guns, and of Bedamini people whose area is being patrolled. Despite its context of heroism in the face of a "primitive" other, the verbatim accounts of the complaints and testimonies (for instance, pp. 48–49) provide a more accurate description and contextualization of anthropophagy than does the above-cited legal judgment. The volume also provides a good feel for the nature, general policies, and attitudes of the Australian colonial officers who were patrolling regions like Strickland-Bosavi in the 1960s and early 1970s. The idea of short prison terms, which demonstrate government stability and power, and returning the "offender" to the community, where he will have a "civilizing" effect on its other members, was current at the time in this area. These attitudes to cannibals are explicit in the dialogue between government officers and the author/photographer.

One of the most insightful sources is a report by a (then) medical student from Perth in Western Australia that appeared in a popular British geographical magazine and is titled "Medical Aid for Bosavi's Cannibals." As it specifically involves people from the eastern part of the Strickland-Bosavi region and is primarily set in Onabasulu communities, I quote from this source at length:

Following my fourth year as a medical student in Perth, I undertook voluntary work in a small bush hospital at Tari in the Southern Highlands of Papua. . . . I found myself determined to return.

The opportunity presented itself when after a few months back in Perth, a letter came from the hospital at Tari inviting me to take part in a medical patrol into the Bosavi region of Papua. Bosavi is one of the last really primitive regions in Papua-New Guinea—an area where payback killings and cannibalism are commonplace. [Bastin 1969:547]

One evening near the end of the patrol, we were invited to watch a sing-sing in the longhouse at Gunigamo [an Onabasulu community]. The only light came from two flickering bark torches, and we could just discern the Bosavi onlookers in the shadows. Dancers, painted with ochre, stood in a line holding arrows. They stamped their feet on the floor in time to a drum beat. Repeating a monotonous chant. Hare[2] translated the chant as "Water for all. Sago is for all. Land is for all". I sat watching but feeling decidedly uneasy and I asked Yehgis [he was a medical assistant that the author had worked with in Tari] why there were five times as many men as women there. He replied that this was because women are eaten in preference to men as their breasts taste sweet. We left early but the sing-sing continued long into the night. [Bastin 1969:551]

Needless to say, this report is an example of the presumptions and predispositions of outsiders to indigenes in this region.

AN ANTHROPOLOGICAL APPROACH TO ONABASULU CANNIBALISM

Despite the exaggerations and unreliability of the above sorts of accounts, the scholarly accounts of cannibal practice in the Strickland-Bosavi regions are consistent and careful, if sparse. That anthropophagous practices occurred among all groups between the Strickland River plains and the Hegigio (upper Kikori) is not in doubt. In general terms, both the practice and context were very much the same throughout the region. These included the following features:

1. In all locations, the victims of anthropophagous activities included—and most usually were—accused and executed sorcerers or witches.
2. There was no specific "ritual" surrounding the acts themselves. The bodies were prepared as was pig[3] and large game, except that the intestines were discarded.
3. Kin persons were never consumed. The necessary distance in relationship appears to be equivalent to that for marriage (as was the case for Onabasulu people).
4. There was no set of explicit beliefs that characteristics of the consumed person were acquired through cannibalistic consumption.

In the context of Onabasulu data I consider these points sequentially in the next section.

The "Topic" of Cannibalism Ethnographically Considered

No ethnographer who has worked in the Strickland-Bosavi region has written specifically about cannibalism. I suspect this is because it is not a topic that presents itself as central to the lives of people in the region. In the case of the Onabasulu, it proved to be, as Lévi-Strauss has suggested, labile (at least in the last instance). Since beginning my research in the area in September 1969, I did not document a single instance of such practice. Undoubtedly, injunctions against it promulgated by both Christian Missions and the Australian colonial administration led to its cessation—especially as these prohibitions were backed up with the threat of imprisonment. However, I would argue that these factors alone cannot totally explain its disappearance. I return below to this question of why cannibalism ceased.

1. *In all locations, the victims of anthropophagous activities included—and most usually were—accused and executed sorcerers or witches;*
2. *There was no specific "ritual" surrounding the acts themselves. The bodies were prepared as was pig and large game, except that the intestines were discarded.*

It is primarily within the context of culturally shaped beliefs in witches that analytic sense can be made of Onabasulu cannibalism. Onabasulu anthropophagous practices, like those across the Strickland-Bosavi region, were thus a part of social actions and understandings of witchcraft/sorcery and threat. As such, they were embedded in beliefs about the nature of persons, sociality, life and death, misfortune, and vengeance. That much of the belief structure and its concomitant practices persisted while cannibalism itself waned indicates that cannibalism was not a necessary part of the structure of witch beliefs and practices.

We are compelled to unfold this broader canvas of beliefs both to illuminate Onabasulu cannibalism in terms of what it meant to the people and to avoid bestowing some misplaced concreteness or centrality to the practice as somehow "emblematic" of Onabasulu history and culture. For example, in a paper for a collection on "Ritualized Homosexuality in Melanesia" (Herdt 1984), Sørum found it necessary to discuss Bedamini male homosexual practices *not* as ritual but in the context of Bedamini sexuality generally (Sørum 1982). This was important, as societies that practiced "ritualized homosexuality" were becoming separate and different from those surrounding them precisely because they were sometimes "metonymically" characterized by the "ritualized homosexuality" (sometimes in combination with "sister exchange marriage"—see Knauft's discussion of this, 1985:188 ff.) epithet. Analogously, it would be misleading to characterize the Strickland-Bosavi social systems with the term "cannibal," as if this signified something axiomatic or central to Onabasulu ideology.

Cannibalism and Witches

In the period just prior to its cessation, the great majority of victims of Onabasulu cannibalism were not those killed in raids on Fasu but people accused of being witches who caused the deaths of others. This pattern is repeated across the Strickland-Bosavi region—with witches/sorcerers having been the primary objects of cannibal practice among the Kaluli (Schieffelin 1976), the Etoro (Kelly 1993), the Bedamini (Hayashi, Isao, personal communication), the Samo (Shaw 1990), and the Gebusi (Knauft 1985). And it is in the context of beliefs about witches that the bases of anthropophagous practices become most clearly discernible.

The Onabasulu witch, or *hinane*, is the close equivalent of the *sei* among the Kaluli (Schieffelin 1976) and the Etoro *mugwabe* (Kelly 1976, 1993). It is, as Kelly points out for the Etoro, "a conceptually egalitarian construct" (1993: 145)—that is, anyone, regardless of gender or age, may be a witch. The defining characteristic of a witch is the presence of a substance that resides in the heart and enables the witch to attack other human beings. This makes them ill or eventually kills them (usually both). The substance will cause the heart to continue beating for a time after death and may be visible in the form of tiny frogs or worms. It imparts to the heart of the witch, when exposed after death, a characteristic glossy yellow appearance. Almost all deaths and much misfortune is attributed to the activity of witches.

The substance of witchcraft, though, is not in itself explanatory of the activities of witches. They are, in the final instance, responsible for their actions because of basic flaws that render them essentially different from other people. Kelly eloquently describes this situation among the Etoro, where the beliefs are virtually identical. Those possessing the flawed character (or soul)

are inherently prone to malicious self-aggrandizement through the consumption of the life force of other persons. This characterological predisposition to selfishness and to the inversion of the values that are central to generosity is held to be expressed in social life as well as supernatural attack. . . . In contrast, a normal person—who lacks this mutation of the soul—is perceived to be governed by *relational* (rather than individualistic) *motivation* and is characterologically predisposed to be helpful, generous, and supportive toward others. The impulse to generosity in helping others is believed to be an inherent component of human nature that is given direction by relational motivation. Only a failure to manifest such impulses requires a deeper explanation, namely a defective spiritual constitution. A witch is different inside. [Kelly 1993:144, emphasis added]

This understanding of relational motivation is part of a basic ontological positioning, not just a definitional statement about the good or proper person. It is as much a part of Onabasulu conceptualizations of what a human *being* is as being able to speak and breathe.

Onabasulu notions of being are further centered in notions of decline and renewal based in the transmission through time of spiritual and physical life forces.[4] The life forces of a person are an aspect of their being called *hame*, which, together with a second aspect, an incorporeal self called *azbane*, constitute what might be called the "soul" of a living person. On death, the *azbane* and *hame* leave the body and rejoin to form a ghost-like being called *gesame*. The state of a person's vitality—that is, their *hame's* well-being—is indicated by the breath, its "physical" manifestation. Shortness of breath is called, onomatopoeically, *hame ha ha*. Vitality declines with age and is part of the passing on of life force through reproduction (in its broadest sense) or through its immoral acquisition by others for augmentation of their own vitality. *Hinane* are such persons. They appear to be very healthy and large, and they achieve their nefarious purposes through attacking the inner and incorporeal beings of others. They are said to finish by removing the liver from their dead victims when the latter are on exposure platforms (later, in underground chambers) and devouring them raw.

Such people are truly reprehensible, and were likely to be executed if their identity was considered certain. The execution was followed by consumption of the body, especially prior to the establishment of "law and order" by the Australian colonial administration in the mid-1960s.[5] After that time, cannibalism all but ceased, and the execution of witches appears to have diminished. In 1966 an Onabasulu man was arrested, along with three Etoro men, for the execution of an Etoro woman who was a witch. The then Southern Highlands District Commissioner said in a letter attached to the report of this patrol that the apprehension of the "four culprits" for the "murder of the aged woman . . . can be classified as the first concrete example of the introduction of Law and Order to the area" (Patrol Report 1/66/67 Komo).

The occurrence of cannibalism related to the execution of witches was part of the experience of many Onabasulu who were of young middle age or older in 1970, and they freely described the generalities and specific acts. As the sending of sickness was (and is) one of the major activities of *hinane*, the periodic epidemics of illness between ca. 1935 and the 1960s (see Ernst 1984:45–51) generated a high incidence of accusations. One man, now deceased, of Orogaiye lineage, was married at roughly the beginning of this period. Claiming that his experience was not unusual, he reported that he was involved in six killings that were seen as connected to executions of *hinane*. Five of those he killed were *hinane*. These included one Onabasulu man who allegedly killed his wife, and one who allegedly killed his classificatory brother. One man was killed for having been responsible for the death of his father. The man himself was badly wounded by the brother (classificatory) of one of the alleged witches he had killed, indicating some serious disagreement at the time over the accusation. The one person killed who was not an *hinane* was the son of one of the *hinane* and was killed accidentally in the attack on his father. Large compensation was paid to the boy's kin. The bodies of all the *hinane* killed were cooked and consumed. Those who were related closely to the deceased usually left the long-house community when the bodies were being prepared and the meat distributed. The meat was distributed to affines and shared with consanguines in the usual fashion of pork or cassowary. The additional element here is that presentations were usually made also to the close consanguines and/or spouses of other known victims of the *hinane* who was killed.

The rationale of the consumption of the bodies of *hinane* is grounded in their understandings of such persons, the nature of their immorality, and beliefs about witchcraft itself. The highly regulated preparation and distribution of the meat makes the consumption of witches a relational act—precisely the opposite of the witches' attacks on others, which are individualistically motivated by the greedy desire to augment their own life forces at the expense of those of their victims. As Knauft points out for the similar anthropophagous Gebusi practices, the consumption of the body is " . . . like the execution itself, is thought to be an apt forced exchange . . . for the degeneration and death of the original sickness-victim" (1985:102). This contrast between social exchange/benefit vs. egotistical accumulation is further manifested in details of the consumptive acts themselves. Cooking the body "like a pig," as it is always described, denies the basic (relationally motivated) humanity of the *hinane*. Onabasulu men frequently retort to what is taken as insult or mistreatment (and thus does not enhance their dignity) by saying, "I am a man, not a pig or a dog."

Consuming the flesh as opposed to the spirit, eating the outside instead of the inside,[6] and consuming the *hinane*'s body cooked instead of raw all represent the contrast of the *hinane*'s actions to those of moral persons'. This discussion goes some way toward illuminating Point B; there was no "ritual" of a specifying sort surrounding the acts themselves. As stated above, "The bodies were prepared as was pig and large game, *except that the intestines were discarded.*" This one contrast with the preparation and consumption of pig is important in this regard. The anthropophagous acts were part of the set of beliefs and practices that surrounded the appropriate treatment of those considered to be the morally responsible agents of misfortune and suffering. Any ritual and mythology surrounding these acts was directed toward the understanding and treatment of such misfortunes—cannibalism *per se* was not the focus.

Cannibalism and Raiding

In the past victims of cannibalism in Onabasulu fell into two categories. The first was *hinane*. The second was people from other ethnic groups who were killed in warfare. These were almost exclusively Fasu-speaking people from across the Hegigio River. These people were, in the past, in a mutual raiding relationship with Onabasulu, and the victims of the raids by both Onabasulu and Fasu were eaten, apparently in the same fashion. Such raids by the Onabasulu were always seen as revenge for raiding by *gisa inoro* (Fasu). The Onabasulu (and the close Kaluli long-house group of Wabamisi) were in a state of permanent enmity with their eastern neighbors, the Fasu (sometimes called Namaporo) across the Hegigio River.

The raiding usually involved a party from either side moving through enemy territory looking for small groups that were hunting or gardening at sago stands. The people were killed, and, if it did not threaten the party's escape, the bodies were carried back to be eaten. Revenge for previous attacks by the Fasu was the reason most frequently cited by Onabasulu for their raids. The largest and most spectacularly successful raid carried out by the Onabasulu against the Fasu took place in the later 1930s or early 1940s—at about the same time as an equally spectacular raid by the Etoro on the Kaluli (Kelly 1977:17; Schieffelin 1976:13). It was carried out by an unusually large party of men from Orogaiye, Sogaise, and Hanoro long-houses, along with allies from Kebi, Sabiasulu, and some Etoro. It was to avenge an attack upon participants in initiation proceedings in a seclusion hut. The men were from Orogaiye and Hanoro, and apparently two were killed. The large Onabasulu party successfully surprised a large Fasu community, managing to kill and bring back, it is said, 15 men and 5 women. If this is so, the party must have contained a minimum of 40 men, given the methods of carrying bodies.[7] Even allowing for exaggeration, this was by far the largest remembered raid the Onabasulu ever mounted and involved many more deaths than usual. Most attacks were against small isolated parties who were engaged in subsistence activities such as gardening or sago washing. This form of attack was said to be favored by the Onabasulu in raids on the Fasu because it lessened the chance of others quickly discovering the attack and counterattacking or inflicting losses during the lengthy Onabasulu withdrawal from Fasu territory. The withdrawal involved a difficult crossing of the Hegigio River, which was dangerous even when not being pursued.

While the frequency of such raids is difficult to determine, it is likely that they were very rare. They were a very real part of the Onabasulu imagination, however. The feeling of terror produced had significant effects on settlement patterns and discouraged people from making individual gardens or building small isolated houses, which, in turn, affected patterns of sago production.

Attacks by Fasu were seemingly random if not unexpected, and such attacks were, therefore, fear-inducing. On a fishing expedition in late 1970, on which there were 19 of us (including 6 children), talk in the temporary lean-to-type shelter was about the enjoyment of the expedition and the reminiscence of the former possibility of ambush in such a situation by Fasu (we had moved closer than any of the longhouses to the Hegigio River, which forms the border with the Fasu). People were exhilarated by recalling their fears. Agibe Fua, one of the party, said to me on the first night: "If you want to understand us, this is how we truly are. And before we would have kept watch for Fasu through the entire night" (Ernst 1984:72).

The thought of a potential attack by Fasu must have been there whenever any small group ventured into the bush for any prolonged period. A group as large as that which was on the fish-poisoning expedition would probably have matched in size smaller raiding parties. A family alone at a sago stand or a garden would have been more certain victims, and there are several cases that were frequently cited, usually with gory or pathetic overtones. For example, a young man and his wife from Wasie were surprised, along with their baby, at a sago stand. The attackers were in turn surprised after they had killed the man and wife but had not yet harmed the baby nor prepared the bodies to be carried back[8] to be eaten. They fled at the sound of the approaching Onabasulu party, which found the baby alternately crying and trying to suckle at its dead mother's breast. Whether the story is true or embellished does not matter in terms of its effects, and those of others like it. Given mutual raiding, anyone in isolation was a potential victim of a similar attack and realized it. That was a very good reason to try to make sure that gardens were communal and sago was adjacent and to seek the sanctuary and relative safety of the longhouse, even if in actual fact Fasu raids were not particularly frequent (my genealogies only indicate deaths from three Fasu raids).

I expect that Onabasulu raids had a reciprocal effect in Fasu. In 1971, a small Fasu party (husband, wife, and infant) passed through the Onabasulu longhouse community of Walagu on their way through to Komo patrol post. That night a *gasa* ceremony was being held in the longhouse as part of the celebration of a marriage. At about 3:30 a.m., a number of men pulled bows and arrows and axes out from under cover and barricaded the doors of the longhouse. They grabbed my torch and began searching. The Fasu family had moved in fear to a corner behind where I was sitting. It turned out that the men were going to execute a witch who had been in attendance, but he had apparently found out and slipped away. In discussing the matter later in the morning with the Fasu man, he indicated that he had been virtually certain that he and his family were going to be the victims of a cannibal attack, "just as before."

The case for the eating of outsiders, especially those in a mutual raiding relationship, is analogous, albeit in attenuated way, to that of *hinane*. These are persons who attack randomly and consume the physical substance of relatives. The attack on an initiation hut that provoked the most memorable and large-scale raid on the Fasu was an attack on the most alive and social of persons at the peak of their powers. The earlier Onabasulu disdain for the Fasu and its foundations is aptly illustrated from the formerly frequently repeated (and empirically unverified) belief that Fasu exchanged their children with one another for purposes of cannibal indulgence to quench the desire for flesh. This is as close as an image can get without the incest-like implications of complete self-closure (devouring one's own offspring), to an individualistically rather than relationally motivated act. The raid on other groups produced a forced exchange, the more direct reincorporation of lost physical substance, and the assuaging of rage that are all archetypically aspects of the execution and consumption of witches.

3. *Kin persons were never consumed. The necessary distance in relationship appears to be equivalent to that for marriage (as was the case among Onabasulu people;*

4. *There was no set of explicit beliefs that characteristics of the consumed person were acquired.*

The notional genealogical distance necessary for two persons to be marriageable among Onabasulu applied equally to the consumption of bodies. One can only eat where one can also marry: both behaviors instantiate a social exchange. This makes logical sense in terms of the fear[9] of "closure" with regard to the distribution of bodily substance and is appropriate for the distribution of pork as well. Beliefs about Fasu child exchange are held to follow similar structural principles. This requirement—that the body of a person could not be consumed unless that person was in the kinship category of *naua*, of stranger (or a threatening nonkin)—helps resocialize the remains of the amoral agent of misfortune and adjust people's understandings of suffering, its causes, and possible rectification.

This resocialization also includes the nutritional reappropriation of the body that was understood to have once thrived on the illicit appropriation of others' being. As such, it was fitting that the nutritional possibilities be there, but that they were the same as those of any meat. As Kelly points out for the analogous Etoro case,

The flesh of the witch is consumed just as the witch consumes the flesh of his or her deceased victims.[10] However, no spiritual elements or personal attributes are transferred in cannibalism, and this view is understandable in so far as the soul of a witch is inherently evil and his or her characteristics totally undesirable. [Kelly 1993:176]

In fact, when asked about the transference of personal attributes in cannibalism during a discussion in Walagu in September 1970, Baliya Mataiya, initially somewhat puzzled by the inquiry, replied with characteristic wit and insight: "When you eat a bird, can you fly?" The nutritional circle created is, however, of importance and is one of a number of aspects grounded in cosmological beliefs.

As Kelly has expressed it: "The basic concept [is] of a circular closed system entailing a reciprocal relation of life and death" (1993:544, n. 19). This is reflected clearly again in the consumption of the bodies of those outsiders with whom the Onabasulu were in a mutual raiding relationship and who were partially sustained by consuming the bodies of Onabasulu—for example, Fasu. As Lévi-Strauss said, "The exo-cannibal reincorporates the virtue of his kinsfolk by ingesting an enemy who has himself eaten them" (1987:111).[11]

CONCLUSIONS

Onabasulu Anthropophagy

Onabasulu cannibalism rapidly disappeared in the 1960s. As Lévi-Strauss suggested of much cannibalism, it appears labile.[12] Certainly its disappearance predated the decline in the execution of *hinane*. In part this was so the deaths of alleged witches could be passed off, if investigated, as accidents. But with the decline in policing and the increase in fighting that has occurred in recent years on the Great Papuan Plateau and surrounding areas, cannibalism does not appear to have reemerged. Similarly, many of the cosmological perspectives in terms of which cannibalism made sense locally have persisted. So too have, in somewhat modified form, the beliefs about *hinane*. The disappearance of anthropophagous practice was most probably due, in large part, to its status as a part of the mechanisms for redressing the suffering of people, but not as central in practice or belief to the general cultural understandings.

To understand what Onabasulu anthropophagy meant to its practitioners, it must be seen as a part of the beliefs and practices associated with witches. These, in turn, are about relating the specific suffering of people to more general cultural understandings of life, death, and being. In this very human project, cannibalism was once important but never central or necessary.

Anthropology and the Ethnography of Cannibalism

Anthropology has historically been ideologically enmeshed with the topic of cannibalism as an exemplar of "exotic" practice. Although various early treatments of it have much in common with those of other "exotic" behaviors like sorcery and magic, it has not received, particularly in more recent times, anywhere near the same amount of anthropological attention. Why is this?

Cannibalism, after all, fits well the picture Kapferer paints as the general setting for the continuing anthropological interest in sorcery and magic:

The investigation of sorcery and magic, indeed the labelling of practices as sorcery and magic, was part of a philosophical and growing anthropological enterprise with huge political overtones. Their study was integral to the more general engagement of knowledge in the legitimation of the imperial domination of the West (the site of reason) over the subordinated rest (the site of unreason). [Kapferer 1997:9]

Unlike some of the anthropological uses of descriptions of sorcery in Kapferer's account, cannibalism *has not been successfully used to disturb or unsettle dominant Western systems of knowledge*. There is no anthropological treatment of cannibalism as a theory-building part of Western science in quite the same manner as, say, Evans-Pritchard's (1937) work on Azande sorcery and related beliefs.

So as anthropologists began to try to distance themselves from direct involvement in the nineteenth- and early twentieth-century colonial enterprises, discussions of cannibalism assumed a minor role in the literature. There was no respectable decentering of established modes of Western thought, as there was with sorcery, and the epithet "cannibal" carried a fascination of horror and crude racist connotations. Extended discussions of cannibalism, with rare exceptions, were left for more popular treatment, where the general themes treat it as either:

1. totally exotic and incommensurable with modern Western understandings of the social world, and in some cases a cultural equivalent to a psychiatric pathology;
2. understandable in terms of the rational need for protein—a derivative of nutritional imperatives and therefore the sociocultural equivalent of cannibalism as survival.

The latter is not too far removed from the more scholarly approaches of cultural materialism in the 1970s (see, especially, Harris 1978). Anthropological approaches could not counter these popular accounts with a capacity to unsettle Western knowledges like those that have emerged from the anthropological study of sorcery. There have, for a long while, been enlightened and humane approaches to the practice that evaluate it within the context of the cultures in which it occurs. In fact, it is arguable that this was the dominant early European attitude and that only as Western colonialism developed was there a movement from noble savage warrior to repulsive ignoble savage.[13] That early developer of the genre of the personal essay, Michel de Montaigne, provides in his essay "On the Cannibals" numerous examples to demonstrate what the translator summarizes thus:

Montaigne's "primitivism" (his respect for barbarous peoples and his admiration for much of their conduct, once their motives are understood) has little in common with the "noble savage" of later centuries. These people are indeed cruel: but so are we. . . . [Screech, in Montaigne 1995:1]

But such approaches, which we saw above in the court case cited, end up being mainly about us. They are antidotes to the usual coarse use of the epithet "cannibal" as a pejorative term used mainly now in racial politics. They run the risk, however, of distorting practices to make them "acceptable" to modern notions of appropriate behavior. However difficult disentangling the notion of cannibalism is both from its conventional connotations and common pejorative uses so beloved in the popular media, such an endeavor is necessary.

There has been no general anthropological or theoretical "payoff" in the treatment of the topic. It has never been decentering in the way that some treatments of sorcery have. This may be an important additional reason so few anthropologists have recently approached the topic at all.[14] While there is usually not a denial of anthropophagy, the omission of discussion of this topic can distort ethnography. Reticence about it can also be subversive of the very subject matter of anthropology—the varieties of ways of being human. It is sometimes said to be omitted to prevent "risk" to the community in which the practices previously occurred, but it is likely that the ethnographer's discomforts are a contributing factor.[15] The popular image of the cannibal from the island of New Guinea is a deeply entrenched one, at least in the English-speaking world, and it seems refractory to any attempts at modification through serious and sensitive analysis. But the response of omission of ethnography because of this popular image—an image that is still a currency in many racially defamatory discourses—is to enhance its power through the denial of cannibalism's historical occurrence. It is sometimes asserted that all reports of cannibalism are unfounded—in fact, the fabrications of observers.[16] But to deny or refuse to disclose material that does not sit comfortably with the historically specific moralities of the investigators and their community factions is also fabrication, and it is one that ultimately effects an analytic that gives weight to that bourgeois tendency to universalize its standards as the only appropriate way of being human.

I would suggest that cannibalism must, however, always be treated contextually. It probably does not lend itself to the theoretical possibilities eventually emergent from anthropological interest in sorcery because its defining feature is not fundamentally anchored to the beliefs that surround it. The *physical* act of ingesting human flesh is inadequate for defining in any general way a category of socio*cultural* meaning and practice. Rather, in each instance the question of what it means for those who practiced it must be asked anew. The questions always need to be asked.

NOTES

Research among Onabasulu has been made possible by grants from the (U.S.) National Institute of Mental Health, the University of Papua New Guinea, and Charles Sturt University. This chapter was written during a generous visiting researcher position at the National Museum of Ethnology, Osaka. I have discussed various issues and material in this chapter with Chun Kyung Soo, Roger Goodman, Yoshida Shuji. Especially helpful were Hayashi Isao and Kerry Zubrinich. I thank them all and attach the usual reminder (which will probably be a relief to them all) that the chapter would be much better if I had listened more carefully to them and that the responsibility for all shortcomings and mistakes is mine alone.

1. The 1902 *Criminal Code Ordinance* (No 7 of 1902) in Papua, which was the adopted Queensland *Criminal Code Act* 1899, also known as the "Griffith Act." It was replaced by *The Papua New Guinea Criminal Code* 1974 and is still in use in Queensland (see Weisbrot 1982:61 ff.).

2. "Hare" is Hale Kale, an Onabasulu politician from Walagu village who was then a government-employed interpreter. He became an important parliamentary representative in the Southern Highlands Province of Papua New Guinea and served in the speaker's position of the provincial parliament before it was dissolved by the federal government amid allegations of corruption and mismanagement.

3. In Onabasulu, this simile was used explicitly and was not initially elicited in response to any questions about the preparation of bodies. Note that it was said that the bodies were *prepared* in this fashion, not the old saw that they were like pig in flavor. No one ever volunteered any taste comparisons, and I never asked for any.

4. Compare these with the almost identical Etoro beliefs in Kelly's extended discussion (1993:146–174; see also Sørum 1982, on Bedamini, and Schieffelin 1976, on Kaluli).

5. Although patrolling had begun earlier, the first patrol to reach all Onabasulu settlements was from Kutubu Patrol Post in 1963. In 1964, the (then) Unevangelized Fields Mission built an airstrip and established a presence in the Kaluli settlement of Dudesa, close to the Onabasulu. In addition to the effects of its presence, this made the region more readily and regularly accessible.

6. It should be recalled here that the one departure from the customary preparation of pork was that the entrails of the *hinane* are not consumed.

7. The bodies were opened and after the intestines were discarded, the trunk was cut in half. Each half was carried by one member of the raiding party, arms or legs being draped over his shoulders.

8. In one version, it was said the man had been disemboweled.

9. Combined with the desire as well. In regard to sexuality, see Ernst (1991), and more generally, Mimica (1991).

10. I would add here that the flesh of the witch is *shared,* though the witch does not share the flesh of the deceased victim.

11. This was in a discussion of the usual classifications of cannibalism, where he pointed out, "The real difficulties begin when one seeks to analyze and classify the various forms taken by cannibalism. The now traditional distinction between exo- and endocannibalism is misleading" (Lévi-Strauss 1987:111).

12. But compare Knauft (1985) on the persistence of Gebusi cannibalism.

13. See, for instance, Arens' (1998) recent review of Lestringant (1998). Arens, incidentally, faults Lestringant for writing "for the cannibals did really exist . . ." implying that this indicates a "polite but distinct form of racism. . . ."

14. There are a few notable recent exceptions. Generally, there is Sanday (1986); for South America, Castro (1992); and for Papua New Guinea, the authors in Brown & Tuzin (1983).

15. In an analogous instance involving another "uncomfortable" aspect of cultural practice, Keesing has written: "I know of several cases where the reporting of male homosexual practices has been a matter of much soul-searching by ethnographers: in one clear case in the Eastern Highlands, the anthropologist has chosen not to disclose such practices in a community that could be placed at risk" (Keesing 1982:10).

16. In collusion with those who tell them the initial stories. Certainly this happens. The paper by Bastin (1969) was dependent in large part on both his readiness to find the savage cannibal of his imagination and in part on Hale Kale's (and others') understanding of this and his sense of humor.

REFERENCES

Anderson, J. L (1970). *Cannibal: A Photographic Audacity.* Sydney and Melbourne: A. H. and A. W. Reed.

Arens, W. (1998). Half-baked Ideas on Cannibalism (a review of F. Lestringant, 1998). *The Times Higher Education Supplement* (4 Sept.), 28.

Bastin, P. (1969). Medical aid for Bosavi cannibals. *The Geographical Magazine* 41 (7), 547–551.

Brown, P., & Tuzin, D. (eds.) (1983). *The Ethnography of Cannibalism.* Washington, DC: Society for Psychological Anthropology.

Castro, E. B. V. de (1992). *From the Enemy's Point of View: Humanity and Divinity in an Amazonian Society* (trans. C.V. Howard). Chicago, IL: University of Chicago Press.

Ernst, T. (1984). *Onabasulu Local Organization.* Ph.D. dissertation, University of Michigan.

Ernst, T. (1991). Onabasulu male homosexuality: Cosmology, affect and prescribed male homosexual activity among the Onabasulu of the Great Papuan Plateau. *Oceania* 62 (1): 1–11.

Evans-Pritchard, E. E. (1937). *Witchcraft, Oracles, and Magic among the Azande.* Oxford: Clarendon Press.

Griffin, J. A. (1972). Is a cannibal a criminal? *Melanesian Law Journal:* 79–81.

Harris, M. (1978). *Cannibals and Kings: The Origins of Cultures.* New York, Vintage Books.

Herdt, G. H. (ed.) (1984). *Ritualized Homosexuality in Melanesia.* Berkeley, CA: University of California Press.

Himmelman, P. K. (1997). The medicinal body: An analysis of medicinal cannibalism in Europe, 1300–1700. *Dialectical Anthropology* 22: 183–203.

Kapferer, B. (1997). *The Feast of the Sorcerer: Practices of Consciousness and Power.* Chicago, IL: University of Chicago Press.

Keesing, R. (1982). Introduction. In G. Herdt (ed.), *Rituals of Manhood: Male Initiations in New Guinea.* Berkeley, CA: University of California Press.

Kelly, R. (1977). *Etoro Social Structure: A Study in Structural Contradiction.* Ann Arbor, MI: University of Michigan Press.

Kelly, R. (1993). *Constructing Inequality: The Fabrication of a Hierarchy of Value among the Etoro.* Ann Arbor, MI: University of Michigan Press.

Knauft, B. M. (1985). *Good Company and Violence: Sorcery and Social Action in a Lowland New Guinea Society.* Berkeley and Los Angeles, CA: University of California Press.

Lestringant, F. (1998). *Cannibals: The Discovery and Representation of the Cannibal from Columbus to Jules Verne* (trans. R. Morris). Berkeley and Los Angeles, CA: University of California Press.

Lévi-Strauss, C. (1987). *Anthropology and Myth: Lectures 1951–1982* (trans. Roy Willis). Oxford and New York: Basil Blackwell.

Mimica, J. (1991). The incest passions: An outline of the logic of Iqwaye social organisation. *Oceania* 62 (1): 13–40.

Montaigne, M. de (1995). *Four Essays* (trans. M. A. Screech). Harmondsworth, Middlesex: Penguin Books.

Sanday, P. R. (1986). *Divine Hunger: Cannibalism as a Cultural System.* Cambridge: Cambridge University Press.

Schieffelin, E. L. (1976). *The Sorrow of the Lonely and the Burning of the Dancers.* New York: St. Martin's Press.

Shaw, R. D. (1990). *Kandila: Samo Ceremonialism and Interpersonal Relationships.* Ann Arbor, MI: University of Michigan Press.
Sørum, R. (1982). Patterns in Bedamini male initiation. *Social Analysis* 10: 42–62.
Weisbrot, D. (1982). Custom and criminal law in conflict. In D. Weisbrot, A. Paliwala, & A. Sawyerr (eds.), *Law and Social Change in Papua New Guinea* (pp. 59–104). Sydney: Butterworths.
Weisbrot, D., Paliwala, A., & Sawyerr, A. (eds.) (1982). *Law and Social Change in Papua New Guinea.* Sydney: Butterworths.

Index

NAME INDEX

Aarne, A., 7
Abler, T. S., 81
Abrams, D., 7
Aiston, G., 59
Akins, N. J., 95
Allen, W., 61
Alvardo, P. de., 3
Amelagos, G., 13, 17, 52, 105
Anderson, J., 54, 145
Anderson, R., 108, 117
Andrews, A., 55
Anglo, M., 13, 52
Arens, W., 13–15, 28, 29, 35–38, 53, 56, 68, 75–77, 105, 117
Armstrong, W. E., 81
Askenasy, H., 4, 5, 13, 52, 67, 92

Bahn, P., 17
Bakhtin, M., 113
Ballard, C., 8, 19
Banfield, E., 64
Barber, I., 38, 81
Barth, F., 30
Barwick, D., 64
Basedow, H., 60, 61, 66
Basso, E., 7
Bastin, P., 146

Bates, D. M., 56, 60
Beaver, W. N., 18
Beecher, L., 7
Bellantoni, N. F., 94
Bercovitch, E., 46
Berdan, F. F., 17
Berndt, C. H., 19, 57, 60
Berndt, R. M., 19, 57, 60
Berry, M. S., 95
Bettelheim, B., 7
Beveridge, P., 57, 59
Block, W. D., 17
Boelaars, J., 130
Bouville, P., 81
Bowden, R., 81
Brady, I., 2, 15
Brew, A., 94
Bridges, B. J., 53, 61, 62
Bridges, P. S., 81
Brockwell, C. J., 53
Brown P., 13, 18, 56
Buckhorn, R., 16,18, 54, 67
Bullock, P. Y., 75, 76, 80
Butterworth, E., 7
Byrne, J. C., 60

Campbell, C. A., 60

Roth, W. E., 59, 60, 66, 81
Rumsey, A., 1, 3, 4, 113, 116, 118
Rushforth, S., 93

Sagan, E., 4, 52
Sahagón, F. B. de., 13
Sahlins, M., 17, 36, 52, 81, 105
Sanday, P., 3, 4, 13, 16, 19, 52, 105
Schieffelin, E., 148, 151
Searcy, A., 60
Sebastian, L., 95
Shankman, P. 4, 54, 56
Shaw, R. D., 148
Shipman, P., 81
Sievwright, C. W., 61
Sillitoe, P., 14
Skate, B., 20
Smidt, D., 124
Smyth, R. B., 53, 54, 59
Snow, C. E., 81
Sørum, A., 148
Sowada, A., 130
Spencer, W. B., 57, 59
Spennemann, D. H., 81
Staden, H., 13
Stanner, W. E. H., 63
Stayt, H. A., 81
Strachan, A., 55
Strathern, A., 3, 4, 8, 16, 19, 106, 107, 119
Strathern, M., 43, 138
Street, B., 7, 63
Sturt, C., 55, 59
Sutton, D. S., 81, 96

Tainter, J. A., 95
Tannahill, R., 52, 81
Taplin, G., 53
Taussig, M., 128
Taylor, M., 18
Titiev, M., 81
Tonkinson, R., 57
Toth, N., 17, 81
Tuck, J. A., 81
Turner, C. G., 76, 77, 78, 79, 80, 84, 90, 93
Turner, J. A., 76, 77, 78, 79, 80, 84, 90, 93
Tuzin, D., 13, 18, 56, 67, 81, 106
Twain, M., 27, 28, 52

Villa, P., 81
Voorhoeve, C. L., 123

Wagner, R., 16, 19
Weiner, J., 19
Weisbrot, D., 145
Westgarth, W., 63
Wheeler, G. C., 53
White, T. D., 15, 17, 18, 80, 81, 84, 85
Whitehead, N. L., 81
Widdowson, J., 7
Wilcox, D. R., 92, 95, 96
Williams, F. E., 19
Wills, W. H., 94
Wormsley, W., 105
Wrench, R., 61

Zegwaard, G. A., 19, 81, 123–138
Zubrinich, K., 2, 3, 5, 130

SUBJECT INDEX

Abau, 30
Anasazi, 15, 75–98
Arapesh, 106, 119
Arawete, 128
Atbalim, 30
Australian Aborigines, 51–68, 81
Azande, 28
Azmat, 81, 123–140

Baktaman, 30
Baya Horo, 7–12
Bedamini, 19, 146, 148
Bimin-Kukusmin, 16, 19, 30, 81, 106
Bodies, 9–10, 136–138

Busama, 81, 96

Cannibalism: anthropology, 2–5, 41–43, 45, 125, 146, 154–156; approaches to, 52; and archaeology, 15, 77–96; and children, 10–12, 109–112, 116; and cosmology, 7–8, 124, 126, 127, 132, 137–138, 153; as discourse, 3–12; and ethics, 38–45, 105, 116, 118; evidence for, 14–16, 29, 33–34, 37, 52, 62–69, 77; and exchange, 40, 106–107, 150, 153; folklore, 8–13; as foreigner, 107–113; headhunting, 123–138; initiation, 133–137; metaphors, 4, 57–58, 68; and morality, 4–5, 29, 45; mortuary